DEBRETT'S

GUIDE
FOR THE
MODERN
GENTLEMAN

Debrett's Guide for the Modern Gentleman
Published by Debrett's Limited
18–20 Hill Rise, Richmond,
Surrey TW10 6UA
United Kingdom

WRITER AND RESEARCHER Tom Bryant

ADDITIONAL TEXT AND RESEARCH Jo Bryant

EDITORIAL CONSULTANT Peter Howarth

HEAD OF PUBLISHING Elizabeth Wyse
SENIOR MANAGING EDITOR Jo Bryant
ASSISTANT EDITOR Sarah Corney

DESIGN AND ART DIRECTION Smith & Gilmour, London
COVER DESIGN Show Media, London
COVER ILLUSTRATION Joel Holland

ISBN 978–1–870520–77–5

Printed and bound by Graphicom – Vicenza, Italy

Visit us at www.debretts.co.uk

DEBRETT'S

GUIDE
FOR THE
MODERN
GENTLEMAN

WORDS OF WISDOM

"THE TRUE GENTLEMAN IS FRIENDLY BUT NOT FAMILIAR;
THE INFERIOR MAN IS FAMILIAR BUT NOT FRIENDLY."
– Confucius (551–479 BC)

"I CAN MAKE A LORD, BUT ONLY
GOD CAN MAKE A GENTLEMAN."
– James I (1566–1625)

"EDUCATION BEGINS THE GENTLEMAN, BUT READING,
GOOD COMPANY AND REFLECTION MUST FINISH HIM."
– John Locke (1632–1704)

"NO MAN WHO WAS NOT A TRUE GENTLEMAN AT HEART,
EVER WAS, SINCE THE WORLD BEGAN, A TRUE GENTLEMAN
IN MANNER, NO VARNISH CAN HIDE THE GRAIN OF THE
WOOD; AND THAT THE MORE VARNISH YOU PUT ON,
THE MORE THE GRAIN WILL EXPRESS ITSELF."
– Charles Dickens (1812–1870)

"A PERFECT GENTLEMAN IS A THING
WHICH I CANNOT DEFINE."
– Anthony Trollope (1815–1882)

"A GENTLEMAN IS ONE WHO NEVER HURTS
ANYONE'S FEELINGS UNINTENTIONALLY."
– Oscar Wilde (1854–1900)

"COURTESY IS AS MUCH A MARK
OF A GENTLEMAN AS COURAGE."
– Theodore Roosevelt (1858–1919)

"I AM NOT A GENTLEMAN.
I DON'T EVEN KNOW WHAT A GENTLEMAN IS."
– *Citizen Kane* (1941)

PREFACE

Today the notion of gentlemanly behaviour is not nearly as clear-cut as it once was. Little wonder then that the twenty-first century editors at Debrett's feel the time is right to re-examine and redefine this most mercurial of definitions of masculinity.

Debrett's has assembled an essential handbook for those who wish to rediscover the art of gentlemanly behaviour for our age. The Guide embraces an eclectic range of topics including: the rules of tailoring; successful seduction; the new chivalry; classic cocktails and martinis; how to fly in style; cuisine to impress; tipping and taxis in far-flung places; how to dress for the boardroom, the beach or the golf course.

This compendium of masculinity is complemented by rare pearls of wisdom from resident mistress of etiquette, Miss Debrett.

This is a book that will entertain and edify. Having read it you will be well-qualified to go forth in to the world in a thoroughly modern, and gentlemanly, manner.

PETER HOWARTH

Editor of *Sunday Telegraph Men's Style Magazine*
and former editor of *Arena* and *Esquire*.

MAN AT WORK

The Quintessential British Suit

SHOULDERS: classically, a British suit fits the body snugly so the shoulders are neither too wide nor too narrow. They are padded, but not excessively so, as they only provide structure; they are not designed to bulk up the shoulder line. There should also be a sharp, 90-degree angle between the shoulder and the sleeve of the suit.

SLEEVES: the length allows for a good finger's width of shirt cuff and should fit neatly, without hugging or gaping, at the wrist.

GORGE: a technical term used to describe the area of the coat where the lapel and the collar meet. British suits tend to have a higher gorge, meaning less shirt is shown. Essentially, moderation is the key with a British suit, so lapels will be neither excessively wide nor skinny.

WAIST: the suit is not too suppressed at the waist, though it is suppressed enough to show off your shape. There should also be a slight flare over the hips.

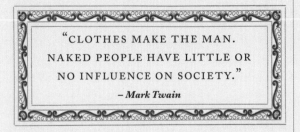

> "CLOTHES MAKE THE MAN. NAKED PEOPLE HAVE LITTLE OR NO INFLUENCE ON SOCIETY."
>
> – *Mark Twain*

BUTTONS: single and double-button suits tend to be more traditionally British. The button should be on your waist. A British suit should be single-breasted even though the double-breasted suit is an English invention.

COAT LENGTH: this should be in proportion to your overall height. A general rule is that the length of a coat should be half the distance between the ground and the top of the coat's collar. This also determines the ideal place for the pockets.

POCKETS: coat pockets were first slanted on British suits because, in the days of hacking jackets, it allowed you to access your pockets more easily while on horseback. A slanted pocket now both references back to those days and contributes to a more stylish look. Ticket pockets, above the main pocket, can make for younger style, but tend to look better on three-button suits and should never be used on a double-breasted suit.

Tailoring Trivia

A coat always used to have a single, central vent, rather than side vents, so that it would sit neatly when worn in the saddle. The central vent would also allow room for a sword to hang backwards from your waist, which is why the left side of the vent will always be over the right.

SIDE VENTS: some houses would disagree, but the most traditional of Savile Row's tailors often insist on side vents for a British suit, while American sack suits will always have a centre vent. Side vents allow you to put your hands in your pockets without disturbing the line of the suit; they are often better for larger people as they will be kinder on the rear.

TROUSERS: the rise between the legs should be as high as is comfortable, while still fitting on the top of your pelvis. This means your legs look longer and, therefore, better. The bigger you are around the waist, the higher you should wear your trousers – this lengthens your legs, making you appear slimmer.

PLEATS: flat-fronted trousers give a longer, slimmer line and are better for those in good shape. Pleated trousers allow you more room and are usually more comfortable. Forward pleats fold towards the fly and are the standard on Savile Row. Reverse pleats are more a hallmark of continental suits. Bigger men should opt for a reverse pleat, as it won't break so much. No-one should ever have more than two pleats.

CUT: while skinny trousers make you look slimmer, remember that the trouser is a practical garment and therefore needs to be cut to allow you room to easily manoeuvre. Trousers should break slightly at the front, but not at the back.

TURN-UP: turn-ups add weight and therefore improve the hang of the trousers, but they can shorten the leg and will not enhance the appearance of a single-breasted suit. They go well with certain fabrics and different cuts such as a double-breasted Prince Of Wales checked suit.

 EXPERT TIP Savile Row tailors call a suit jacket a coat. Sound like a pro and impress them by doing the same.

DOUBLE-BREASTED SUITS add width, while single-breasted suits make you look taller and slimmer. Bigger, shorter men should avoid double-breasted suits as they make you look boxy. Ideally, they fit slim and athletic men who want to make the most of their physique.

THREE-BUTTON SUITS add a little width to the chest as they tend to concentrate the eye on that part of the body. As a general rule, it's best to only do up the middle button, but the top button can be fastened too. Never do up the lowest button.

TWO-BUTTON SUITS draw the eye to the waist and tend to work best on those with a medium build. Technically, the lower button is superfluous – it is just there for the look. It should never be done up as it pulls the coat out of shape, meaning your suit looks wrong.

ONE-BUTTON SUITS are simple and stylish, creating clean, stylish lines. The fit and button draw the eye to the waist – often the narrowest part of the body – meaning the suit, effectively, stretches the body upwards and inwards, making them ideal for shorter men.

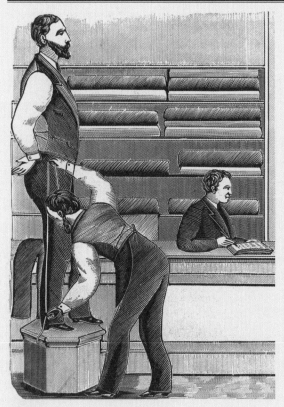

WHY GO BESPOKE?

A bespoke suit will give you confidence. Knowing that you are wearing a suit that has been created specifically to make you look good will allow you to leave an instant impression. People will naturally look at you. Well cut and perfectly fitted suits are rare so, if you wear one, you will instantly stand out.

Your suit should improve with age. If well made, it will gradually mould itself to your body as the effect of your body temperature will be to slowly press it from the inside out. That means it will look better and better. Once a tailor has created a pattern of your shape, he should keep it on file. This means that, provided you don't change shape, he can – if necessary – make you a suit without you even having to spend time being refitted.

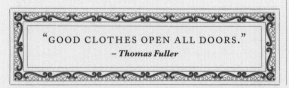

> "GOOD CLOTHES OPEN ALL DOORS."
> – *Thomas Fuller*

AT THE TAILOR

{1}

Tell your tailor where, how and when you will be wearing your garment. They can make alterations depending on the temperature of the places you might be, the type of work you might be doing, your posture, and much more.

{2}

Tell your tailor what your suit is for: is it a deal-making suit, an everyday suit, a leisure suit, for a special occasion or to wear on television? The more detail you give, the more likely you'll be able to get the suit you want.

{3}

What will you be keeping in your pockets? Your phone, wallet or keys ruin the lines of a suit, but spaces can be found for them if you tell your tailor what you usually carry around.

{4}

Do you put your hands in your pockets? It affects the slant of the pocket, the venting and fit of the coat.

{5}

Be honest. There's no point sucking in your stomach and pushing out your chest in front of a tailor: the finished suit won't fit and it will be your own fault. And they always know anyway. You should relax with your tailor as, the more tense you are with them, the more unnaturally you'll stand, which makes fitting your suit impossible.

{6}

Tell your tailor whether your weight tends to fluctuate. While losing and gaining weight will obviously change the fit of your suit, it will also alter your balance and posture, which can lead to badly fitting suits.

{7}

You are the customer. If you don't like something your tailor is suggesting, tell him.

{8}

Don't be offended by the truth. If your tailor tells you something looks awful, it probably does. A tailor wants you to look your best when you leave his shop, so trust his judgement. It's his name on the suit, after all.

{9}

Look at what your tailor is wearing. If you don't like his suit, don't ask him to make you one as, nine times out of ten, that is roughly the sort of suit he'll make for you. Some houses have a strict style too, and may not be able to cut you the suit you require.

{10}

Remember, rules are meant to be broken. While guidelines are important, never stick too fast to them as creating your own style is of far more importance than following everyone else's.

KNOWLEDGE HOW TO BUY A BESPOKE SUIT

{1} FIND A TAILOR YOU LIKE. Look at the suits he makes and wears and, if he is part of a house, at the other suits in that range. Trust reputation too. Savile Row and Jermyn Street are gossipy places – if someone is well-respected then they are invariably good.

{2} ONCE YOU HAVE FOUND a good tailor, meet for a consultation. This is your chance to tell him exactly what you want. It will give him a chance to quiz you on your style too. At the meeting, wear a suit and shirt you like, along with the shoes you are likely to wear with your new suit. This will give your tailor an idea of your taste.

{3} YOU SHOULD DISCUSS weight of cloth, patterns, colours and styling of your suit at this stage. Choose carefully and take your time as there will be many different options.

{4} YOU WILL BE MEASURED and, from that, your tailor will create a pattern. At the higher end of the market, this will be created specifically for you. Further down, this will be a generic pattern adjusted for your measurements. The pattern is then applied to the fabric, which will be cut to fit. Allow at least an hour for the first consultation and fitting session.

{5} YOUR FIRST FITTING should allow you to try on your suit in the fabric you have chosen. Often there will be no lining at this stage. All aspects of the suit's fit, from sleeve length to button height, will be checked here. You will get at least three or four fittings for your first suit but, if you return to the same tailor for more suits, he should be able to cut that down to two.

{6} AT YOUR FINAL FITTING you should be trying on a virtually finished suit; the only things left undone at this stage will be the hand-stitching that will finish the suit.

{7} THE HAND-STITCHING WILL TAKE around five hours so you should be able to leave with your suit two to three days after your final fitting and, roughly, eight to ten weeks after your first consultation. It should take a tailor about 60 hours, in total, to make your suit.

SEVEN TAILORING FAUX PAS

Never say to a tailor, "You're the expert, go off and make me a suit". They will make something they like but which you may not.

•

If you don't know exactly what you want, at least know what you don't want.

•

Don't ask for something they don't do. A traditional Savile Row tailor is unlikely to be too wacky.

•

If they can't make what you want, a good tailor will direct you elsewhere; a bad one may make it for you but it probably won't be quite right.

•

Be flexible. Just because you have your heart set on a certain style doesn't mean it's right for you.

•

Don't expect your suit overnight. The longer it takes, the better it will be.

•

Once you have found a tailor you like, stick with him; it takes time to build up another relationship. Equally, don't feel compelled to stay with someone whose suits you dislike.

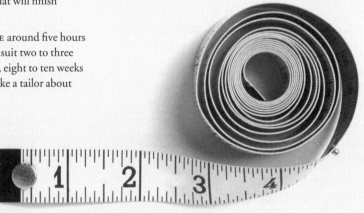

GET IT RIGHT: TAILORING TERMINOLOGY

BESPOKE: the term bespoke has been watered down to include products that aren't really bespoke – from kitchens to cars. For a fully bespoke suit, you should be starting with absolutely nothing, a blank sheet on which to build. The rule is that, if you don't ask for it, you won't have it included, as this is a process in which you will be in complete control. For a truly bespoke suit, you will be consulted on every aspect of your garment, from fit, shape and style, to the height and depth of the pockets. The cost of a bespoke suit will rise according to your choices and fabrics. With care, however, it should last for 20 years or more, so is well worth the indulgence and the investment.

•

CUSTOM: a custom, or semi-bespoke, suit is one for which a style already exists. You can choose fabrics, textures, colours and a few things besides but, essentially, the cut of the suit will not change. Trouser size can be altered, but they will not be made specifically for you, just tailored to fit. There is still a wide choice with a custom suit, including the amount of buttons required, double or single-breasted, pleated or flat-fronted trousers. What won't be changed are style details such as the slant of the pockets or the width of the lapels. For most people, this is perfectly adequate, especially as a custom suit will cost half as much as a bespoke one. It is also a good way to buy well-fitting suits that can be changed to follow fashion.

•

BITS HAND-FINISHED: standing between a custom and a ready-to-wear suit, this is an off-the-peg garment on which the cuffs and buttons have not been finished. This means the button height, which is important, can be altered to fit you, as can the sleeve length.

•

READY-TO-WEAR: designed to fit an average chest size and height, it will look fantastic on anyone lucky enough to be of those average proportions. Sleeve lengths can be adjusted, waists can be taken in and general alterations can be made but, essentially, what you see is what you get. Nonetheless, this can work very well for a good number of people, particularly because a ready-to-wear suit will be a fraction of the price of a bespoke or custom suit.

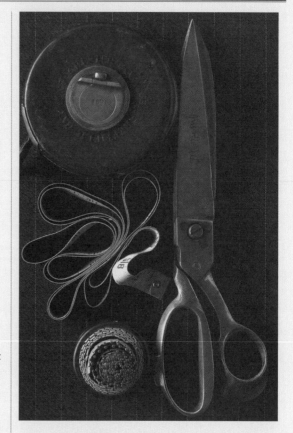

STYLE GUIDE HOW TO WEAR A SUIT

{1}

A suit – and certainly a bespoke one – should be designed to make you look impressive even when you are relaxed, so make sure you stand at ease. This is important because if you are wearing a suit all day, you don't want to permanently feel at attention.

{2}

A suit should improve your posture as it will give you a structure within which to stand. Without a suit on, you are more likely to slouch.

{3}

Never think of your suit as a uniform. It should be worn with individual flair, not as something you have to wear for work.

{4}

When you sit, pull your trousers up at the top of the knees. It will lessen the strain on the knees. You should also unbutton your coat, especially if wearing a double-breasted suit.

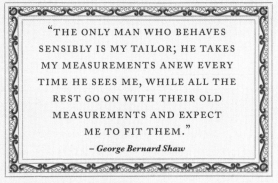

Perfect Patterns

TEXTURE: a plain suit can look fantastic with texture added to it through the weave. A coarser fabric will create a matt finish, while different weaves will create different effects. A twill weave will give your suit a nicely cut finish with a slight sheen. Dinner jackets classically have a barathea weave, which kills light, meaning that they will appear matt. Experimentation with other weaves, basket or birdseye for example, can effectively bring a plain coloured suit alive.

STRIPES: there is an almost infinite number of stripes out there, from wide to narrow, and bold to subtle. In general, vertical stripes will add height, but your body shape will determine how wide or narrow the stripe should be. As a general rule, the bigger you are, the wider the stripe you can pull off. Avoid going too bold, you don't want your suit to drown you. Diagonals, meanwhile, are very classic but be careful as they tend to look old-fashioned.

CHECKS: there is a wide array of checks, from the bold and bright to those that are more demure. The Prince Of Wales, named after Edward VIII, and Glenurquhart Plaid are the classic checks but not everyone can get away with them so, if you are more of a wallflower, these should be avoided. A good alternative to check is herringbone, as it will add depth up close but, from a distance, will appear more plain.

CLOTH COUNTS

Know what weight of cloth you want. If you get it right, you'll always impress your tailor. 12-ounce cloth is the best all-round weight for year-long wear in Britain. 8-ounce cloth is good for the tropics but not for the UK. 14-ounce cloth is fine for the middle of winter, but may be too heavy for other seasons.

ESSENTIAL WARDROBE

THREE BUSINESS SUITS OF VARYING COLOURS.
TWO BLAZERS; ONE TRADITIONAL, ONE CASUAL.
ONE DINNER JACKET.

Tailoring Trivia

On a bespoke suit, the buttons on the sleeve will actually undo (though of course you shouldn't leave them undone). Originally, this was because ships' surgeons didn't remove their coats when performing operations, but needed to roll back their sleeves – hence the name: surgeon's cuff.

BEST PRICE

It is worth asking your tailor if he has offered you his best price. Most do this as a matter of course, but some don't and few will be offended. Be careful though as, if pushed, they may bring the price down by lowering the quality of your suit fabric.

WAISTCOAT RULES

{1}

Three-piece suits, while perhaps less common, still look good.

{2}

With the coat off, a waistcoat gives your upper half structure as it works in a similar way to a corset.

{3}

A waistcoat lengthens the body – it allows you to wear a flattering fabric from neck to toe – so works well on larger men or those with shorter legs.

{4}

Waistcoats should have six or seven buttons, but the lowest should always be left undone, especially as most are cut in such a way as to make it impossible to fasten.

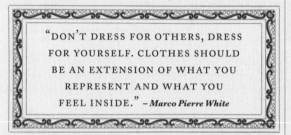

"DON'T DRESS FOR OTHERS, DRESS FOR YOURSELF. CLOTHES SHOULD BE AN EXTENSION OF WHAT YOU REPRESENT AND WHAT YOU FEEL INSIDE." – *Marco Pierre White*

SUIT CARE

Frequent dry-cleaning will ruin your suit very quickly. Even if you are wearing your suit at least once a week in the office, you shouldn't have it dry-cleaned more than twice a year. Wool is a natural fibre and therefore naturally repels dirt, so a simple brush and press is often all that is needed to clean your suit.

Belts and Braces

BELTS SHOULD NEVER be worn with suits. They will give the appearance of cutting you in half, ruining both the lines of the suit and your appearance. They also give people the impression that your trousers don't fit properly, which is hardly the sort of statement you'd wish to make. Besides, with a bespoke suit, why would you need one?

BRACES ARE FAR BETTER, provided they are button-on rather than clip-on. As they fall from the shoulder, the trousers will be allowed to hang, creating natural movement, which is exactly what you're after.

BRACES AND, if you must, belts should be worn as a detail rather than as something functional – you really shouldn't need anything to keep your trousers up other than your waist. You could wear belt and braces together, but only if you've taken leave of your senses.

STYLE GUIDE POCKET SQUARES

Pocket squares are a chance to add individual flair to your suit. There are multiple ways to fold your silk square but most of these, essentially, fall into two categories – the square top and tufted (pointed) top. Pocket squares suit most men except those with large chests, who should divert attention elsewhere. They should always be worn with a tie, but the square should never match the tie.

SQUARE TOP: lay your square flat with the top corners horizontal. Fold the left side over the right side to make a rectangle. Fold the bottom up, just short of the top. Tuck into your jacket pocket.

TUFTED TOP: lay your square flat, with one corner at the top and one at the bottom, making a diamond shape. Fold the bottom corner to meet the top corner. Fold the left corner half-way across the triangle, and repeat with the right, creating a shape like a square, open envelope.

LININGS

Suit linings are a chance to add a dash of flair to your suit and, given that no-one else will really see them, they should be designed with individual style in mind. For the more flamboyant, it is appealing to go with a bold colour inside. For a more subtle approach, bold flashes can be added to the tops of inside pockets, rather than to the entire inside of the jacket. When choosing a lining, be sure to pick a colour that will work with the colour of shirt you will most often wear with your suit.

Historical Style

Thought to be responsible for the tradition of leaving the lowest button on a waistcoat undone – because his expanding waistline prevented him from fastening it – Edward VII also introduced turn-ups to suits, as he would often roll up the bottom of his trousers when walking across his estate. Rumour also has it that, after being caught in a rainstorm on such a walk, he sought sanctuary in a woodsman's house. To dry his trousers, the woodsman's wife ironed them. But, thinking that as the king, his trousers would be ironed differently from her husband's, she put a crease in the front, rather than on the side. Edward liked the look, and it has stuck ever since.

THE ANATOMY OF THE SHIRT

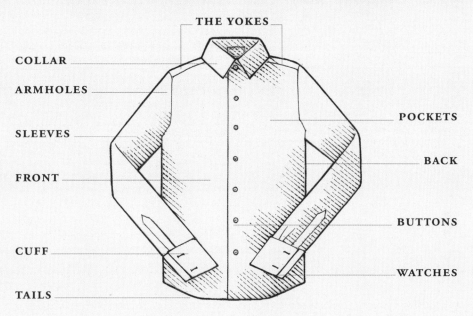

THE YOKES

COLLAR

ARMHOLES

SLEEVES

FRONT

CUFF

TAILS

POCKETS

BACK

BUTTONS

WATCHES

THE YOKES: the whole shirt hangs from here. If this doesn't fit, then the shirt won't fit.

ARMHOLES: not so high as to hit the front and back of the arm.

SLEEVES: these must be long enough to show enough cuff at the end of the suit jacket. They should be tight enough to look good, but loose enough to allow plenty of movement. Wear the jacket you will be wearing with your shirt when you buy.

FRONT: unless you have a large stomach, the front should be close-fitting and flat, as the fullness of a shirt should be contained in the back. A larger waistband may mean more room is required at the front of the shirt.

CUFF: generally, the cuff should end four and a half inches from the end of your thumb. Cuff linings can add flair and structure. Double cuffs fit cufflinks and can be altered to accommodate any type of cufflink from square to round, mitred to bar. Bring the cufflink you intend to wear with your shirt when you have it fitted.

TAILS: a shirt should be long enough to ensure that it never pops out of the waistband during the day. Take advice from your tailor on the appropriate length.

COLLAR: collar shape depends on shape of face, shoulder slope, style of jacket and size of tie-knot. A narrow tie will suit a more traditional collar, while anyone who insists on footballers' tie

knots will require a wide, cut-away collar. If the style of tie you wear changes, your tailor can change your shirt's collar to accommodate this. To check whether your collar fits, you should be able to fit three fingers under it at the side of the neck. Always wear a collar stay, too, unless you are wearing a button-down shirt.

POCKETS: pockets spoil the line of a shirt and unless you require them for a specific reason – as somewhere to carry your credit cards or glasses for example – steer clear of them. If you must have pockets, then have one on either side to balance the shirt. It won't look good with a suit but will work more casually.

BACK: shoulder pleats will allow for fullness in the back and permit free movement. For a slim-fit shirt, a centre pleat is required. A baggy shirt won't do your profile any favours.

BUTTONS: four-hole buttons are generally sewn on with a machine and, therefore, lessen the bespoke impact of your shirt. Some tailors will hand-sew three-hole or six-hole buttons – and use brightly coloured thread – to highlight the shirt's bespoke qualities. Buttons can be hidden by a fly-front, if necessary, though the shirt may look oddly bare.

WATCHES: a made-to-measure shirt can be styled to allow for slim, medium-sized and large watches. Wear the watch you intend to wear with your shirt at the fitting.

TEN REASONS TO
GO BESPOKE

{1}
A bespoke shirt will actually fit you.

{2}
A bespoke shirt can be made to suit your needs
– be they warmth, coolness, physical activity
or even the way you sit and stand.

{3}
Tailors know what looks good; they can advise
you on what suits you and what doesn't.

{4}
If you're not sure what you want, make use
of your tailor's expertise.

{5}
If you look after it, a bespoke shirt will last
for 10 years or more.

{6}
Just because a shirt is from a good label,
it doesn't mean it will fit properly.

{7}
A bespoke shirt makes a statement.

{8}
When you walk out of the door, you are an
advert for your tailor. He wants you to look
your absolute best.

{9}
It should be the most comfortable item
of clothing you own and, if you're wearing
it in the office all day, that is important.

{10}
If you are wearing clothes made for you, your
confidence will be high and you may achieve more.

What Your Shirtmaker Needs to Know

{1} Your exercise regime. Regular weightlifting will change your body shape over time.

{2} Whether you are having physio or doing yoga. Again, this will change your body shape and posture.

{3} Whether you are on a diet or prone to putting on weight.

{4} What you will be using your shirt for. For example, if your job involves you being active, then a tight shirt will wear quickly.

{5} The climate in which you will be wearing your shirt.

{6} Where and how your shirt will be cleaned. If it will be regularly subjected to hotel laundries, a tougher fabric may be required.

{7} Whether you tan easily. If you are likely to wear your shirts in hot climates, then the shirt's colour will need to make allowances for your change in skin tone.

{8} Never tell your tailor you've got better shirts elsewhere. They will hate you.

When Bespoke Won't Suit

{1} If you need a shirt quickly, buy a ready-to-wear shirt. If necessary, it can be altered to fit better at a later date.

{2} If you have seen a shirt you like that fits, then there's little point in having one made.

{3} If you want a shirt that is the height of fashion, buy one off-the-peg. A bespoke shirt should be timeless rather than temporary and therefore doesn't necessarily move with the times.

{4} If you want to buy a shirt cheaply, don't go bespoke. Remember, though, that it may not last as long nor is it likely to be of the same quality.

{5} Some people will never look good in a shirt, no matter whether it is bespoke or not. If you are one of these, and if you have to wear a shirt, save your money and buy one off-the-peg.

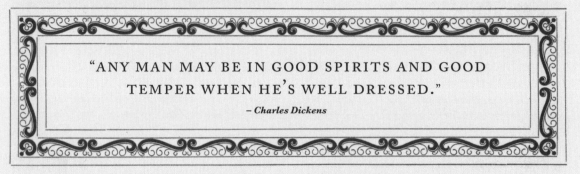

"ANY MAN MAY BE IN GOOD SPIRITS AND GOOD
TEMPER WHEN HE'S WELL DRESSED."

– *Charles Dickens*

KNOWLEDGE FABRICS

{1} The higher the number (thread count), the finer the fabric.

{2} For most people, either two fold 140 weight cotton or two fold 120 is the best for business shirts – both fine and tough, they are still fairly versatile.

{3} The 120 weight fabric is better for anything demanding; the 140 for an office-only job.

{4} Two fold 100 is the best weight for anyone in a more physical job as it is a stronger and less fine fabric.

{5} Two fold 200 weight shirts are about the highest weight that is practicable.

{6} Although 240 weight and higher does exist, they require hand-laundering and can't be worn regularly.

COLOUR RULES

{1}
First match colours to skin tone.
{2}
Then match colours to your suits.
{3}
For your first bespoke shirts, play it safe with white and blue before experimenting later.
{4}
If you want a white shirt, make it textured. It's just more interesting.

STYLE GUIDE MONOGRAMS

A MONOGRAM should only be your initials. It should be embroidered on your cuff or by your waist only.

MONOGRAMS ON CUFFS wear out quickly; monograms on the chest are vulgar. Signatures can occasionally be acceptable, but only if you have the pizzazz to pull it off.

A MONOGRAM ON THE WAIST of your shirt is a stylish choice and, as you reach into your jacket pocket when the bill arrives, people will be able to see who's paying…

 EXPERT TIP If you have any problems with your shirt, or if your body shape changes, take your shirt back to your tailor for it to be mended or re-fitted. Often tailors build their shirts to allow for a change in body shape.

Tailoring Trivia

Shirts used to have long tails because they were used as nightshirts as well as day shirts. The tails were designed to maintain the wearer's decency when in bed before they were tucked into trousers during the day.

GET IT RIGHT: READY TO WEAR SHIRTS

TALL BUILD: if you are tall and lean, a fitted shirt can make you appear scrawny. Cut away collars will make you look broader and, therefore, more evenly shaped. If, however, you are tall and muscular, a fitted shirt can make you look more powerful.

•

ROTUND BUILD: avoid fitted shirts and opt for those with pleats in the back to allow room for movement. Long collars can make you appear taller, drawing attention away from the waist. Big checks look better on bigger men while vertical stripes may make you appear taller rather than wider.

ATHLETIC BUILD: wear a fitted shirt to show off your physique. Those with broad shoulders can pull off bigger collars, but anyone with a short neck should have a smaller collar.

•

SHORT BUILD: a fitted shirt can make you appear more square and, therefore, less short. If, however, you are short but rotund, a fitted shirt will do you no favours at all. In that case, go for one with pleats and a traditional collar as this will draw the eye up and down, making the most of your stature. Vertical stripes will also help you to appear taller, but big checks will drown you.

Tie Trivia

It is rumoured ties were either invented by Mongolians, who used them to attach prisoners to their horses, or by the Chinese emperor Shih Huang-ti whose Terracotta Army all have cloth wrapped around their necks. There is also evidence to suggest that some Roman soldiers wore ties as a mark of their prowess in battle. The modern tie is the successor of the cravat, worn originally by Croat soldiers who sported theirs as a mark of identification.

To tie or not to tie?

AS OFFICES GET ever more casual, and as the trend slips towards wearing suits without ties, the question of whether to go open-necked or not becomes more and more important. The rules, however, are relatively simple and are all about gauging the situation.

IF YOU ARE HEADING into a business meeting with a senior and more formal colleague, take your cues from him. If he's to be the man to promote you, he'll want someone he can relate to. By the same token, if this is a meeting with equals, you can perhaps afford to be more relaxed, as being tie-less suggests a more friendly, less fussy nature – a look which can pay dividends in a creative environment but can lose you marks in a more intense, business-orientated office.

THERE ARE SOME PLACES, of course, where a tie is essential. Many traditional members' clubs insist on one, as do some of the calendar's social events – The Stewards' Enclosure at Henley, for example – and such rules must always be upheld.

MEANWHILE, ALWAYS REMEMBER that a tie can be both the making of a suit and an essential dash of flair as they will serve to draw another's eye.

CLUB TIES

The origins of club ties are disputed. Some believe that I Zingari, the amateur cricket club formed by old Harrovians in 1845, was responsible, designing ties, blazers and caps themed on their black, orange and gold flag. Others theorise that club ties were a natural development from the 'old school ties', which originated when public school sporting teams began to tie the coloured bands from their boaters around their necks in the mid-19th century. Since then school, club and regimental ties have been used to denote membership of a set and as the identifying tags of social status. Stripes on British ties always start high on the left and slope to the right. American striped ties slant in the opposite direction.

TI(M)ELINE

1950
Club tie
AS WORN BY: Bankers

1955
Bootlace
AS WORN BY: Teddy boys

1960
Skinny tie
AS WORN BY: Mods

1965
Kipper tie
AS WORN BY: Hippies

1970
Psychedelic tie
AS WORN BY: Hippies

1975
Wide tie
AS WORN BY: Disco dwellers

1980
Skinny tie
AS WORN BY: Punks, mods

1985
Leather tie
AS WORN BY: Pop stars

1990
Bold, bright tie
AS WORN BY: Bankers

1995
Novelty tie
AS WORN BY: Idiots

2000
Skinny tie
AS WORN BY: Indie bands

2005
No tie
AS WORN BY: Prime Ministers

STYLE GUIDE KNOTS

FOUR IN HAND

THE LOOK: classic

YES OR NO: can leave your neck looking bare but will never be wrong.

HOW TO:
{1} Start with the wide end of the tie hanging a foot below the narrow end.
{2} Bring the wide end up and through the hole at the neck, then thread it through the knot.
{3} Pull the knot up to the neck to tighten.

HALF WINDSOR

THE LOOK: contemporary

YES OR NO: perhaps the most useful knot because it's wide enough to fill a shirt collar without making you look like an estate agent.

HOW TO:
{1} Adjust your tie so that the wide end is on the right, hanging a foot below the narrow end.
{2} Cross the wide end over the narrow and then back underneath.
{3} Next, bring the wide end up and then down through the loop.
{4} Bring the wide end across from left to right.
{5} Turn the wide end up, through the neck loop and then down through the knot in front.

WINDSOR

THE LOOK: footballer

YES OR NO: "the mark of a cad," according to James Bond.

HOW TO:
{1} Start with the wide end on the right, a foot and half below the narrow end.
{2} Take the wide end over the narrow end, from right to left, and then up through the middle of the neck loop, before returning it to the left.
{3} Take the wide end from the left to the right, behind the narrow end.
{4} Take the wide end up through the middle of the neck loop and then across the front from left to right.
{5} Take the wide end up and through the neck loop and then down through the knot.

TIE RULES

DO buy silk ties with a wool interlining. It will feel classier, look better and last longer.

DO wear a tie clip to add a little extra to your tie.

DO remember that wool ties can create a different and intriguing look.

DO experiment. Ties serve no practical purpose, so they may as well serve a sartorial one.

DO roll ties up, but never fold them, when packing. Should they emerge wrinkled, hang them in a steamy bathroom rather than iron them.

DON'T tuck your tie into your trousers. It should reach just above the waistband, but never be inside it.

DON'T match your tie to a pocket square. It couldn't be more wrong.

DON'T leave your tie at half-mast. A tie, when worn with a suit, should be properly done up.

DON'T be too extreme. Too wide and you look like a wind-sock, too narrow and you'll look a country and western singer.

DON'T ever go novelty. Flowers, stripes and bold colours are fine, The Simpsons is not.

Tiesight

THE AMERICAN JOURNAL OF OPHTHALMOLOGY in 2003 found that tying a necktie too tightly could increase pressure on the eyeballs by constricting the jugular vein. As a result, their findings indicated that, over time, this pressure increase could lead to glaucoma.

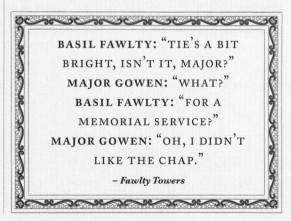

BASIL FAWLTY: "TIE'S A BIT BRIGHT, ISN'T IT, MAJOR?"
MAJOR GOWEN: "WHAT?"
BASIL FAWLTY: "FOR A MEMORIAL SERVICE?"
MAJOR GOWEN: "OH, I DIDN'T LIKE THE CHAP."

– Fawlty Towers

KNOWLEDGE
HOW TO BUY A WATCH

A brand name should be a guarantee of quality. The more respected the brand, generally the better the watch, though be aware that you may well have to pay for the privilege.

Buy your watch from a place renowned for selling timepieces. A brand that has a rich history of telling time will often provide a better watch than those which are new to the game.

Ensure you know what you want. Like buying a bespoke suit, there are companies which will be only too happy to discuss the minutiae of the watch's movement, its mechanisms and details. There are also those whose watches will be built for short-term fashion rather than long-term quality.

Choose carefully. For a watch to retain its magic, you should be able to develop a lasting relationship with it. There's nothing worse than being bored with your watch six months after you've spent a lot of money on it – you should still be fascinated by it and feel good when wearing it year after year.

Research your watch. Find out what it stands for and its heritage. These are the things that allow you to develop a rapport with it.

Try on a lot of watches. What looks good in the shop may not look good on your wrist.

If you're buying a serious watch, you should be buying a mechanical one. There are one or two collectable digital watches but, mostly, they should be confined to the gym.

Trust your instincts. It's likely that you've been wearing a watch for most of your life. All that experience means that you probably, if only subconsciously, know exactly what you're looking for.

A watch is never about just telling the time. Buy into a brand and indulge in the luxury. Take the time to look at the heritage of the company too – it will usually be reflected in their watches.

MONEY MATTERS:
WHY SPEND MONEY ON A WATCH

THE ARGUMENT THAT WATCHES are the only item of jewellery it is acceptable for men to wear is perhaps beginning to wear thin in an age when male rings, bracelets and even necklaces are becoming more prevalent. Watches are becoming less and less essential given the accurate time-telling capabilities of mobile phones, pdas and other devices that are now essential to modern day living. And so, as the watch becomes less useful for telling the time, the fact that it is not essential makes it, once again, the luxury object it used to be.

REMEMBER THAT MEN have a side of their brain that is logged into the functioning of mechanical objects. As a portable mechanical object, there is nothing better than a wristwatch, so start collecting. As such, a serious watch should be mechanical, rather than digital or radio-controlled. Having so many hundreds of moving parts all working accurately on your wrist is precisely where the appeal lies.

Investing in Watches

While investing in watches can be lucrative, it is also something of which to be wary as there are no guarantees. The big name watch brands are often the safest places to put your money as their lengthy history would suggest they will continue to be desirable. As with most collections, rare is good.

Fashion watches are far more hit and miss as what is in fashion today may never be in fashion again. With that in mind, never buy something that you dislike solely because you think it may be valuable in the future. If its value plummets, you can at least get some wear from a watch you genuinely like.

"FAR OUT IN THE UNCHARTED BACKWATERS OF THE UNFASHIONABLE END OF THE WESTERN SPIRAL ARM OF THE GALAXY LIES A SMALL, UNREGARDED YELLOW SUN. ORBITING THIS AT A DISTANCE OF ROUGHLY 92 MILLION MILES IS AN UTTERLY INSIGNIFICANT LITTLE BLUE-GREEN PLANET WHOSE APE-DESCENDED LIFE FORMS ARE SO AMAZINGLY PRIMITIVE THAT THEY STILL THINK DIGITAL WATCHES ARE A PRETTY NEAT IDEA." – *Douglas Adams, Hitchhiker's Guide to the Galaxy*

STYLE GUIDE WATCHES

MATCH YOUR WATCH to your outfit. For example, if you are wearing a dinner jacket, you don't want something huge and overly-noticeable on your wrist.

HAVE MORE THAN ONE WATCH. You wouldn't go for a work-out in your suit and, by the same token, there are certain watches that are wrong for certain occasions.

MAKE SURE YOU HAVE FUN with your watches. Women are allowed to do so with their handbags and accessories, so why shouldn't men do exactly the same with what they wear on their wrists?

WATCHES ARE NAMED AFTER FILM STARS and explorers for a reason. There's nothing wrong with feeling like Steve McQueen when you slip yours on.

POCKET-WATCHES ARE FINE as an affectation, but you need a big personality to pull them off. They're fun but possibly a little contrived.

DIAMONDS ARE A GIRL's best friend. Not a man's.

HOW TO STORE YOUR WATCHES

Storage is an important aspect of caring for your watch. If you have paid four or five figures for a watch, it is likely to be one of your most valuable possessions. Look after it and don't just sling it in a drawer.

Some watches require very special care. A perpetual calendar watch – which will tell the day, month, year and even the phase of the moon for years to come – requires a great deal of attention as resetting them, if they aren't worn for a week, will be enormously fiddly and time consuming.

It is a good idea to carefully store such watches in a watch-winding box. There's not much point in having a moon-face indicator that is inaccurate because of incorrect storage.

Getting your watches serviced regularly is important. It is normally adequate to take them in once every three years so that the moving parts can be lubricated, the seals can be replaced, and the balance wheel can be checked.

If you are likely to swim in a watch, you should get its seals checked once a year. If water gets inside your mechanism, you will be facing a hefty bill.

 EXPERT TIP If you're going to start collecting watches, then a secure safe is vital investment. Also, make sure that they are covered by your insurance policy.

Wedding Rings

Once, wedding bands were the preserve of women alone. It took the Second World War to change things when men, away from home on the front, took to wearing one to remind them of their wife. Slowly times have changed and now it is common for most married men to wear one – though it is certainly not compulsory.

The key to wearing a wedding ring is in picking one that is right for you – neither too wide for your fingers, nor so slender as to appear feminine. Unless you are absolutely set on a gold ring, platinum is by far the best option. Though more expensive, it is strong, durable and hypo-allergenic. It will last longer than silver or white gold as the metal, when scratched, is just displaced rather than worn away. Platinum rings also wear down to a suitably satisfying dull sheen.

MALE JEWELLERY

{1}

Accent your current look, rather than draw attention to something new.

{2}

As a general rule, understatement is key.

{3}

A chunky ID bracelet will look more Del Trotter than globetrotter.

{4}

Beaded necklaces suit surfers, not suit-wearers.

{5}

Anything encrusted with diamonds should be for your other half, not you.

SIGNET RINGS

Originally, the signet ring was used to imprint the wearer's coat of arms in the wax seal on the back of an envelope or scroll. Now, however, the signet serves no real practical purpose whatsoever and is used more frequently to denote membership of a family or club. Worn, generally, on the little finger of the left hand, they should be made of gold and have a crest on the flat surface. The best are those with actual meaning; crests should not be invented purely for the adornment of fingers.

KNOWLEDGE SHOE TYPES

BROGUES

The classic office and business shoe, perfect with a suit and can also be matched, less formally, with jeans when in brown. Easily identified by the distinctive patterns across the toe, and available as a full or half-brogue, these are perhaps the most essential shoe in the wardrobe.

OXFORD

The epitome of English style, understated, classic and perfect with a suit – so much so that they have always been James Bond's shoe of choice. Similar in shape to a brogue, though without the patterned toes, these are plain and simple. They should be of black or brown polished leather; more casually, or with flannel trousers, they can also look good in suede.

DERBY

Less formal than the Oxford or the brogue, though similar in shape, these are unfussy in either brown or black. Often with only two or three eyelets for lacing, they are an ideal way to dress down a suit. They can also be worn more casually with jeans.

MONK SHOE

Halfway between a formal Oxford and a loafer, the monk shoe is generally built fairly high to accommodate the buckle, so can impact on the fall and hang of suit trousers. They look best cut quite narrow, matched with slim cut trousers.

DRESS SHOES

Traditionally, these should be patent leather pumps, worn with a dinner jacket, but it takes a bold man … More recently, it has been fashionable to wear dress shoes with jeans. They should be polished to a dazzling gleam.

LOAFER

Loafers are one of the most informal and convenient shoes, but wear with caution. An American innovation, developed by Italian shoemakers, they represent a continental style and are best paired with chinos or jeans.

ANKLE BOOT

The ankle boot tends to look wrong with a formal suit and should, therefore, be avoided for strict dress codes. However, with slim cut suits, they can create a mod-like look which will work in less formal situations.

 EXPERT TIP Try matching a pinstripe suit and brown suede shoes for a stylish, classically English look.

HOW TO SPIT AND POLISH

SPIT AND POLISH WILL CREATE THE BEST POSSIBLE SHINE ON A SHOE. IT IS A SHINE ACHIEVED WITHOUT BRUSHES, BUT WITH JUST A CLOTH, SOME POLISH, WATER AND ELBOW-GREASE. {1} WITH A MOIST CLOTH, THOUGH NOT OVERLY WET, APPLY POLISH TO YOUR SHOE. {2} RUB A SMALL AREA BRISKLY UNTIL IT IS NO LONGER CLOUDY. {3} REPEAT MANY TIMES OVER DIFFERENT, SMALL AREAS. {4} STAND BACK AND CHECK YOUR REFLECTION IN THE TOE CAP.

Lace-Up

There are multiple ways to lace a shoe, but there are three that are the most effective. The strongest, and best looking, is to have the laces crossing parallel to one another. A basic criss-cross is also sturdy, though doesn't tend to look quite as good. A more stylish option is to criss-cross the laces over the top, and then feed them up and underneath the eyelets, rather than across the tongue.

Laces, generally, should be of the same colour as the shoe. An eye-catching look can be created by adding either off-white laces to brown shoes, or by sporting brightly coloured ones.

GET IT RIGHT: SOCKS

There is one essential rule for socks: they should always be long enough. That means that, when you cross your legs as you sit down, an inch or two of calf flesh should not suddenly appear underneath your trousers.

In terms of colour and pattern, however, there are two schools of thought. One is that, no matter what, your socks should be plain, unpatterned and preferably black (unless, you are wearing a brown belt, in which case they should be brown or possibly grey).

The other opinion is that they are a chance to add some sparkle. Some people like to have a bit of fun, and add some flash. It is, however, really up to you, but go for spots or stripes and never wear novelty pairs featuring cartoon characters.

Socks can also be matched with your jacket and tie; some say you should also match them to your belt, but that's not to everyone's taste.

While, once, the rule used to be 'wool for winter and cotton for summer', good quality, thin, cotton socks should be adequate for most of the year.

POLISHING RULES

{1}

Polishing regularly but briefly will give better results than polishing sporadically but vigorously.

{2}

It is best to use shoe polish or wax, though good quality shoe cream can be effective – avoid the sponge-like devices that claim to contain polish.

{3}

Black shoes, being colourless, should reflect as much light as possible; however, the tone of brown shoes should be emphasised, so polish them with a wax of slightly lighter colour than the shoe itself.

SHOE CARE

Ideally, you should own a different pair of shoes for every day of the week. While this sounds impractical, remember that a good pair of shoes should last you most of your life if cared for properly, hence an investment now will spare one later. Leather shoes ought to be rested for at least a couple of days after they are worn in order for them to dry out. If you have five pairs, you can apply a coat of polish to your shoes each night. Without buffing, allow the polish to absorb into the shoes, thus feeding the leather, over the course of the week. The shoes can then be given a quick polish before leaving the house.

•

As soon as you remove a shoe, place a shoe-tree inside it as the leather is at its most malleable when warm – i.e. when it's been on your foot. The shoe tree should be made of unvarnished cedar, too, as this will draw out any excess moisture from inside the shoe.

•

If your shoes are wet, fill them with newspaper as soon as possible to absorb the moisture as they dry. Never leave them near a source of heat, like a fire or radiator, as this will instantly dry out the leather and warp the shape of the shoe.

•

Dirt should be removed carefully with a damp cloth and should never be soaked out. For suede shoes, remove any mud with a stiff brush and then bring up the nap with a suede brush. If possible, don't wear suede shoes in the rain.

•

Your sole should be made of leather, which should be replaced when they become worn down. This may cost £60 to £70 but, once done, essentially leaves you with a brand new pair of shoes.

•

Never add stick-on soles or metal clips to either the toes or the heels as these will upset the balance of your shoe. You'll also make a racket while walking down the street.

SHOE TRIVIA: Holes were first placed in brogues in Ireland to allow water from walking through peat bogs to drain away from the shoe. However, when Goodyear Welt was invented – the waterproof technique of bonding a shoe's sole and its upper – the holes became obsolete except as a style statement.

ELEVEN CLASSIC COATS

{I} *Bomber Jacket*
Who wears one: The Clash, James Dean
Identify it: similar to a Harrington (see below) but fuller and more like a blouson. They should always have a ribbed cuff.
Why wear one: both classic and contemporary, it's a coat that will never go out of style.

•

{II} *Chesterfield*
Who wears one: Roger Moore's James Bond
Identify it: thigh-length, double or single-breasted, woollen and often in grey herringbone.
Why wear one: an alternative to the Crombie, it is a versatile, smart, formal coat that, again, can be worn more casually.

•

{III} *Crombie*
Who wears one: Morrissey
Identify it: thigh-length, single breasted and occasionally with a velvet collar.
Why wear one: the classic English town-coat. A wardrobe essential; can be paired with both a suit and more casual attire.

•

{IV} *Duffel Coat*
Who wears one: Field Marshal Montgomery, Paddington Bear
Identify it: thigh-length, hooded, navy blue, brown or black, toggles essential.
Why wear one: classic, warm and quirky. A good way to dress down a suit.

•

{V} *Harrington*
Who wears one: Steve McQueen, Frank Sinatra
Identify it: short, fitted to waist-length, lightweight and essential to any wardrobe.
Why wear one: effortlessly cool and, despite being 70 years old, they still feel contemporary.

•

{VI} *The Mackintosh*
Who wears one: Columbo, Michael Caine
Identify it: made of rubber, this is the original waterproof jacket.
Why wear one: perhaps a more styled waterproof than a wax jacket, this is both versatile and eminently useful. Fantastic for a downpour but not so good in warmer weather.

{VII} *Parka*
Who wears one: Liam Gallagher
Identify it: with a fur-lined hood and capacious body and pockets, it's both warm and practical.
Why wear one: while it is a great look when paired with casual clothes, it tends not to work so well with suits.

•

{VIII} *Pea Coat*
Who wears one: Marlon Brando in *On The Waterfront*
Identify it: hip-length, double-breasted and navy blue. Think of sailors.
Why wear one: can double up as both a smart and casual jacket. Plus it's warm.

•

{IX} *Shearling Coat*
Who wears one: Arthur Daley, John Motson
Identify it: leather on the outside, lamb's wool on the inside, often with big wool collar.
Why wear one: warmth, and just the right side of geezer.

•

{X} *Trench Coat*
Who wears one: Humphrey Bogart
Identify it: long, waterproof and often lined, it is built for turning up the collar and avoiding the elements.
Why wear one: originally designed for British soldiers, it is practical, warm and functional.

•

{XI} *Wax Jacket*
Who wears one: Guy Ritchie, Royalty
Identify it: frequently green or brown, it is warm, dry, eminently matter-of-fact and strikingly British.
Why wear one: the quintessential waterproof jacket. Look after it and it will last you a lifetime.

Are Pac-a-Macs Acceptable?

A jacket should always perform. There is nothing worse than dealing with that awkward time of year – when it might be warm one minute, then rain the next – if you don't have a jacket that can cope.

Cagoules and pac-a-macs are practical, lightweight, stowable and allowed to be creased. They may not always look fantastic, but they will rarely let you down.

HATS: WHO'S WHO

THE SAMUEL L JACKSON
The backwards, baggy, beret is a tough look to pull off but one which actor Samuel L Jackson has made his own. It says casual cool and *laissez-faire*; it is ideal for dressing down a look.

THE DEAN MARTIN
A descendant of the fedora and the boater, the 'pork-pie' – named after the food – has always had a jazz and musical connection. Dean Martin, for one, was a fan of its broad brim and flat top, while musicians from jazz saxophonist Lester Young to the mods of the early 80s were also fans.

THE FRANK SINATRA
Elegant and simple, a fedora remains a classic hat. Pinched at the front, with a crease along the middle and medium brim, it speaks of both Humphrey Bogart and, more recently, Pete Doherty. But the classic wearer was Frank Sinatra who pushed his back on the head and bent the brim forward.

THE JAMES BOND
Similar to a fedora, the trilby is essentially a more pared down version of the same hat. With a narrower brim and made of a softer felt, it creates a more restrained and British look.

THE CHARLIE CHAPLIN
Outdated now, the bowler hat, immortalised by Charlie Chaplin, has maybe had its day. Conjuring evocative images of early-to-mid 20th-century businessmen commuting to work, it's a hat that denotes formality, city conformity and uniform. A hard hat, they were originally intended to protect gamekeepers from blows around the head from poachers but soon became a signifier of the middle-class, representing the middle ground between the top hat of the upper classes and the flat caps of the lower.

THE GODFATHER
Bigger, broader and without the pinched sides of the fedora and trilby, the homburg is a larger hat than both its contemporaries. Popularised by Edward VII but popular with the 1920s gangsters of America, it now conjures up connotations of modern jazz musicians.

THE MAGICIAN
The traditional top hat is now only worn with morning dress, evening dress or by magicians and guitarists. Made of black silk, it should be worn on the front of the head.

SCARVES

Scarves serve two purposes. The first, obviously, is as a means of keeping you warm. The second, more sartorially, is almost as an alternative to the neckerchief. Silk or cotton scarves are the best for the latter. Available in an infinitesimal range of patterns, they can be ideal for wearing inside the office to brighten up your look. Cashmere and wool-knit scarves are for keeping you warm, but that doesn't mean they shouldn't look good too. Like ties, it is often best to gauge the flamboyance of your scarf with your personality. Big, bold characters can get away with brighter scarves, while the more reserved might prefer something in a sleek, pinstriped grey.

Meanwhile, tying your scarf couldn't be simpler. There may be myriad different ways, but simply folding your scarf in half, placing it behind your neck and tucking the loose end into the folded end under your neck will always work well.

GLOVES

WHILE MODERN-DAY CARS, WITH THEIR HIGHLY-DESIGNED STEERING WHEELS AND EFFECTIVE AIR CONDITIONING SYSTEMS, MAY MAKE DRIVING GLOVES OBSOLETE, THEY DON'T MAKE A PAIR MADE OF SOFT LEATHER ANY LESS DESIRABLE. YOU MAY NOT NEED THEM FOR WARMTH, BUT YOU WILL CERTAINLY NEED THEM FOR THAT FEELING OF HERITAGE AND LUXURY.

•

OUTSIDE OF THE CAR, GLOVES ARE ESSENTIAL IN THE COLD WINTER MONTHS. AVOID MITTENS AS THEY MAKE DOING ANYTHING AT ALL IMPOSSIBLE. INSTEAD, ENSURE YOUR GLOVES ARE LEATHER OR SUEDE, WITH A WOOL, CASHMERE OR SILK LINING.

STYLE GUIDE PENS

IN THE AGE OF THE EMAIL and the computer, pens make a style statement. A fountain pen speaks of tradition, it also suggests care and attention and, for someone who craves luxury, what could be more bespoke than a pen whose nib moulds itself to your individual handwriting – so much so that the pen may become unusable for anyone else?

WRITING IN PEN also focuses the mind. There is no delete button, no backspace, so words must be considered and chosen carefully before being committed to paper, making their meaning all the more succinct. Fountain pens should be filled from an inkwell because, though cartridges are more efficient, there is something inexpressibly pleasing about drawing ink through your pen's nib.

BIROS AND BALL-POINTS are a different matter and, if possible, gentlemen should have two: one for the desk and something slimmer and more lightweight for the inside jacket pocket. Disposable biros, meanwhile, are for writing shopping lists only.

Modern Technology

Worker bees and magnates argue that, in this era of 24/7, minute-by-minute developments, their careers are at stake if they do not keep up – via a wireless handheld device – when they're out of the office. Yet the sight of someone at a dinner table, casting furtive glances at their little friend, lined up beside their plate like a modern-day napkin, is a little obsessive and off-putting. Those in the know refrain from checking their gadgets when in company. They don't make their friends feel like they are hanging around their desk, talking to them while they are trying to work. Well-behaved addicts will only have a double date with their electronic gizmos in the privacy of their own home or office.

MP3 ETIQUETTE

Be aware that your music – distorted, tinny, percussive, maddening – may be audible to those around you from your headphones. Adjust the volume accordingly, or invest in a good quality pair that won't force you to share your musical preferences with the rest of the train carriage.

TEN LONGHAND
WRITERS

Martin Amis • Paul Auster • J.G. Ballard
Truman Capote • Ernest Hemingway
Hanif Kureishi • Elmore Leonard • Ian McEwan
Michael Ondaatje • Philip Pullman

By Hand

Just like the demise of the book, the death of handwriting should not be assumed. The dangers of rushed email or the bashed-out, impersonal "R U OK? I am gr8" ugliness of texting – all these fade into white noise beside the stylish, deliberated simplicity of the handwritten note.

•

Crisp vellum stationery, the elegant flow of letters pouring across a clean page: these are the building blocks of our civilisation. Yes, we now have the printed word, but do we really want future civilisations to believe that ours was an age of bank statements and bureaucracy?

•

Handwritten notes are both personal and permanent; postcards survive to amuse well beyond the first "Wish you were here" impulse. And remember, a love letter is worth a thousand texts.

THE PEN IS MIGHTIER THAN THE SWORD.

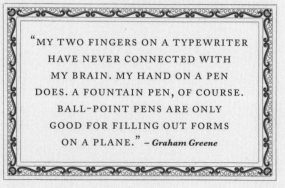

"MY TWO FINGERS ON A TYPEWRITER HAVE NEVER CONNECTED WITH MY BRAIN. MY HAND ON A PEN DOES. A FOUNTAIN PEN, OF COURSE. BALL-POINT PENS ARE ONLY GOOD FOR FILLING OUT FORMS ON A PLANE." – *Graham Greene*

BAG MEN

BRIEFCASE: in most offices, dress codes have relaxed to a level where briefcases have become outdated. In formal offices, however, a briefcase still makes a statement. It should be made of black or brown leather.

LAPTOP BAG: the successor to the briefcase, the laptop bag is now perhaps the most useful work-wear bag. However, cheap, nylon cases are ubiquitous and seem to be *de rigueur*. Instead, stand out from the crowd and buy a structured, padded, leather bag that offers its cargo protection.

DOCUMENT CASE: more formal than the laptop bag, less stiff than the briefcase, the document case is a business classic that affords you a touch of individuality. Most can now be bought with a leather strap that allows them to be worn over the shoulder or strapped across the body.

MESSENGER BAGS: similarly sized to a laptop bag – or smaller and neater – the so-called 'man-bag' is now not so much accepted as essential. Casual enough to be worn at weekends, but useful enough to be crucial for work, this is the ideal dumping ground for a phone, pda, mp3 player, camera, notebook and pen.

RECORD BAGS: an alternative to the messenger bag, the record bag – slung casually over a shoulder – is a practical, cool, casual and versatile.

SHOPPER OR TOTE: a leather shopper or tote is the perfect alternative to a messenger bag or the formality of a briefcase. Spacious and versatile, they offer a practical and stylish choice.

Wallet Wise

CREDIT CARD, BILLFOLD: the classic, fold-in-half, four credit card-carrying, fit-in-your-trouser-pocket wallet. Buy in black or brown leather; canvas wallets won't last as long and don't feel as good in your pocket.

COIN PURSE, BILLFOLD: similar to the classic wallet but with a pouch for carrying small change. Will have to be hard-wearing in order to cope with the extra weight of the money stored within.

COAT WALLET: slim, tall and designed to fit inside your inside jacket pocket. A more formal, and more old-school, style of wallet. Bigger than pocket wallets, they have more room for credit cards and sometimes even cheque books.

SLIMLINE WALLET: credit cards are rapidly taking over from paper money, so wallets catering solely for plastic are a popular choice. They may contain debit or credit cards and your swipe pass for work, while the unobtrusive styling means your tailor will thank you for preserving the lines of your suit.

TRAVEL WALLET: bigger than a standard wallet and designed to fit your passport, boarding pass, traveller's cheques and foreign currency. Those with zips are often the most secure and practical.

MONEY CLIP: lighten your load with a leather credit card case in one pocket and money clip in the other. Beware though – money clips may suit larger-than-life movie Mafiosos, but they look considerably less stylish in the local.

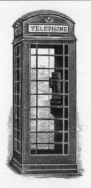

Mobile Manners

First and foremost, don't let your conversation disturb other people.

•

Observe a church-like silence in 'quiet zones' on trains.

•

Carriages of commuters really aren't interested in your business.

•

Avoid intimate conversations – unless you want to broadcast your secrets.

•

Switch off your phone when you are going into meetings, theatres, cinemas etc. and avoid ringtone embarrassment.

•

Zany, intrusive or comical ringtones are rarely amusing.

•

Turn off your phone in face-to-face social situations, or you may soon find yourself condemned to interfacing with your gadgets.

•

Don't put your phone on the dining table, or glance at it longingly mid-conversation.

If you have to take a call when you are meeting someone socially, apologise in advance. If you don't warn them, they'll feel justifiably marginalised.

Never take a call in front of other people in social situations; why import your private business to the dinner table? Excuse yourself and withdraw somewhere private to make or receive calls.

THE A–Z OF GETTING AHEAD

A is for Arrogance: superiority doesn't make for success.
B is for Blunder: minor, keep quiet; major, confess.
C is for Conduct: be professional.
D is for Deliver: hit deadlines.
E is for Eating: don't comment on others' dietary habits.
F is for Flirting: never in the office.
G is for Gossip: avoid rumour and lies.
H is for Honesty: use with caution.
I is for Internet: surf with care.
J is for Jokes: keep them clean.
K is for Keenness: enthusiastic, not desperate.
L is for Listen: be all ears.
M is for Mood: avoid extreme swings.
N is for Nosiness: remember the boundaries.
O is for Over-Familiarity: they're colleagues, not mates.
P is for Personal Space: respect it.
Q is for Quiet: keep the peace.
R is for Respect: remember the pecking order.
S is for Sex: always a risky business.
T is for Tea: get your round in.
U is for Underdressed: keep it smart.
V is for Visionary: express your ideas.
W is for Waffle: stick to the point.
X is for X-Rated: after hours only.
Y is for Yawning: never a good look.
Z is for Zzzzz: never at your desk.

INTERVIEW SUCCESS

- Dress appropriately for the formality of the company.
- Shake hands firmly, sit up straight, maintain eye contact.
- Don't cross your arms, hunch your shoulders, fiddle or fidget.
- Speak clearly, and respond immediately to what is being said.
- Prepare – know about the organisation.
- Enthuse about your achievements; keep it relevant to the job.
- Always ask questions – they stimulate good conversation.
- Listen to the answers.
- Be honest and never name-drop.
- Never flirt.
- Promotion favours the polite: be well-mannered.
- Whatever the outcome, your response should be gracious.
- Never burn bridges.

Handshakes

Be firm, but don't clench in a bone-crushing grip.
Never offer a limp or sweaty hand.
Your fingers should grip the other person's palm.
Don't crush their fingers.
Make eye contact for full impact and sincerity.

How to Ask for a Pay Rise

DON'T BE SCARED: if you don't ask, you don't get.
DO IT PROPERLY: book an official meeting with your boss.
DO YOUR RESEARCH: check the going rate for
similar roles and assess what you're worth.
TIME IT RIGHT: don't choose a time when
your boss is very busy or stressed.
ARE YOU WORTH IT? check that your
performance/input has increased.
CHOOSE A FIGURE: think about what you'd
really like and ask for a bit more.
AVOID ULTIMATUMS: don't threaten to leave
(unless you're serious) – they may just say okay.

HANDLE THE BOSS	BE THE BOSS
Be efficient.	Listen to your staff.
Don't argue.	Recognise strengths.
Be pleasant.	Don't unduly criticise.
Don't flatter.	Understand procedures.
Be willing.	Set reasonable goalposts.
Don't grovel.	Don't shift parameters.
Be capable.	Offer encouragement.
Don't boast.	Deliver praise promptly.
Be patient.	Give rewards when due.
Don't despair.	Keep professional morale high.

STYLE GUIDE MANAGEMENT

David Brent vs Alan Sugar

SUGAR: "I don't like liars, I don't like cheats. I don't like bullshitters. I don't like schmoozers. I don't like arse-lickers."
BRENT: "Avoid employing unlucky people – throw half of the pile of CVs in the bin without reading them."

SUGAR: "I can tell you where every screw, nut and bolt is in my company. I know everything [in my business]. Never, ever, underestimate me."
BRENT: "Those of you who think you know everything are annoying to those of us who do."

SUGAR: "There's only room for one bigmouth in my organisation, and that's me."
BRENT: "I suppose I've created an atmosphere where I'm friend first and boss second and probably entertainer third."

SUGAR: "I gotta tell ya, you're fired!"
BRENT: "If you treat the people around you with love and respect, they will never guess that you're trying to get them sacked."

TEN RULES OF EMAIL ETIQUETTE

> Close attention should be paid to spelling and grammar.
> Classify your email with an informative subject line.
> Be careful of sending messages written in haste.
> Avoid sarcasm and subtle humour unless you know that the reader will 'get it'.
> Err towards the polite and formal.
> Where there is more than one recipient, list them according to hierarchy.
> If you send an email in error, phone the recipient immediately and ask them to ignore/delete the message.
> Check all recipients carefully before hitting 'reply to all'.
> Reply to emails promptly – a simple acknowledgement will buy you time.
> Never send inappropriate, indecent or pornographic emails to colleagues.

SIX MEETING RULES

{1} **Be prepared.** Check the agenda carefully and establish the goals of the meeting.
{2} **Be punctual.** No one wants to wait for you, no matter how important you (think you) are.
{3} **Turn off** your pda/mobile phone.
{4} **Refer to people by name** – make everyone feel included.
{5} **Don't interrupt.** Wait for others to finish their point.
{6} **AOB.** Don't waffle. Stick to what's important.

IT'S ALL IN THE FONT

SERIF: a slight projection finishing off the stroke of the letter. Serifs help the eye to stick to the line, and thus facilitate reading. They are therefore ideal for continuous prose.

OLD STYLE (15TH CENTURY): Renaissance typographers blended Carolingian scripts and Roman uppercase letters to create a new font type better suited to Gutenberg's new printing technology. Characteristics: consistent width of strokes and serifs; cove serifs (forming curves where they join the main strokes); serifs with rounded ends; diagonal stress to imitate handwriting. Classic Old Style Font = Garamond.

TRANSITIONAL (18TH CENTURY): greater contrast (vertical strokes are thicker than horizontal); coves are more exaggerated (appearing triangular); serifs are short and sometimes pointed; design is linear and austere. Classic transitional fonts = Times Roman; Baskerville.

MODERN (19TH CENTURY): dramatic increase in contrast (vertical/horizontal strokes); long hairline serifs; lack of coves and rounded corners. Classic Modern Font = Bodoni (**New Century Schoolbook** is a later derivative).

SANS SERIF: ('without serif'): became prominent in the 1920s and 1930s, especially with the advent of the Bauhaus movement and Russian constructivism. Widely used in signage, titles, labels, logos etc. Classic sans serif types = Gill (1927); Futura (1928); Helvetica (1957); Frutiger (1976).

WHAT YOUR FONT SAYS ABOUT YOU

Baskerville: straightforward, conventional, traditional.
Bodoni: self-consciously old-fashioned; mannered; foppish.
Frutiger: modern, forward-looking, unconventional.
Palatino: elegant, civilised, gentlemanly, a lover of fine art and antiquities.

N.B.: If in doubt, your default font should always be Times Roman: it's functional, clear and uncontroversial. Never ever use script fonts (imitating handwriting – for example Comedy, Lucida Calligraphy etc.).

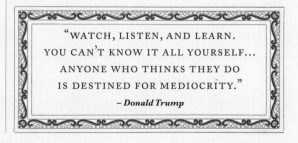

"WATCH, LISTEN, AND LEARN. YOU CAN'T KNOW IT ALL YOURSELF... ANYONE WHO THINKS THEY DO IS DESTINED FOR MEDIOCRITY."
– *Donald Trump*

TEAM SPIRIT *A good team player can…*

GET ALONG WITH COLLEAGUES

COMMUNICATE EFFICIENTLY

KEEP EMOTIONS IN CHECK

ACCEPT RESPONSIBILITY

AWARD PRAISE WHERE DUE

KNOW STRENGTHS AND WEAKNESSES

BE WILLING TO COMPROMISE

STAY CALM AND NOT PANIC

NEVER BLAME TEAM MEMBERS

BE FLEXIBLE

THE OFFICE PARTY

· Be smart and sociable, but know when to draw the line.
· Circulate and socialise, but keep it upbeat and general.
· Ask about families, children and holidays.
· Don't gossip, spread rumours or confess your sins.
· Steer clear of mistletoe and dirty dancing.
· Keep goodnight kisses innocent; wake up alone.
· Never pull a sickie the day after.

Business Trips

Business trips with colleagues seem to re-draw the lines of office etiquette; you're suddenly sleeping with your workmates (or rather snoozing next to them on the plane), breakfasting with them, even sunbathing with them around the hotel pool. But remember that work hierarchies remain. Your boss is still your boss, even when he's in his trunks brandishing an umbrella-ed cocktail. Be flexible and tolerate whatever situation you find yourself in, be it a strip club in Frankfurt, a bathhouse in Istanbul or a karaoke bar in Tokyo. If round-the-clock proximity to your workmates makes you feel claustrophobic, the exercise card is a blameless time-out option. Top tip: if possible, travel to and from the trip separately from your colleagues.

TEN WAYS TO LOOK BUSY
BY GEORGES COSTANZA OF *SEINFELD*

{1}

NEVER WALK WITHOUT A DOCUMENT IN YOUR HANDS

{2}

USE COMPUTERS TO LOOK BUSY

{3}

KEEP A MESSY DESK

{4}

USE VOICE MAIL

{5}

LOOK IMPATIENT AND ANNOYED

{6}

LEAVE THE OFFICE LATE

{7}

USE SIGHING FOR EFFECT

{8}

OPT FOR THE STACKING STRATEGY

{9}

BUILD YOUR VOCABULARY

{10}

DON'T GET CAUGHT

THE LAW OF LIFTS

There is an invisible boundary around people.

·

Be silent, or talk in hushed tones.

·

Allow people to get out before you try to get in.

·

Accept when it's full and wait for the next one.

·

Press buttons for others when you're near the control panel.

·

Activate the 'doors open' / 'doors close' button when required.

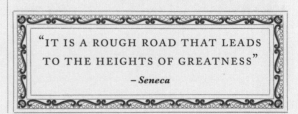

> "IT IS A ROUGH ROAD THAT LEADS TO THE HEIGHTS OF GREATNESS"
> – *Seneca*

Blue Sky Thinking

THE PROBLEM WITH JARGON Let's all be proactive about the way we interface, give it some face-time, run it up the flagpole and kick the tyres, then come up with a value-proposition that really shows we're tasked with thinking the unthinkable and so on. At the end of the day, it all comes down to what you bring to the table. Isn't it time we closed the circle, and concentrated on our core competencies? We need to build a soup to nuts solution, and that means rolling out a seamless paradigm shift. With a world-class approach, and the right synergy, we can take it to the next level. It's win-win. So why not think ouside the box?

THE SOLUTION Don't use jargon to disguise ignorance, wrong-foot colleagues and clients, or conceal ineptitude. Think carefully about what you are trying to say. It is never a mistake to write, and speak, in plain, jargon-free English. You will be praised for the sheer incisiveness of your thinking, and rewarded for your ability to communicate.

OFFICE ROMANCE

Think carefully before hitting on a colleague.

•

Office life will never be the same again once you take the plunge.

•

You could lose your job – are they worth it?

•

Liaisons between bosses and subordinates are usually problematic.

•

Keep it quiet until things get serious.

•

Avoid public displays of affection in the office.

•

Mixing business with pleasure usually ends in tears.

WATER-COOLER SUCCESS

{1} Strike a balance between talking and listening.
{2} Make others feel like you are listening (and interested).
{3} Throw in the occasional non-creepy, genuine-sounding, well-placed compliment.
{4} Ask about weekends, family, children and other-halves.
{5} Gentle humour or a harmless in-joke will oil office politics.
{6} Never talk about money, race, religion, salary, sex, politics, illness or death.
{7} Familiarity comes with time – be aware of unspoken barriers.
{8} Bluffers and serial liars always get their come-uppance. Name-droppers and braggers bore everyone.

MISS DEBRETT *The Man in the Office*

JUST BECAUSE YOU'RE OUR BOSS doesn't mean we have to respect you. But we're more likely to do so if you don't patronise us. Don't boast: it might make you feel big to regale us with tales of your high-flying exploits – boardroom battles, career triumphs, big bucks, business accolades – we will just see you as a sad workhorse who doesn't have a life.

DON'T TRY TO CHARM US: compliments on our appearance (beyond a generalised "You look smart") are risky; nosiness about our personal life is creepy; attempting to be one of the girls by telling off-colour anecdotes is simply offensive. Social flirting is acceptable amongst equals, but beware: if you get the tone even slightly wrong we will fear that you are making a pass, and if we're not interested you will be entering very dangerous (possibly illegal) waters. A better option is to go for an air of relaxed camaraderie.

LISTEN CAREFULLY to what we're saying, don't bully us or talk over us, and defuse all situations with easy-going irony and humour. And remember that, despite the glass ceiling, the boot is increasingly on the other foot.

SO IF YOU END UP with a female boss, treat her with professional respect. Don't for a moment think you can get round her by flirting with her, and ease up on manifestations of old-fashioned chivalry – if you leap to your feet whenever she enters the room you will only serve to emphasise the gender difference.

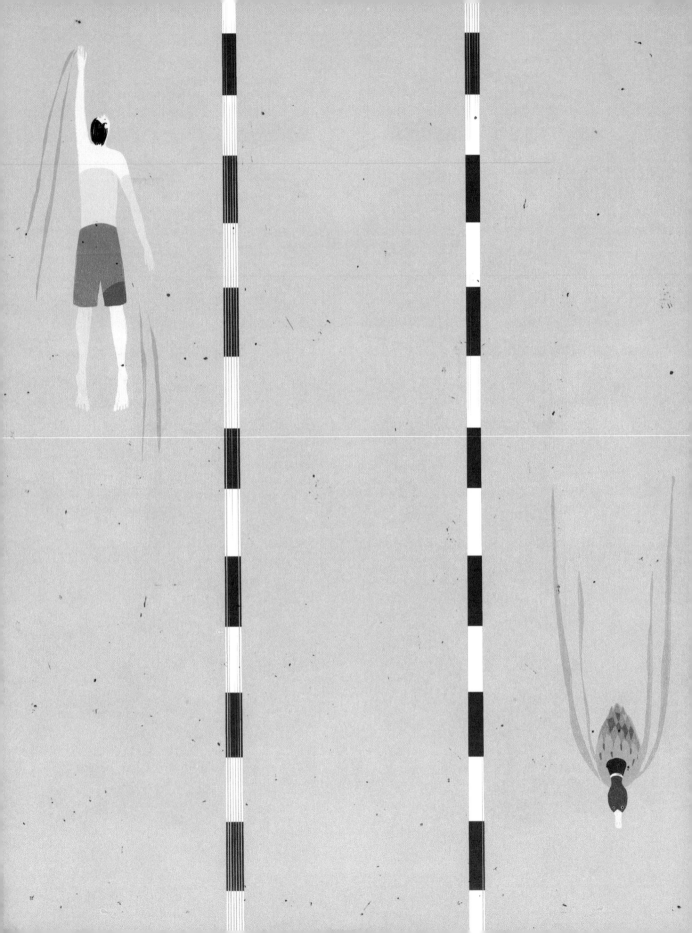

MAINTENANCE

HOW TO GET A HAIRCUT

{1} Be realistic. If you're no longer in your twenties, and if your hair is thinning, the latest style may not be for you.

{2} Your barber wants you to look your best when you leave. You're an advert for his business, so trust his advice.

{3} You can tell your barber that you want your hair to look like a certain actor in a certain film. It makes his job easier, but remember they're not miracle workers.

{4} A barber will gauge your style on your appearance. If you regularly wear a suit, for example, he will tailor your haircut towards that, so wear what you spend much of your time in at the hairdressers.

{5} Tell your barber what you do for a living, what you like to do in your spare time, and as much detail about yourself as you're comfortable with. It all helps tailor your haircut specifically to your life.

{6} You should look after your hair, which means getting it cut once every five weeks or so. Remember, also, that you get what you pay for.

{7} If you prefer not to spend money regularly on a haircut, you should still visit a high-end salon once. Then, before the lines of your haircut have grown out – i.e. after about three or four weeks – go to your usual, cheaper place. They can then use your previous haircut as a guide.

{8} If your barber gets out his clippers before his scissors – unless you have a shaved head – leave immediately.

THE THREE BASIC HAIRCUTS

The Steve McQueen

The Elvis Presley

The Peter Fonda

ESSENTIALLY THERE ARE three simple haircuts: the short, medium, or long – or, The Steve McQueen, The Elvis Presley and The Peter Fonda. These are the basis for virtually every hairstyle.

WHILE YOUR CLOTHES can be changed on a daily basis, you wear your hair seven days a week, 24 hours a day. It is, therefore, one of the most important things to get right about the way you look. There's little point in donning a bespoke suit and pairing it with a badly-cut barnet that doesn't suit your clothes or your lifestyle .

BY THE TIME YOU HIT your thirties, you should know how your hair behaves and, more crucially, what it is likely to do over your remaining years – fall out, go grey or stay much the same.

MUCH OF WHAT SUITS you will be determined by your hair-type and face shape. Talk to your hairdresser about what will suit you; they have seen many more heads than you and will know all the tricks to make sure you walk away with the right cut for your hair and face. Spend some time and work out what makes you look, and feel, good.

Barber Etiquette

BARBERS AND HAIRDRESSERS spend a lot of time in close contact with strangers. As a result, they are often skilled at reading signals. They can assess moods quickly and, if they are experienced, they will react accordingly. If you've had a bad day and don't want to talk, that's fine, as long as you're not silent to the point of rudeness. Alternatively, if you fancy a chat, then go for it, but don't hold up the barber.

SOMETHING THAT IS GUARANTEED to irritate the person cutting your hair is talking on the phone. The odd call is fine, and your barber should stand back and let you take it. However, repeated phone calls make your hairdresser's job impossible and your haircut is likely to suffer.

KNOW ROUGHLY what you want when you sit in the chair. Talk to your barber; tell him your style, your likes and your dislikes. The first time you go to a new barber, you should have a fairly detailed chat with them before they get started. This is important as it will establish what you have in mind for the cut, and gives you the chance to ask some questions. Never simply say, "do what you think is best". You won't end up with a haircut that you want, but one your barber wants to give you.

IF YOU'RE HAPPY with your haircut, then tip – usually around 10 per cent. In salons, you can tip the person who washed your hair, rather than the person who cut it; one will be earning considerably less than the other.

AT A TRADITIONAL BARBERS, it is okay to wait for the person you want to cut your hair to be free, even if others are available. It's your money, after all.

UPKEEP

SHORT HAIR

Keep short hair in check with a matt paste. It will add texture and control to your hair. It should also be water-soluble so that it can be easily rinsed out. Avoid heavy waxes as they are hard to wash out of your hair, meaning they will block your pores and cuticles.

•

MEDIUM HAIR

Medium length hair should have a natural flow to it, so heavy products should be avoided. Instead, use something gel based that will add texture but won't stiffen your hair. The gel should be malleable and easy to apply.

•

LONG HAIR

Hair with length shouldn't need too many products. However, many people with long hair tend to leave it to look after itself. To keep it in good nick, use a leave-in conditioner in the same way that shorter-haired people use hair gel. It will create some hold, but won't go crispy or rock hard. It is a quick and easy way to look after your hair.

All hair types

YOU SHOULDN'T WASH YOUR HAIR too frequently as you wash out the body's natural nutrients. On the other hand, many people don't feel clean unless their hair is clean – no-one wants sweaty, dirty and greasy hair .

IT IS THEREFORE BEST TO USE a very good quality, mild shampoo in small doses. A five pence piece-worth should suffice, unless you have very long hair.

CONDITIONER FEEDS YOUR HAIR and keeps it nourished. For longer hair, it should be used once or twice a week, and left on for as long as possible – a leave-in conditioner is ideal. Conditioner is not totally necessary for anyone with shorter hair, providing that their hair is kept well cut and is in very good condition.

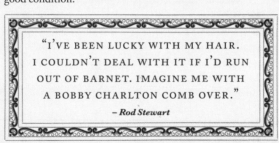

> "I'VE BEEN LUCKY WITH MY HAIR.
> I COULDN'T DEAL WITH IT IF I'D RUN
> OUT OF BARNET. IMAGINE ME WITH
> A BOBBY CHARLTON COMB OVER."
> – *Rod Stewart*

HOW TO WASH YOUR HAIR

WET HAIR WITH WARM WATER. SQUEEZE A FIVE PENCE PIECE WORTH OF SHAMPOO INTO PALM.

•

RUB PALMS AND START A LATHER, SMOOTH OVER HAIR AND SCALP. MASSAGE WITH FINGERTIPS IN SMALL CIRCULAR MOTIONS. RINSE UNTIL WATER RUNS BUBBLE-FREE.

•

WORK A SMALL AMOUNT OF CONDITIONER THROUGH HAIR. LEAVE AS LONG AS POSSIBLE, THEN RINSE THOROUGHLY.

How to go bald

{1} Get a good haircut. Not everybody has the head-shape to shave all their hair off, and not everyone who's losing it wants to make such a bold mover either. It's more important to keep hair short and neat if it's getting thin.
{2} Keep your hair at an even length all over – it will make you look sharper.
{3} Don't live in denial.
{4} Never, ever get a comb over. Everyone knows what you're up to and you'll be a laughing stock.
{5} At all costs avoid adverts in the back of the paper that promise growth, hair weaves and other similar remedies.

How to go grey

{1} Accept it, then learn to love it.
{2} George Clooney should be your guide.
{3} Be cautious of dyeing your hair all over but, if you must, then make sure it looks subtle and natural.
{4} Bear in mind that most hair dyes can be very harsh and will look as unnatural and as obvious as a comb-over. Steer clear, or get a professional job.
{5} Go for a more subtle approach. Fly colour your hair by putting dye through it on a comb. It won't remove all of the grey, but should take about half away. This simple method usually creates a natural look.
{6} Keep your hair shorter. Grey hair always looks better when cut regularly and kept in trim.

HOME SHAVING

It would be great to be shaved professionally every morning but, in reality, shaving is frequently done in a rush before leaving for work. There's no real way to avoid this, but treat yourself to a good shave at weekends.

{1} Open up your pores by soaking a flannel under the hot tap until it is steaming, and then hold it against your face for a minute. Alternatively, shave in a hot bath and allow the steam to do the same job.

{2} Use a shaving cream or soap. It is simply not possible to get as good a shave with a shaving gel.

{3} For those with sensitive skin, use a moisturiser instead of a shaving cream. Something like aqueous moisturising cream will work just as well and won't cause skin reactions.

{4} Using a circular motion, apply the soap to your skin with a brush. Your stubble will stand on end making the shave easier and closer.

{5} Generally, modern, multi-blade razors are extremely good if kept clean; never use disposable razors.

{6} An electric razor will not shave you as closely as a multi-blade razor: like a hovercraft, they tend to buzz over the surface but never get to the root.

{7} Check which way the hair on your face grows. Shave in the direction the hair grows, especially if you have sensitive skin or if you are prone to bleeding. The growth direction changes on different parts of the face, especially on the neck.

{8} For a close shave, put another hot flannel on your face for a minute to open up your pores again.

{9} Brush on another application of shaving cream, and then shave in the opposite direction to which your hair grows.

{10} Once finished, run your flannel under very cold water and hold it against your face. This will close up your pores and help seal your skin.

{11} Moisturise as soon as possible with a moisturiser, a shaving balm or aftershave gel.

QUICK TRICKS

SHAVING CUTS: stem the flow with a styptic pencil dipped in water, not dabs of tissue. Costing next to nothing, they last for years and are the most effective way to seal up cuts.

RAZOR RASH: buy an alum block, dip it in water and rub it on your face. It will instantly soothe, reducing redness and irritation.

POGONOPHOBIA
A FEAR OF BEARDS

Beard Care

{1}
Look after it. Use shampoo to keep it in good condition and place hot flannels on your face to steam the skin underneath. Moisturise regularly.

{2}
Use clippers to keep your beard neat. They are also useful for keeping stubble at a consistent length.

{3}
Draw an imaginary line from the top of your sideburn to the corner of your moustache. There should be no hair above this line.

{4}
There should be no hair on your neck, just on the underside of your jaw above your Adam's apple.

{5}
Goatees and their variants are never acceptable.

 EXPERT TIP A cut-throat shave is not recommended for those who normally use electric shavers as the skin will not be conditioned sufficiently.

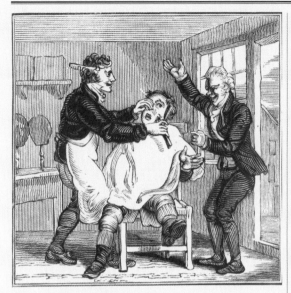

In the chair

The cut-throat shave should be done by a professional in a barbers. It should serve as an education for home-shaving and, as masculine exercises go, there are few better.

First, hot towels are applied to the face to open up the pores. Then shaving soap is applied with a brush. The barber then shaves with the grain of the beard, preferably in as few strokes as possible.

For a very close shave, a second application of hot towels and shaving soap follows, before the barber then shaves against the grain. Afterwards, a cold towel, shaving balm and aftershave is applied to close the pores.

TEN FAMOUS BEARDS

Confucius
Fidel Castro
Charles Darwin
Sigmund Freud
Che Guevara
John Lennon
Abraham Lincoln
Karl Marx
George Bernard Shaw
ZZ Top

HOW TO LOOK RUGGED WITHOUT LOOKING ROUGH

THIS IS AN ESSENTIAL KNACK if you are of the work hard, play hard school of thinking. Take your cues from someone like Steve McQueen who looked craggy but still managed to appear groomed.

THE MOST IMPORTANT THING to concentrate on is your face. It creates first impressions, does most of your communicating and it's what other people spend the majority of their time looking at. Hence, you can get away with those old jeans and battered biker jacket if your face looks healthy.

IT IS ESSENTIAL TO LOOK AFTER YOUR SKIN. A glow about your skin and hair will make you look good no matter what's going on underneath – it can mask a multitude of sins. A daily moisturiser will keep your skin healthy, while a toner can also be useful. Steam your face once a week to allow moisture in and grease out. For those prone to dark rings under the eyes, there are gels available. Don't forget to have a glass of water before you go to bed.

Beard Trivia

A beard grows approximately five inches per year. The longest beard on record was grown by Hans Langseth of Norway. When he died in 1927, his beard measured 17.5 feet (5.3 metres). His beard is on display at the Smithsonian Institution, Washington DC.

HOW TO BE HAIRY

{1} The hair on the back of your neck should be kept to a minimum. Shave it. No-one should have to guess where your haircut stops and where your back starts.
{2} Back hair should be waxed off. It may be painful but it is essential. No exceptions.
{3} If it's a huge problem, have it lasered. It is permanent, effective and relatively cheap.

Eyebrows, ears and noses

{1} A mono-brow can be shaved easily, but it's more effective to pluck between your two brows. Make sure you don't over-pluck as, over time, the hair may not grow back – and you don't want to look permanently startled. If in doubt, get it done by a professional.
{2} Nasal-hair trimmers are a cheap, effective and essential piece of gear. Use them.
{3} For ears, see {2} and substitute 'ear' for 'nasal'.

KNOWLEDGE SPA STARTER

Most men are naturally anti-spa, seeing it as a more feminine pursuit. Those same men, however, are often sold after trying just one treatment.

The best place to start is with a sports massage after a work-out, game of squash or round of golf. The deep tissue massage will ease aches and pains and get you used to the spa ambience.

On top of the recommended daily intake of two litres of water, you should drink plenty of water before a treatment – being hydrated is essential to the effectiveness of massage. You'll often find that you will feel thirsty after a treatment too, so make sure you keep up your water intake.

The night before a treatment, avoid excessive amounts of alcohol. You don't want to be hungover and dehydrated and, in some cases, the massage can lead to you feeling unpleasantly drunk again. Additionally, no spa therapist wants to be exposed to your morning-after alcohol fumes.

EXPERT TIP When buying a treatment for your wife, partner or female friend, you should buy two. It's a much more enjoyable to go with somebody else, and makes the day more memorable. It's expensive but you'll look better and extra-thoughtful.

MANICURE MATTERS

Other than the face, the hands are often the only part of a man's skin that is visible, so you should want them to look good. They display the more obvious signs of ageing, so keeping them in good nick is important.

Nails should always be kept clean and short but, every now and again, treat your hands to a professional going-over – removing calluses, softening and removing cuticles, nail-filing and shaping, moisturising and a hand massage. With well maintained hands you can gesticulate with confidence.

EIGHT TREATMENTS TO TRY

Indulge in a range of treatments that can be as beneficial to you physically as they are relaxing. Switch off and get pampered…

{1} **SPORTS MASSAGE:** good for athletes, sportsmen, golfers or anyone who has been using their muscles. It is a strong massage that can be tailored to target specific areas. Therapists must have special qualifications in order to carry out this kind of treatment as it can be damaging if performed wrongly.

{2} **SWEDISH MASSAGE:** another strong massage, this uses basic and firm techniques that will leave you relaxed rather than targeting specific problem areas. It is excellent for improving circulation.

{3} **AROMATHERAPY:** very relaxing, this is beneficial for the skin above all else. Different essential oils can be chosen to help different conditions, from dryness and dehydration to insomnia and digestive problems. Generally an aromatherapy session should be preceded by a consultation to ascertain the ailments to be targeted and soothed.

{4} **SHIATSU MASSAGE:** a traditional Japanese massage relying on finger pressure and stretching rather than muscle-kneading. Intended to benefit both mind and body, the aim is to encourage a natural energy flow. It is often said to benefit breathing, blood-circulation and nerves, while also relaxing, de-stressing and improving flexibility.

{5} **THAI MASSAGE:** a deep massage that involves stretching while firm rhythmic pressure is applied to the body. Often, no oil is used. The person being massaged will be manipulated into various shapes to aid the massage process. It can also involve hot poultices, making it an effective de-stress massage.

{6} **HOT STONE:** heated stones are applied to the body, which is drizzled with oil. It will help ease aching muscles, making it a good treatment for active people, golfers or people who work out frequently.

{7} **REFLEXOLOGY:** every organ in your body has a referral zone in your foot. For example, if you cross your two big toes, it represents your head. Massaging the feet, therefore, can be a way to treat other more inaccessible areas of the body, such as the stomach. You may worry that it will be ticklish, but in reality it's not.

{8} **FACIAL:** although it is usually considered the least masculine treatment, this is the treatment that most men will return to most often after their first try. A facial usually involves cleansing, exfoliating and moisturising the skin on the face, as well as paying attention to the neck, upper-chest and scalp.

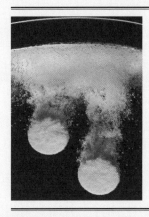

ESSENTIAL MEDICAL KIT	**ESSENTIAL EQUIPMENT**	**ESSENTIAL PRODUCTS** *You spend money on smelling good, so look good too…*
Antiseptic cream	Alum block	Cleanser
Antidiarrhoeal medicine	Clippers	Eye gel
Cold and flu remedy	Electric toothbrush	Exfoliating face wash
Condoms	Flannel	Fragrance
Cough linctus	Nail brush	Intensive moisturiser
Hangover remedy	Nail clippers	Toner
Ibuprofen	Nasal-hair trimmer	Shaving cream
Indigestion tablets	Razor	Shower gel
Paracetamol	Scales	SPF moisturiser
Plasters and bandages	Styptic pencil	Sun cream
Thermometer	Tweezers	

Spa Etiquette

ARRIVE IN GOOD TIME for your appointment, preferably 15 minutes before.

ALWAYS WEAR UNDERWEAR or swimming trunks. Once you are lying down on a table, areas not being worked on will be covered with a towel. Use the robes and slippers provided. That's why they're there.

LEAVE YOUR MOBILE PHONE or other electronic gadgets in the changing room. You're supposed to be relaxing.

REMOVE YOUR WATCH and any jewellery apart from your wedding or signet ring.

BE CLEAN. No exceptions.

YOU'LL BE ASKED to fill out a consultation form; be honest and don't lie.

TELL YOUR THERAPIST about any allergies, problems or injuries. These can be accommodated or treated.

RELAX. You will get greater benefit if your body is loose. The therapist isn't trying to hurt you, so let them do their job.

DON'T FEEL THE NEED for small talk during relaxation treatments. Enjoy the peace.

IT'S OK TO YELP when getting your back waxed. It hurts: you're allowed to show pain. Rest assured, it does get easier.

DON'T BE EMBARRASSED about using the bathroom. It's a fairly normal reaction after a treatment, especially reflexology.

YOU'RE GOING FOR A MASSAGE or a treatment. Never ask for anything else or be suggestive.

SUNBEDS

Sunbeds are not safe tanning. Harmful UV rays from sunbeds can be stronger, increasing the risk of skin cancer and causing premature ageing. There is no safe way to 'build up' exposure; equally, irregular, intense UV exposure from the odd sunbed is extremely damaging and dangerous. Never use a sunbed after sunbathing, more than twice in 24 hours, or if you are fair, freckly, prone to burning or have lots of moles.

SAFE TANNING

ALWAYS USE A BROAD SPECTRUM, WATER RESISTANT SUNSCREEN OF SPF 15 OR HIGHER.

•

APPLY GENEROUSLY UP TO 30 MINUTES BEFORE EXPOSURE; REAPPLY AT LEAST EVERY 2 HOURS.

•

SUNSCREENS HAVE A SHELF LIFE OF 2–3 YEARS.

•

A TAN DOES NOT PROTECT YOU; IT IS NOT A SUNSCREEN.

•

PEELING IS YOUR BODY'S WAY OF GETTING RID OF DAMAGED CELLS.

KNOWLEDGE UV

UVB has a shorter wavelength than UVA, penetrating the upper layer of the epidermis. UVA has a longer wavelength; it penetrates deeper, damaging elastin and causing ageing. A broad spectrum sunscreen protects you from both UVA and UVB rays.

Scent Trivia

The nose associates good smells with good things, and vice versa. Vanilla-based fragrances are popular because they remind the nose of childhood ice-creams or custard. It is also why the smell of cut grass is alluring – in many people's heads, it symbolises the arrival of summer.

GET IT RIGHT: WEARING FRAGRANCE

Fragrance should be sprayed onto body areas that are naturally warm. Your body warmth will allow the scent to develop to its full potential. The first area should be your pulse points – your wrist and around your neck – as these are warm places where the blood is close to the skin.

Spray a quick burst onto your chest after a shower. Apply no more than two or three squirts after you've dried yourself – you will already be warm from washing and so, as the cologne heats up under your shirt, it will really open up.

Your nose adapts to familiar smells, making them seem less strong. If a smell has been around you for a while, your brain will assess it and, if it is safe, will regard it as part of the background 'noise'. It's a primitive function that means recognisable smells seem less strong than new and potentially dangerous ones. You will therefore not be able to smell your fragrance as clearly as you did on the day you first wore it, so resist the urge to splash it on more thickly.

Apply the right amount. The smell ought to complement your own skin odour and character, rather than overpower you. Apply two or three squirts to the chest and neck, depending on the strength of the perfume. If you can still smell the fragrance five or ten minutes after applying, then it's about right. If you can't smell it, add some more. Eau de toilette is stronger than aftershave as the latter is designed to be applied to raw skin, so contains less ethanol.

HOW TO BUY FRAGRANCE

FACED WITH A WALL OF DIFFERENT FRAGRANCES, often the temptation is to start spraying willy-nilly. Don't go into sensory overload: it is best to try a maximum of just five different scents. Choose ones that you think you like and spray a few squirts onto a paper scent strip.

TAKE IT AWAY and smell it again 20 minutes later. By then, the top notes will have gone and you'll be left with the heart and base notes, which is how it will generally smell on you. If you still like it, then spray it on your skin and see how it combines with your own skin. If you're impressed: buy it.

IF YOU WANT TO SHOW OFF, or if you want to let the person behind the counter know you're serious, sniff the crook of your elbow deeply in between smelling different products. Smelling your own skin or familiar scent of your clothes acts as a reset button for your nose, sending it back to its default setting. In some shops they will offer you coffee beans for the same purpose, but often their smell is too overpowering.

ASIDE FROM ITS SMELL, it's also worth taking a look at what a particular eau de toilette is trying to say. It's perfectly acceptable to buy a brand if you are attracted by its image, say of adventure and exploration. A lot of market research goes into scents, and the packaging and brand image will often be replicated in its smell.

SOME COMPANIES NOW OFFER BESPOKE FRAGRANCES, where you can choose the ingredients to make up the base, heart and top notes. There are, however, around 900 new fragrances launched every year, so you should be able to find one in the shops that you like. There are some single perfume ingredients – such as vetiver and cedar wood – that some fragrance aficionados love to wear alone – but only confident 'noses' would go down that road.

THERE IS ALWAYS, HOWEVER, one failsafe method of testing whether a fragrance is right for you: if your partner doesn't like it, bin it.

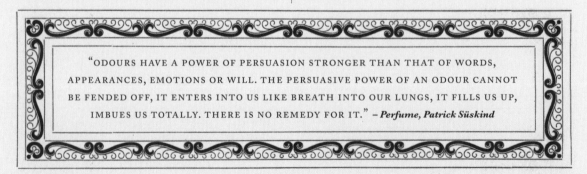

"ODOURS HAVE A POWER OF PERSUASION STRONGER THAN THAT OF WORDS, APPEARANCES, EMOTIONS OR WILL. THE PERSUASIVE POWER OF AN ODOUR CANNOT BE FENDED OFF, IT ENTERS INTO US LIKE BREATH INTO OUR LUNGS, IT FILLS US UP, IMBUES US TOTALLY. THERE IS NO REMEDY FOR IT." – *Perfume, Patrick Süskind*

Why You Should Wear a Fragrance

Gone are the days when a man who wore fragrance was liable to have his sexuality questioned. In fact, the balance has now swung so far in the opposite direction that those who don't wear it are the anomaly.

Most men now have four or five different fragrances for different occasions. While women often wear perfume as a reflection of who they are, men tend to wear it as an accessory.

Your fragrance is the finishing touch to the clothes you choose to wear. It is an accessory in the same way that your cufflinks might be. You should, therefore, have a wardrobe of scents to fit with your mood, the occasion and your clothes.

A scent will increase your personal space, too, as your fragrance will extend the area you inhabit. It is also a great confidence builder – especially when you get that admiring look from someone as you sidle past.

TIME AND PLACE

Some fragrances will suit different times of day better than others. In the office, a lighter fragrance is generally more suitable; a heavier fragrance is best at night. Bear in mind that, if eating out, there are some scents – like fougère fragrances – which will overpower the plate in front of you. Oriental fragrances with vanilla or other edible notes, however, often go well with food. Wear the smells of the seasons, too. The smell of incense and wood is out of place in the summer, while citrus and fresh flower notes make little sense around the fire in the winter.

THE EVOLUTION OF A SCENT

CITRUS AND TOP NOTES: fragrances will, for the first 20 minutes, be dominated by the fresh, fruity and citrus notes. These are the instant hit, the first odour you'll smell, but they are short-lived – they are there as the scented handshake to welcome you.

HEART NOTES: after 20 minutes, the heart notes will begin to emerge from the citrus notes. They were always there, but were just overpowered at first. These are the flowery, spicy and woody smells and they should last for two or three hours. Essentially, this is what your fragrance will smell like for most of the time that you wear it.

BASE NOTES: once the heart notes have evaporated, the base notes are left. Often there to act as fixatives for the skin – they can be vanilla, musky, woody or smoky notes – these are the smells that are noticeable on your clothes the morning after.

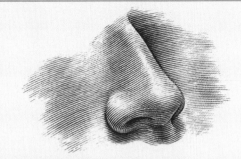

STYLE GUIDE FRAGRANCE

CITRUS COLOGNES: fresh and energising, they will smell initially appealing but they will not last long. These have been worn by men for centuries to give refreshment, though they really started to be worn as a statement in the 1960s, when men started to wear fragrance on a daily basis.

AROMATIC FRAGRANCES: lavender or herbal driven scents. They became more prominent in the late 1960s, as people sought fragrances with a more distinctive, fresh character.

AQUATIC FRAGRANCES: a development in the 1990s, these are based on marine notes and can often be identified by a maritime theme in their name and a watery character in the scent. They are fresh, cooling and transparent.

FOUGÈRE FRAGRANCES: meaning 'fern' in French, these are woody and mossy. When men's fragrance became more acceptable in the 1960s, most wore fougères. Fresh, powerful and unapologetically masculine, they are the traditional and sophisticated fragrance choice of gentlemen.

CHYPRE FRAGRANCES: a mainstay of the 1970s, featuring warm, leathery notes combined with citrus freshness. They were originally intended to capture the smell of Cyprus – dry warmth, tree resins, citrus and a hint of white flowers – with a long-lasting and complex result. Today, all fragrances of this type are variations on the original theme.

ORIENTAL FRAGRANCES: inspired by 'mysterious' Eastern smells, these are fragrances with big characters that often combine woody notes, and incense and spices. They came into prominence in male perfumery in the mid 1990s. Since then, the level of vanilla has increased in Oriental fragrances for men.

HOW TO STORE FRAGRANCE

Avoid heat and sunlight. The bathroom is a challenging place to keep fragrance because of the fluctuations in temperature. A cool and dark place such as a cupboard is ideal. Failing that, keep it in its box. Citrus colognes can go off quite quickly – normally within a year – while more complex fragrances (like Oriental) last much longer, sometimes years.

WASHING SYMBOLS DECODED

Machine wash (with max temperature)

Do not wash

Hand wash only

Iron: one dot = cool;
two dots = warm; three dots = hot

Do not iron

Do not tumble dry

Do not bleach

Suitable for dry cleaning

Specialist dry cleaning

IN THE WASH

Separate darks, colours, whites etc.

Empty pockets; zip-up zips.

Take note of garments' care labels.

Never wash anything at a higher
temperature than stated on the label.

Don't overload the machine, and
don't use too much powder.

Don't leave the load in the machine
for too long after it's finished.

Never use bleach.

SHIRT CARE

WASHING: wash your shirt after each time you wear it at 40 degrees. Remove collar stays, undo the buttons and turn inside out (to protect the buttons).

DRY CLEANING: dry cleaning will wear your shirts out quickly, particularly under the arms where deodorant will not be removed. It is better to wash them at home (always check the care instructions) and then take them to the dry cleaner for pressing (except for special shirts such as those made of silk).

BESPOKE CARE: you should wash a bespoke shirt three times before wearing it to allow it to shrink and soften. If you wash it once a week, it will require new collar and cuffs in three years (which your tailor can easily replace) but the rest of the shirt should still be in perfect condition. A bespoke shirt should last 10 to 15 years with proper care.

KEEP IT CLEAN STAIN REMOVAL

BALLPOINT INK: dab with methylated spirits.

BLOOD: soak in salted cold water (not hot) and then wash as usual.

CANDLE WAX: place a few sheets of kitchen roll over the wax, and press with a warm iron, allowing the wax to be absorbed into the paper.

CHEWING GUM: freeze the garment and then carefully pick off the hardened gum.

CHOCOLATE: if the chocolate is soft, place the garment in the fridge and then scrape off.

CURRY: dab with a solution of biological detergent, then wash as usual.

DEODORANT: rub with white wine vinegar and wash as usual.

GRASS: wash in biological detergent; dab any stubborn stains with methylated spirits.

LIPSTICK: rub fabric against fabric with washing-up liquid, and then wash as usual.

PERSPIRATION: soak in a solution of white vinegar and water. Rinse, then wash as usual.

RED WINE: dab with carbonated water, and then wash as usual.

SHOE POLISH: dab with white spirit, and then wash as usual.

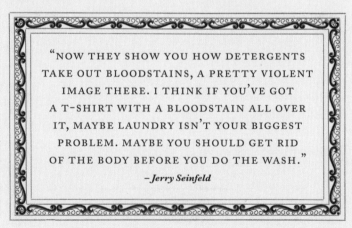

"NOW THEY SHOW YOU HOW DETERGENTS TAKE OUT BLOODSTAINS, A PRETTY VIOLENT IMAGE THERE. I THINK IF YOU'VE GOT A T-SHIRT WITH A BLOODSTAIN ALL OVER IT, MAYBE LAUNDRY ISN'T YOUR BIGGEST PROBLEM. MAYBE YOU SHOULD GET RID OF THE BODY BEFORE YOU DO THE WASH."
– *Jerry Seinfeld*

SIX STORAGE SECRETS

{1}
Do use suitably shaped hangers, never wire.

{2}
Don't overfill your wardrobe or drawers
– clothes need to breathe.

{3}
Do empty pockets before you hang up jackets or trousers.

{4}
Don't put anything away when it's wet or damp.

{5}
Do put hanging covers over rarely worn garments.

{6}
Don't store clothes in direct light (don't forget
about garments in the back of the car).

Cashmere Care

- HANDWASH IN LUKEWARM WATER WITH A MILD SHAMPOO.
- REMOVE EXCESS WATER BY GENTLY SQUEEZING THE GARMENT IN A TOWEL.
- DRY FLAT – NEVER HANG TO DRY.
- GET YOUR CASHMERE DRY CLEANED IF YOU ARE UNSURE.
- USE A CASHMERE COMB TO REMOVE PILLING.

 EXPERT TIP Never dry clean your suit more than twice a year. If it's looking shapeless, get the dry cleaner to press it, but not clean it.

HOW TO IRON A COTTON SHIRT

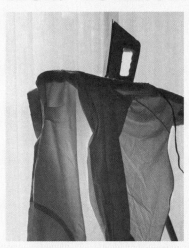

Develop a practised routine. It's personal choice, but the sequence of collar, cuff, sleeve, yokes, back and, lastly, the front is recommended.

The shirt should be damp (preferably from the wash) – never try to iron a dry shirt because the creases will not be removed effectively. The shirt should be unbuttoned, and any collar stays removed.

{1} COLLAR: iron the underside first, then the outside from the point of the collar to the centre. This will prevent any creasing at the tips.

{2} CUFFS: iron unbuttoned and with double cuffs unfolded. As with the collar, start with the inside, and then do the outside.

{3} SLEEVES: work from the top to the cuff. The addition of a crease is a matter of personal choice.

{4} YOKE: fit the shirt over the narrower end of the board.

{5} BACK: the easiest bit because it's button-free. Utilise the wide end of the board.

{6} FRONT PANELS: iron around the buttons and pay special attention to the panel with the buttonholes, which will be on show when the shirt is worn.

LEATHERCARE

- Leather is a skin; keep it fed and moist – allow it to breathe.
- Never store leather in plastic bags or non-porous containers.
- Use leather conditioner occasionally to prevent it from drying out or cracking.
- Spray items with a protector.
- Avoid any products containing silicone or wax.
- Hang leather jackets on wide or padded hangers.
- Use shoetrees in leather shoes.
- Stuff leather bags with tissue to maintain their shape.

MOTH RULES

Protect wool and cashmere from moths by putting cedar blocks in your drawers and wardrobe.

•

Make sure knitwear is clean before it's put away and store for longer periods – such as the summer months – in sealed containers.

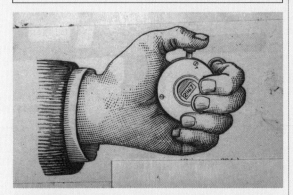

IMPORTANT Before starting any kind of training, you should consult a fitness or medical professional.

HOW MUCH EXERCISE DO YOU NEED?

HOW OFTEN? The government advises that, to sustain your level of health, you should be active for 30 minutes, five days a week. This increases to 60 minutes of activity, five days a week, if you want to lose weight.

HOW MUCH? Unless you have health problems, cardiovascular activity should range from a minimum of fast walking for 30 minutes to a maximum of running for an hour and half. Once you are in the habit, the time will be easy to find. If you have only an hour a day, you should incorporate both cardiovascular and resistance training into your programme: aim for 40 minutes of cardio and 20 minutes of weights.

TRAINING RULES

{1}
TRAIN WHEN IT SUITS YOU: you are more likely to stick with a programme.
{2}
TIMING IS PERSONAL CHOICE: some people get better results in the morning, some in the afternoon and some in the evening.
{3}
BREAKFAST TIME: if you are training first thing, and your time is limited, it is convenient to simply get up and get going, saving breakfast for afterwards. Ideally, though, you should eat something before training – but food requires about an hour and a half to be digested.
{4}
HYDRATION: you should be drinking about a litre of water per hour of exercise. You should continue to drink water after exercise too.

GET IT RIGHT SPORT SHOES

Owning the right pair of shoes is vital – different shoes are needed for different activities • Having the ideal pair will enable you to get the best results and ward off potential injuries • Visit a specialist gym or running shop and get fitted properly • Each person's foot can roll a different way when running; shoes that will support one person may work against another • For most gym activities, you should have two pairs of shoes • A dedicated pair of running shoes should be the most important item in your collection.

{1} **RUNNING SHOES:** if fitted correctly, these will provide support and balance tailored to your running style. They are perfect for both treadmill and outdoor running but, because they are a little higher and more built-up than other trainers, they are less stable for gym work such as weight-lifting. *N.B. This is the least versatile shoe: it should only be used for running and nothing else.*

{2} **CROSS-TRAINING SHOES:** for most other gym based activities, like aerobics or other classes, cross-training shoes are the most useful. They are tailored to cushion impact, but allow your foot to change direction more easily than a running shoe. *N.B. This is a good all round shoe – as good for indoor football as it is for weights work.*

{3} **SQUASH SHOES:** squash shoes have a wider base, like a skate-shoe, enabling balance and stability during the frequent changes of direction required when playing squash. *N.B. A squash shoe and a cross-trainer are probably interchangeable, though neither should be used for running.*

{4} **WEIGHT-LIFTING SHOES:** these are slightly weighted at the back to provide optimum stability when you have a large load on your shoulders. *N.B. Only serious body builders need invest.*

FAT BURNING

For anyone wishing to burn off a lot of fat, then regular, low-intensity and long runs of over 90 minutes are ideal. If you don't have that sort of time, then interval runs are extremely effective. In a 40-minute period, try 16 repetitions of one minute's hard running and one minute's walking (plus a warm-up and cool down). The key to losing weight, however, is regular exercise almost every day.

 EXPERT TIP It is better to do an hour a day, rather than two hours every other day – resistance training relies on working the same muscle group two days in a row.

Essential Exercise Gear

SHORTS: one of the most important items of clothing in the kit bag. Tracksuit trousers are heavy, they hold sweat and will heat you up far too quickly as gyms are generally quite warm. For longer runs, ensure that your shorts do not chafe, while long, Lycra trousers are useful in the winter. Tight, buttock-hugging Lycra shorts are fine under another pair of shorts but, alone, they won't earn you many friends in the gym.

VEST: whether a t-shirt or a sleeveless top, these should be made of a material that wicks sweat away from your body; cotton is not a good idea as it gets heavy and can chafe your skin.

JACKET: for colder weather, when running outside, a dry-fit jacket is essential to both wick sweat away from the body and also for keeping the wind and rain out. Garish colours, though good for warning traffic and pedestrians of your presence, aren't generally a good look.

SOCKS: sports socks have evolved hugely. Get some that provide cushioning if you are doing a lot of running, and that absorb the sweat from your foot.

HEART-RATE MONITOR: these are perfect for letting you know exactly how hard you are training (or, indeed, if you need to push yourself harder). They are reasonably priced, effective and very useful. There are also lots of gadgets about – from GPS watches to shoes with micro-chips – that will supply information to your wrist or portable digital player that would normally only be available on a treadmill.

HOW TO KEEP MOTIVATED

{1} Before you start training, set some goals – whether it's simply to get fit, get a good beach body or something more specific like running a marathon.

{2} Keep your goals in mind as you train and you will find that, despite a hard day at the office, you will still be inspired to hit the gym.

{3} You should set short, medium and long-term goals so that, as you achieve something, you have another to keep you going.

{4} Make sure your goals are reasonable. No-one is going to look like Arnie within just 12 weeks.

{5} Take a photo of yourself before you begin training and look at it whenever your will is flagging. Continue to take photos of yourself (in the same light) to see your progress.

{6} Take body measurements and watch them either grow or decrease depending on your aims.

{7} If fitness is your goal, find a test that is fairly simple – like running a mile – and then do it monthly to see whether your times are improving.

MAXIMUM HEART RATE

For a rough rule of thumb, your maximum heart rate can be approximately worked out by subtracting your age from 220. So, if you are 35, your maximum heart rate could be around 185. This is only a guide – there are more specific ways of finding this figure out; for proper assessment, you should speak to a qualified fitness professional or a doctor.

FITNESS TERMS EXPLAINED

AEROBIC: essentially, this means working with the presence of oxygen – so it includes all cardiovascular exercises. It will improve your fitness.

ANAEROBIC: exercising muscles without the presence of oxygen is anaerobic and is generally used to build power and strength. It is often not possible to work anaerobically for long.

BODY MASS INDEX (BMI): a scale that compares your height and weight. Many fitness professionals believe it is outdated and sometimes inaccurate, but it can be a useful guide.

BASAL METABOLIC RATE (BMR): the number of calories burnt doing nothing. The more muscle the higher the BMR.

CARDIOVASCULAR: a fat burning and essential form of exercise that will improve your heart (cardio) and lungs (vascular) while also improving your body shape, fitness and endurance.

ELECTROLYTES: minerals like sodium, potassium, calcium and magnesium that are lost through sweat when working out.

PERCEIVED EXERTION: a rough guide to determine how hard you are working out, based on a scale of 0–10 which rates how difficult you find an activity.

PRONATION: the natural inward roll of the foot, from heel to toe, during running. An excessive inward rolling is called overpronation. The correct running shoes are essential in dealing with this. *See also Supination.*

RESTING HEART RATE (RHR): essentially, the lower your resting heart rate is, the fitter you are. Your heart rate should be discussed with a doctor before attempting to change it.

SUPINATION: also called underpronation, this is when the foot does not roll inwards enough when running. *See also Pronation.*

> **IMPORTANT** Before starting any kind of training, you should consult a fitness or medical professional.

PERSONAL TRAINERS: PROS

{1} MOTIVATION: when you're flagging, it's all too simple to ease off when alone. That's never an option with a trainer. When you start training, you may see good results very quickly. However, that improvement will slow down over time, which is when a personal trainer can step in and encourage you and liven up your programme.

{2} GOOD ADVICE: you may know your body, but a personal trainer will know exactly how and when to improve it. They'll also know the right way and the wrong way to exercise, which will allow you to make the most of your gym time and help you avoid injuries.

{3} CONFIDENCE: most trainers say that the majority of people who fail when exercising do so because they don't have enough belief in what they are doing. A personal trainer will ensure that can't happen.

{4} RESULTS: a personal trainer's reputation is often based on word of mouth. If they don't get results, they don't get work. Therefore, if you hear of a good personal trainer, the chances are they should be able to work wonders for you. Check that they are listed on the Register of Exercise Professionals before you sign up.

{5} CHANGE: a personal trainer will know how to change your routine. You should be moving on to something new every six to twelve weeks or so to prevent you finding regimes both easy and, occasionally, boring. You should stick with a routine long enough to get the benefit but your body needs to have different muscle groups challenged, so change is essential. A personal trainer will know when the moment is right.

PERSONAL TRAINERS: CONS

{1} RELIANCE: with a personal trainer, it can be easy to just to assume that your one session a week with them is all the exercise you need, meaning you rely solely on their input. You should still be exercising alone between sessions.

{2} EXPENSE: really, the only equipment you need to get fit is a pair of running shoes. They will frequently cost less than just two sessions with a trainer.

{3} OVER-WORKING: if your only aim was simply to get in shape, then a personal trainer may take that too far into body building. This shouldn't happen, though, if you lay out your goals at your first meeting.

Gym Etiquette

Wipe down your equipment each time you use it. No-one wants to sit in your sweat. Carry a towel with you wherever you go.

•

Make sure your kit is clean before you even set out for the gym.

•

Be courteous to other members. You're not the only one working out.

•

Leave your mobile and pda in your locker.

•

Don't hog the machines. If you're waiting to use something, let the person who is on it know you are waiting. They should ask you whether you would like to work in with them between sets.

•

Check your personal hygiene. In an atmosphere where people will frequently be gasping for breath, no-one wants a whiff of whatever is lurking in your armpits.

•

Keep your clothing modest. You may be cooler in skimpier gear, but others won't want to be near you when you're lunging. Never go bare-chested or barefoot.

•

Mirrors are for honing your technique; they are not an opportunity for you to vainly admire your body.

•

Music through earphones should only be audible to you.

•

Return your weights. Just because you can lift a house doesn't mean the next person who wants to use the dumb-bells can.

•

Be sensible. Don't stack up the weights on a machine to impress others nearby. You'll injure yourself and no-one will care anyway. You might also drop the weights which is dangerous.

•

Keep noise to a minimum and keep your grunting to yourself. Don't get distracted by or stare at girls working out.

 EXPERT TIP When it comes to lifting weights, the less machine work the better. Lifting free weights will encourage the development of core strength as more muscles come into play, so a good collection of dumb-bells is essential for the home gym.

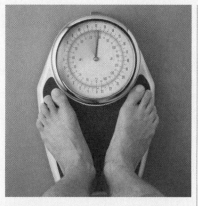

COUNTING CALORIES

Activity	Calories used in half an hour*
Badminton	125
Basketball	255
Climbing stairs	300–500
Cycling	150
Driving	50
Fast walking (4.5mph)	200–240
Football	306
Golf	110
Horse riding	255
Jogging	300–450
Judo	360
Mountain climbing	270
Rowing	380
Sitting at a desk	50
Skiing	250
Swimming	250
Tennis	260
Watching television	50

approximate: amount can vary according to body weight

ALCOHOLIC CALORIES

Drink	Calorific value
Glass of champagne	(120ml) 90
Glass of red wine	(175ml) 120
Glass of dry white wine	(175ml) 130
Pint of lager	120
Pint of Guinness	170
Pint of bitter	180
Pint of dry cider	200

HOW TO GET A BODY LIKE BOND

DIPS: using your own body weight is tough but effective. Add weights around your waist when the repetitions begin to feel easy.
MUSCLES WORKED: chest, triceps and shoulders.

PULL-UPS: incredibly effective in terms of adding strength. Use an overhand grip for good results.
MUSCLES WORKED: back.

SQUATS: can improve leg strength exponentially if done correctly. Squats also help the shoulders and abs.
MUSCLES WORKED: quads, legs.

PRESS-UPS: easy to perform anytime, anywhere.
MUSCLES WORKED: chest, triceps.

LATERAL RAISES: useful for exhausting a muscle before overloading it to gain good results. Use carefully.
MUSCLES WORKED: shoulders.

GEAR HOME GYMS

FOR THE BASIC HOME GYM, all you need is a set of dumb-bells, an exercise ball, a chin-up bar and a pair of running shoes. With those, you can cover all the bases.

FOR A BIGGER HOME GYM, get an adjustable cable pulley machine as well. Highly versatile, a cable pulley machine will allow you to work most of the core muscle groups (avoid multi-gyms as they won't work all your muscles as effectively).

FOR AEROBIC ACTIVITY, a rowing machine, a running machine and a bike are all very useful, as can be a cross-trainer.

CORE STRENGTH EXPLAINED

Your core muscles are your deepest, underlying muscles – the ones you can't actually see – which keep your posture correct. If they are working properly, they will keep your body in the best shape possible when running, sitting at your desk or watching television. While they won't enable you to get a flashy body, they are thought to greatly reduce the risk of problems like back injuries in later life. Core training is currently recommended by fitness professionals as the most essential form of training. That means working less on machines and more with exercise balls, free weights and cable pulleys. Your core muscles will come into play as they enable you to balance on the ball as you lift a weight.

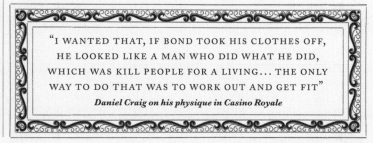

"I WANTED THAT, IF BOND TOOK HIS CLOTHES OFF, HE LOOKED LIKE A MAN WHO DID WHAT HE DID, WHICH WAS KILL PEOPLE FOR A LIVING... THE ONLY WAY TO DO THAT WAS TO WORK OUT AND GET FIT"
Daniel Craig on his physique in Casino Royale

> **IMPORTANT** Before starting any kind of training, you should consult a fitness or medical professional.

Walking

PROS: if you have medical problems, or if you have simply let your fitness lapse, walking can be a good place to start. Easy, free and, if done regularly, it can be a good first step.
WHAT IT WORKS: cardiovascular ability and stamina can be improved.
CONS: it will take you a long time to get fit from walking alone. If your fitness is already at a reasonable standard, walking will not raise your heart rate to a sufficient level to do much good.

Running

PROS: perhaps the best form of exercise for weight loss, it's easy to do, free and will make you feel good thanks to the release of endorphins, while it will also hugely benefit the heart and lungs. Those training for marathons or 10km runs, they should seek specific advice, however for general training, most people should be running at least three times a week with their heart rate at 70–75 per cent of its maximum. Running on grass is the best surface possible, and machines will also cushion impact to an extent. Road running is the hardest form of running and comes with the highest risk of injury but, if you are running road races – such as marathons – you will need to run on pavements to train. You can replicate road running conditions, to an extent, on a machine by setting the gradient to 1.5 degrees.
WHAT IT WORKS: heart, lungs, legs and stamina.
CONS: there is a high risk of injury to knees, shins and backs among other things because of the impact of pounding the pavement. Running can shorten muscles, too, unless you stretch properly before and afterwards.

Swimming

PROS: there is no impact when swimming, so there is a lesser risk of injury. It is also great for joints and flexibility as swimming requires you to constantly stretch as well as strengthen. While it will build up fitness, it will also build up power and physique as swimming develops longer, leaner muscles than lifting weights.
WHAT IT WORKS: cardiovascular, endurance and all major muscles group are worked and improved.
CONS: most people don't have the technique or ability to swim for long enough to do a proper work out. Even if you can swim well, it's worth getting some lessons to ensure you are swimming properly enough to improve your condition.

Rowing

PROS: brilliant for improving fitness, cardiovascular ability and strength, it can also be fairly pleasurable if done on the river. Even on a rowing machine the benefits are multiple.
WHAT IT WORKS: great for building up lower body and leg strength, it will also improve cardiovascular ability.
CONS: you need a boat, an ergometer or rowing machine to undertake it. Rowing machines can be boring, but it is also important to learn the proper techniques before stepping into a boat in order to get the most benefit while also avoiding common problems like back injuries.

Cycling

PROS: another excellent form of training, this is a low impact way of greatly improving fitness and cardiovascular ability. It also won't necessarily require gym membership, so it can be done anytime, anywhere. Alongside swimming and running, this can make the basis of an excellent cross-training regime.
WHAT IT WORKS: leg strength and cardiovascular ability are all huge beneficiaries from cycling.
CONS: you need to buy a good bike first, while there is also a risk from traffic on the road.

Resistance Training

PROS: lifting weights, essentially, will build up strength. Though it won't necessarily allow you to build up size, it will improve muscle power. Increasing your muscle mass will also speed up your metabolism, meaning that you will burn more calories on a day to day basis.

> "LACK OF ACTIVITY DESTROYS THE
> GOOD CONDITION OF EVERY HUMAN
> BEING, WHILE MOVEMENT AND
> METHODICAL PHYSICAL EXERCISE
> SAVE IT AND PRESERVE IT." – *Plato*

WHAT IT WORKS: which muscles are worked will depend on your training routine. However, you should aim to have a programme that concentrates on all aspects of the body, especially core strength.

CONS: there is a high risk of injury if exercises are not performed correctly.

Circuit Training

PROS: a fairly traditional technique, this really hasn't changed much from most people's school days. As a means to achieving general fitness it is still good, though.

WHAT IT WORKS: depending on the routine, it can work the majority of major muscle groups. It is also good for cardiovascular ability.

CONS: circuit training can be an imbalanced way to work out, because certain muscles groups may not be worked while others are overworked.

Team Sports

PROS: football, rugby and other active team sports are one of the best ways to get fit. Gyms can be boring, so team sports will provide both the mental and physical stimuli that you need. They can also improve hand-eye coordination and there are myriad social advantages too. Though cricket and golf will help your fitness, they should not be your only exercise of the week.

WHAT THEY WORK: it varies according to the sport but, generally, cardiovascular ability, leg strength, upper-body strength and overall fitness will all benefit.

CONS: there is a high chance of injury as you will not be able to control the conditions in which you are exercising. You will also need to make sure your fitness (and ability level) is of a reasonable standard before starting.

Racket Sports

PROS: squash, in particular, is very good for the heart. However these are not sports (like many of the above) that should be attempted at anything other than a basic level unless you are fit in the first place.

WHAT THEY WORK: heart and lungs will get great benefits, though there will be no strength building.

CONS: there is a chance of injury (e.g. tennis elbow), while squash is a high-impact sport – both your knees on the ground and, occasionally, your opponent's racket in the face.

Exercise Classes

AEROBICS: great for cardiovascular ability and for improving fitness, the only problem may be that your pride could take a dent as they tend to be designed more for women than men. They can also be done in the water as an aquarobics class, which is good for people returning from injuries but is generally quite a female-dominated activity.

BODYPUMP: combining aerobic exercise with hand-weights, this involves high-repetitions with low-weights, making it great for toning and fitness.

BOXERCISE: a safe way of letting off some aggression as you won't get hit back, it is nonetheless a tough work-out that will improve cardiovascular ability.

PILATES: good for building up core strength and improving flexibility, this will also help you when it comes to lifting weights in the gym.

SPINNING: a high-intensity cycling class that will improve fitness but it is quite specific: it will develop your ability on a bike but not necessarily as a runner.

YOGA: though yoga classes are often seen as a woman's domain, they are excellent for building up suppleness – even more so than pilates. This is essential for warding off movement problems in old age.

BOXING CLEVER

Perhaps one of the toughest forms of exercise, boxing is nonetheless extremely effective for getting you into shape. Good for your physique, strength and for your fitness, it is ideal for those concentrating on aiding their heart and lungs and for those looking to lose weight. The downside to boxing is the obvious risk of being hit, combined with some boxing clubs' reluctance to take on people who are simply looking to get fit, rather than people looking to fight.

Improved strength, suppleness, balance and co-ordination. Enhanced clarity of thought and improved mental focus.

Standing styles

Focus: punching, kicking and blocking using various stances, footwork and combinations; more about speed than power.

KARATE – 'EMPTY HAND' An art of self-defence as well as a sport. Training usually places equal emphasis on basic techniques, sparring and 'forms' or stylised patterns of attacks and defences.

KUNG FU – 'SKILL AND EFFORT' Many different styles: some use punches and kicks with hard, linear movements, whilst others use soft and circular movements with less emphasis on combat. Some schools may use weapons.

TAEKWONDO – 'THE WAY OF HAND AND FOOT' A modern martial art characterised by fast, high and spinning kicks. It combines four disciplines: patterns, sparring, self-defence and break test. Places greater emphasis on sport than art.

KICKBOXING Started in the United States during the 1970s. Competitors fight with boxing gloves, foot pads, head guards and gum shields. A great way of improving fitness.

MUAY THAI Often referred to as Thai boxing. Also known as the science of eight limbs – fighters used hands, feet, knees and elbows. New rules and protective wear had to be introduced when it became too dangerous.

Ground Fighting or Grappling Styles

Focus: the 'wrestling' aspect of combat, but not limited to ground-based movement.

JIU-JITSU – 'GENTLE ART' Relies on turning an opponent's force against himself. Students learn to gauge the force of their opponent's attack and use it against him, evade attacks and attack nerve and pressure points.

BRAZILIAN JU-JITSU A modified version of the Japanese art. Ground fighting techniques and submission holds feature strongly, with the aim of dominating an opponent and forcing a submission.

CAPOEIRA This art resembles a stylised 'dance' with emphasis on ground fighting, but not grappling or locks. Relies heavily on leg techniques and leg kicks for attacks and defence, rather than hands, which are mainly used to maintain your position on the ground.

SAMBO (pronounced *sombo*) A grappling-based style with an emphasis on real-life self-defence and practical ways to neutralise a threat. Combat Sambo is the martial art version used by Russian elite forces, and is often practised wearing military fatigues.

Throwing Styles

Focus: throws, trips, locks or other methods to disrupt the opponent's balance, starting from a standing position.

JUDO – 'THE GENTLE PATH' The most widely practised of the martial arts. Consists mainly of throws, pins, chokes and arm-locks. Despite a strong element of grappling, it does not require great power or size to do well.

AIKIDO – 'THE WAY OF HARMONY WITH THE SPIRIT' Based on principles of harmony and non-resistance to one's opponent. The circular movement of the opponent's force is diverted and turned back on himself. Size does not matter.

KEMPO OR KENPO A style of karate developed in the West. The former refers to more traditional forms and the latter to more contemporary versions. It differs from karate as throws are an important element and it also incorporates punches, strikes and kicks. At more advanced levels, defence against weapons may also be taught.

Weapons-Based Styles

Focus: the culture and tradition of martial arts (although some, such as Kali, do emphasise self-defence or combat).

IAIDO Students learn to recognise difficult situations and avoid them becoming a problem or engaging the conflict before it becomes a significant matter. Beginners start with a wooden sword and progress to real weapons once the basic skills are mastered. The overall aim is to become so good that you never have to draw your sword in the first place.

KENDO – 'THE WAY OF THE SWORD' Derives from the two-handed sword-fighting techniques of the samurai. Fighters use the *shinai*, a four-foot bamboo sword with a cord running along one side, and the aim is to strike the opponent with the side opposite the cord. Protective clothing is worn to cover the head, wrists and abdomen.

KALI – 'BLADED WEAPON' Originates from the Philippines. Unlike many other martial arts, weapons training is introduced first followed by hand and foot techniques. In addition to sticks, bladed weapons may be used.

KYUDO – 'THE WAY OF THE BOW' Often considered the purest of all martial arts. Emphasis is placed upon posture, balance, concentration, composure, physical awareness and motion.

Meditative Styles

Focus: breathing, posture and controlled, slow movement to build internal and external strength.

T'AI CHI – 'THE SUPREME CHALLENGE' The underlying principle is that the mind, body and soul must be unified for wholeness and complete health. Students learn how to channel potentially destructive energy (in the form of a kick or a punch) away from themselves and in a direction where it is no longer a danger. The pace is slow, graceful and seemingly effortless, but strength and flexibility are improved greatly.

CHI KUNG (QIGONG) Combining meditation with exercise, Chi Kung is based on correcting the flow of energy that runs through your body. There are many variations, but most tend to involve breathing techniques, moving exercises, still postures and mental training. Chi Kung is good for correcting posture and improving balance – it may also be practised on a daily basis.

TEN CLASSIC MARTIAL ARTS FILMS

Drunken Master (1979)
Jackie Chan

•

Fist of Legend (1994)
Jet Li

•

Crouching Tiger, Hidden Dragon (1999)
*Michelle Khan, Chang Chen,
Zhang Ziyi, Chow Yun-Fat*

•

Enter the Dragon (1973)
Bruce Lee

•

The Chinese Connection (1972)
Bruce Lee

•

The Shaolin Temple (1982)
Jet Li

•

Shaolin Master Killer (1983)
Gordon Liu

•

Supercop (1992)
Jackie Chan, Michelle Yeoh

•

The Karate Kid (1984)
Ralph Macchio, Pat Morita, Elisabeth Shue

•

Rumble in the Bronx (1996)
Jackie Chan

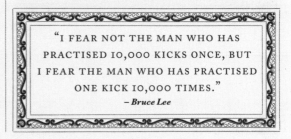

"I FEAR NOT THE MAN WHO HAS PRACTISED 10,000 KICKS ONCE, BUT I FEAR THE MAN WHO HAS PRACTISED ONE KICK 10,000 TIMES."
– *Bruce Lee*

AT HOME

Colour Schemes

A COLOUR WHEEL

A COLOUR WHEEL DEMONSTRATES THE IMPORTANCE
OF THE PRIMARY COLOURS. IT IS A SIMPLE WAY TO
THINK ABOUT MIXING AND MATCHING COLOURS.

SCHEME 1 *Tonal:* use one colour from the colour wheel
at varying degrees of intensity for a simple, elegant look.
SCHEME 2 *Harmonious:* use colours that sit well together,
usually found next to each other on the colour wheel, but
don't mix warm and cool colours.
SCHEME 3 *Complementary:* combining contrasting yet
tonal colours, found opposite each other on the colour
wheel, makes a statement and creates an impact.

Warm colours: red, orange. Look best in artificial light,
so suit rooms that are used in the evenings, such as a dining
room, creating an intimate feel.
Light colours: green, blue. Create a bright and airy feel –
use to complement rooms benefiting from daytime use
and natural light, such as a kitchen.
Neutral tones: grey, beige, cream. Recessive colours
that complement woods and natural materials; best for
rooms where the emphasis is on striking furniture, art etc.
*N.B. Use details in the room, such as cushions or rugs,
to pick out – or introduce – colour.*

 EXPERT TIP Always use a tester of paint on
the wall before you buy; don't rely on colour
cards. Then buy enough paint for the whole
job as different batches can vary in colour.

Five Rules of Light

{1} **VARIETY:** use various table lamps and standard
lamps. Light from different sources, at varying heights,
creates atmosphere.
{2} **MOOD:** dimmer switches for main lights are essential.
Bright overhead lights are an instant mood-killer.
{3} **UPLIGHTERS:** lit corners, using uplighters, create
warmth and cosiness.
{4} **NATURAL:** utilise natural light in a room. Don't arrange
furniture too close to the window. Mirrors help spread light
around a room.
{5} **DETAIL:** light shades are a statement. Choose one
that fits with the style of the room; make sure it doesn't
lose its intensity of colour or look too pale when lit up.

 EXPERT TIP Small rooms look bigger
with a dark floor, light coloured walls
and an even lighter ceiling.

SPATIAL AWARENESS

DO establish a focal point – fireplace, TV, bed, coffee
table – and build the rest of the room around it.

DON'T push all the furniture up against the wall,
especially sofas.

DO measure up carefully before you buy furniture, taking
note of permanent features such as radiators and windows.

DON'T overcrowd the room with too much furniture
– sometimes less is more.

DO arrange objects in threes or odd numbers.

DON'T draw attention to the corners of a room.

 EXPERT TIP Mirrors give the illusion
of space, especially if hung on a wall
opposite a window.

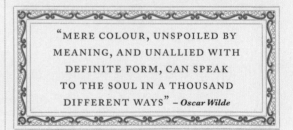

"MERE COLOUR, UNSPOILED BY
MEANING, AND UNALLIED WITH
DEFINITE FORM, CAN SPEAK
TO THE SOUL IN A THOUSAND
DIFFERENT WAYS" – *Oscar Wilde*

GET IT RIGHT: *Elements*

PROPORTION

Furniture and objects must be of a similar scale.

BALANCE

Arrange furniture and objects equally in the space.

CONTRAST

Use colour and pattern to blend and create a mood.

HARMONY

Choose complementary colours, patterns and textures.

Details: Room Furniture

Before you furnish a room consider the impact that is made by decorative details: architraves, skirting boards, cornices, door furniture. These should harmonise with your overall decorative scheme and the interior style of your home.

For Georgian and early Victorian classicism, opt for hinged shutters, geometric cornicing, deep skirting boards and silver or brass door furniture.

Late Victorian and Edwardian style schemes are enhanced by dado rails, elaborate – frequently floral – cornices, tongued and grooved panelling, and brass or porcelain door furniture (knobs and finger plates).

The more modern the look the more simple the room furniture: minimal architraves and skirting boards, and geometric, chrome door handles.

EXPERT TIP Create interest in a room with a 'feature wall', using patterned wallpaper on just one wall.

PLANT LIFE: SECRETS OF SUCCESS

SUNLIGHT: most plants like a well-lit position; some prefer shadier spots. No plants like very dark conditions.
WATER: soil should be kept damp and not allowed to dry out.
DRAINAGE: plants left sitting in water die; don't over-water.
DUST: leaves should be dust-free so they can photosynthesise.
FEED: give plants a feed occasionally; read the instructions to prevent over-feeding as it can do more harm than good.
READ: check the plant's label or a book for care advice.

PLANTS: EASY TO GROW SPECIES

{i} *Yucca elephantipes* (Yucca)
{ii} *Euphorbia ingens* (Cowboy Cactus)
{iii} *Sansevieria trifasciata* (Mother-in-Law's Tongue)
{iv} *Spathiphyllum wallisii* (Peace Lily)
{v} *Zamioculcas zamiifolia* (ZZ Plant)
{vi} *Dracaena marginata* (Madagascar Dragon Tree)

MAKING PATTERNS

VERTICAL STRIPES MAKE A WALL LOOK TALLER.
HORIZONTAL STRIPES MAKE IT LOOK WIDER.
SMALL REPEATED PATTERNS MAKE AN AREA LOOK
BIGGER THAN LARGER REPEATED DESIGNS.
GEOMETRIC PATTERNS MAKE AN AREA LOOK LARGER.

GET THE LOOK: *Six Interior Styles*

Gothic Revival

Exposed beams – metalwork lighting – arches – stone fireplace – dark floorboards – heavy wood furniture – stained glass – dark red and gold patterned wallpaper

Japanese Modern

Tatami matting – sliding screens – low-level furniture – futon – bamboo/cane – black lacquered furniture – paper light shades – orchid – bonsai

Victoriana

Polished wood floorboards – rugs – patterned tiling – overcrowded rooms – velvet curtains – plump sofas/chairs – porcelain ornaments – floral wallpaper – cast iron fireplace

Modernism

Plain walls – under-furnished rooms – blinds – tubular steel furniture – black leather chairs – simple fireplace – low-level fitted shelving/cupboards – cacti

60s Retro

Shag-pile rug – futuristic shaped furniture – psychedelic patterns – drapes – tie-die fabrics – inflatable furniture – retro telephone – loud clashing colours

Modern Scandinavian

Laminated floorboards – white walls – contrasting primary colours – plain sleek sofa – modern art – blonde wood furniture – architectural plants

TWELVE CLASSIC CHAIRS

{I} *Bibendum Chair* c.1925
Eileen Gray (1878–1976)
Named after its similarity to the 'Michelin Man',
the Bibendum chair, and Gray herself, went unnoticed
until interest surfaced in the 1970s when many
pieces of her work went to auction.

•

{II} *Wassily Chair* 1925–27
Marcel Breuer (1902–1981)
Inspired by the shape of bicycle handlebars, the Wassily
Chair was designed and created for artist Wassily
Kandinsky. The use of the tubular steel frame is hailed as a major
breakthrough in furniture design.

•

{III} *Grand Confort Chair, Model No.LC2* 1928
Le Corbusier (1887–1965)
This Bauhaus design classic – soft leather cushions,
contained in an angular tubular steel frame – famously
combines function and style. It was inspired by a club chair
manufactured by the English furniture company Maples.

•

{IV} *Barcelona Chair* 1929
Ludwig Mies van der Rohe (1886–1969)
The leather and chrome Barcelona Chair was designed for
the interior of Mies van der Rohe's iconic German Pavilion
(known as the Barcelona Pavilion) at the 1929 Barcelona
International Exhibition

•

{V} *Prouvé Standard Chair* 1930
Jean Prouvé (1901–1984)
Designed with ultimate precision to balance, function,
strength and comfort, the Standard Chair features a
moulded plywood seat and back. Its versatility, style
and lightweight look have given it longevity and
a place in modern design history.

•

{VI} *Bent Plywood Chair* 1943
Gerald Summers (1899–1967)
Summers produced this sleek, aerodynamic-looking
chair from a single sheet of bent plywood. Subsequently
described as "organic" and "biormorphic", only 120
were produced. Today, this chair is a rare, collectable
and much sought-after item.

{VII} *Tulip Chair* 1955–56
Eero Saarinen (1910–1961)
The curved base and pedestal (or 'stem') of the Saarinen
Tulip Chair inspired its name. This was a revolutionary
design, taking away the legs of the chair or, as Saarinen
called it, "the slum of the legs".

•

{VIII} *Eames Lounge and Ottoman* 1956
Charles (1907–1978) and Ray Eames (1912–1988)
This leather upholstered cushion, encased in a curved
veneered shell, and accompanying ottoman, was designed
by this husband and wife team as a birthday present
for director Billy Wilder. These design classics are part
of the permanent collection at MoMA, NY.

•

{IX} *Panton Chair* 1959–60
Verner Panton (1926–1998)
Originally named the S Chair or Stacking Chair, the Panton
Chair's instantly recognisable shape is a masterpiece of sleek,
modern yet practical design. This was the first cantilever
chair, made out of one piece of plastic.

•

{X} *Ribbon Chair* 1961
Cesare Leonardi (1935–) and Franca Stagi (1937–)
Made from fibreglass and chrome-plated tubular steel,
this complicated looking chair represents a classic
example of 1960s design. The curved shape of the
twisted ribbon-like seat is canterlivered on a
small, triangular steel base.

•

{XI} *Air Chair* 2000
Jasper Morrison (1959–)
This one piece, made from gas-injected polypropylene,
is stackable, lightweight and suitable for outdoor use.
The practically stylish Air Chair comes in a wide range
of colours, including fuchsia, sky blue and white-ivory.

•

{XII} *Louis Ghost Armchair* 2002
Philippe Starck (1949–)
This transparent single-mould polycarbonate chair is
inspired by Louis XVI. Modern technology, combined
with historical Baroque design, created an instant
postmodern classic that quickly obtained cult status.

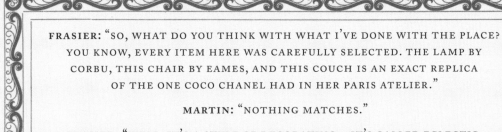

FRASIER: "SO, WHAT DO YOU THINK WITH WHAT I'VE DONE WITH THE PLACE? YOU KNOW, EVERY ITEM HERE WAS CAREFULLY SELECTED. THE LAMP BY CORBU, THIS CHAIR BY EAMES, AND THIS COUCH IS AN EXACT REPLICA OF THE ONE COCO CHANEL HAD IN HER PARIS ATELIER."

MARTIN: "NOTHING MATCHES."

FRASIER: "WELL, IT'S A STYLE OF DECORATING – IT'S CALLED ECLECTIC. THE THEORY BEHIND IT IS, IF YOU HAVE REALLY FINE PIECES OF FURNITURE, IT DOESN'T MATTER IF THEY MATCH – THEY WILL GO TOGETHER."

– Frasier, 'Give Him the Chair!'

"A CHAIR IS A VERY DIFFICULT OBJECT. A SKYSCRAPER IS ALMOST EASIER. THAT IS WHY CHIPPENDALE IS FAMOUS."

– Ludwig Mies van der Rohe

EIGHT DESIGN CLASSICS

Create a shrine to iconic design with some modern classics:

FLORENCE KNOLL SOFA
ARNE JACOBSEN EGG CHAIR
ISAMU NOGUCHI COFFEE TABLE
LE CORBUSIER LC6 DINING TABLE
EILEEN GRAY SIDE TABLE
LOUIS POULSEN PH 3/2 TABLE LIGHT
AALTO VASE
ARNE JACOBSEN ROMER CLOCK

FOUR CLASSIC DESKS

Albini Desk
Nelson™ Swag Leg
Alfieri Desk by Calligaris
Florence Knoll Table Desk

LIGHT STYLE

TABLE Isamu Noguchi Akari
DESK Type 75 Anglepoise
FLOOR Arco
PENDANT Le Klint LK172

MISS DEBRETT *What Your Place Says About You*

YOU MAY HAVE PUT A LOT OF MONEY and thought into your home décor: state-of-the-art electronic equipment, the latest flatscreen TV, collectable furniture and fittings. You will be proud of your bachelor pad, but beware, because your female visitors will be crawling all over it with a different agenda in mind.

WHILE WE MAY APPRECIATE your design values, our main interest is sleuthing – looking for evidence that you're one of the good guys. And that means signs that you're a sentient being, with your own taste, style and sense of humour. We like books (though beware science fiction and fantasy), pictures, interesting art and quirky objects that come with a slice of history attached. A family photograph is fine – but avoid lovingly displayed images of your mother or your ex. Signs that you were once a child (an old toy, your favourite adventure story, a wacky picture) will be appreciated, but only in strict moderation. Signs of sad bachelordom (just-discarded games consoles, an extensive and much-loved collection of *Top Gear* DVDs, a perfectly aligned collection of CDs arranged in fetishistic genre order) will be ruthlessly mocked.

IF YOU CAN DEMONSTRATE that you enjoy the sensual pleasures (cushions, fluffy towels, smart toiletries, fine quality cotton sheets) it will count in your favour.

FILMS YOU MUST OWN

Action
Bullitt (1968)
Die Hard (1988)
Dirty Harry (1971)
Seven Samurai (1954)
The Terminator (1984)

·

Classics
8½ (1963)
A Clockwork Orange (1971)
12 Angry Men (1957)
Citizen Kane (1941)
Singin' in the Rain (1952)
The Third Man (1949)

·

Comedy
Airplane! (1980)
Blazing Saddles (1974)
Dr Strangelove (1964)
Monty Python's Life of Brian (1979)
Some Like it Hot (1959)
This is Spinal Tap (1984)
Withnail & I (1987)

·

Drama
Fargo (1996)
Goodfellas (1990)
Once Upon a Time in America (1984)
Reservoir Dogs (1992)
Scarface (1983)
Vertigo (1958)

·

British
Chariots of Fire (1981)
Goldfinger (1964)
Great Expectations (1946)
Trainspotting (1996)

·

Romance
Brief Encounter (1945)
Casablanca (1942)

Gone With the Wind (1939)
The English Patient (1996)
Lady and the Tramp (1955)
Love Story (1970)
When Harry Met Sally (1989)

·

Horror
Deliverance (1972)
Don't Look Now (1973)
The Exorcist (1973)
Halloween (1978)
Psycho (1960)
Rosemary's Baby (1968)
The Shining (1980)
The Texas Chainsaw Massacre (1974)

Classic Trilogies
The Bourne Triology (2002–07)
The Dollars Trilogy (1964–66)
The Godfather (1972–90)
Indiana Jones (1981–89)
Lord of the Rings (2001–03)
Star Wars (1977–83)

·

War
Apocalypse Now (1979)
Das Boot (1981)
The Eagle Has Landed (1976)
The Great Escape (1963)
Lawrence of Arabia (1962)
Platoon (1986)

·

Western
Butch Cassidy and
the Sundance Kid (1969)
High Noon (1952)
The Magnificent Seven (1960)
Once Upon a Time in the West (1968)
The Searchers (1956)

·

Sci-Fi
2001: A Space Odyssey (1968)
Alien (1979)
Blade Runner (1982)
Close Encounters of the
Third Kind (1977)
E.T. The Extra Terrestrial (1982)
The Matrix (1999)

> "THE LENGTH OF A FILM SHOULD
> BE DIRECTLY RELATED TO THE
> ENDURANCE OF THE HUMAN BLADDER."
> – *Alfred Hitchcock*

IN THE KNOW COLLECTING VINYL

{1} The Beatles are the most collectable band in the world. Elvis Presley is second.

{2} The rarity of a record, rather than its quality, is what gives it value.

{3} If a record sold thousands of copies on release, it's unlikely to be worth much now.

{4} For modern bands, promo copies can be worth five times more than full commercial releases.

{5} For future returns, invest in limited edition releases now.

{6} No matter how rare, if a record is scratched, it's worth a lot less.

{7} Signed records are worth more.

{8} Running your fingers through a shop's record racks always beats browsing online.

REDUCE THE RISK OF RSI

EXERCISE YOUR THUMB: squeeze a squash ball five times between your thumb and index finger three times a day.

STAY LOOSE: keep your fingers bent in as natural a position as possible.

JOINT CUSTODY: keep your wrist joints relaxed but also straight.

SIT UP STRAIGHT: good posture means the nerves that run down your arms will be in good shape.

GET OUT MORE: put down your controller occasionally.

> "BE NICE TO NERDS. CHANCES ARE YOU'LL END UP WORKING FOR ONE." *– Bill Gates*

Collectable Toys

The most valuable antique toys are those that proved the most popular in their day, as they can claim the most sentimental value. However, the most popular toys tend to be the ones that were played with the most, meaning they are also in the poorest condition. Condition is everything, so a boxed 1970s' Action Man will be worth at least four times its original cost – and often more – as few people bought one to leave in its packaging. Generally, the rarer a toy the better, while anything younger than 30 years old tends not to have attracted much value yet. That means, however, that 1980s' toys – such as Transformers and action figures – are coming into vogue, as those who were fans as children now want to buy back a nostalgic slice of their past.

ELEVEN ESSENTIAL GAMES

Grand Theft Auto: Vice City

•

Gran Turismo 3

•

Halo: Combat Evolved

•

Medal Of Honour Frontline

•

Pro Evolution Soccer

•

Resident Evil 4

•

The Sims 2

•

Street Fighter II

•

Super Mario Galaxy

•

Tetris

•

Wii Sports

FIVE RULES OF GAMING

{1}

No laps of honour or raised arms

{2}

You are not on Centre Court, playing the FA Cup Final or battling zombies – despite appearances to the contrary.

{3}

More than two hours at a sitting counts as an obsession.

{4}

Once the console has been switched off, you are not indestructible: adapt to real life immediately.

{5}

Computer games are not an adequate girlfriend/wife substitute.

HOW TO RIG UP A ROOM

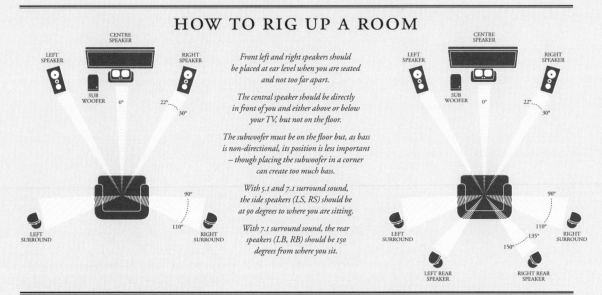

Front left and right speakers should be placed at ear level when you are seated and not too far apart.

The central speaker should be directly in front of you and either above or below your TV, but not on the floor.

The subwoofer must be on the floor but, as bass is non-directional, its position is less important – though placing the subwoofer in a corner can create too much bass.

With 5.1 and 7.1 surround sound, the side speakers (LS, RS) should be at 90 degrees to where you are sitting.

With 7.1 surround sound, the rear speakers (LB, RB) should be 150 degrees from where you sit.

WHY SPEND MONEY ON A TOP-QUALITY AV SYSTEM?

Film and music collections take both time and money to accumulate. They are also, frequently in the case of music, reminders of a certain moment in your life – the album that recalls a particular summer, the single that reminds you of a particular girl – so why dilute memories with fuzzy pictures and dodgy sound? No matter how much you deny it, you spend considerable amounts of your time sat in front of the box, or reclined in front of your stereo. The better the system, the better the quality of your escape.

WHERE TO SPEND YOUR MONEY

{1} CD/DVD player: the most important part of a system. A good disc player will extract as much information as possible from a CD; good sound relies on good information.

{2} Processor: the sound processor is the second most important part of a system; good processors can improve the information sent by the CD player.

{3} Projector: the quality of a projector is an essential element of the home cinema experience.

{4} TV: as above, it's about both decoding and presenting information; the better the quality, the better the viewing.

{5} Speakers: they are the least useful in terms of improving sound quality, and the easiest part of a system to upgrade later.

PORTABLE DIGITAL PLAYERS

Sound quality from a portable digital player (e.g. an mp3 player) is never as good as from a CD because the sound is compressed to allow room for greater storage. Make sure you transfer your music onto your digital player in an uncompressed state – this takes up more room but will give you more satisfying results. As a general rule, however, portable digital players are best for music on the move, rather than in the home.

Vinyl or CD? What it Says About You . . .

Record collectors will tell you that nothing compares to the sound of vinyl. And while they may have had a point in the early days of CDs, the technology has now progressed to such a point that there is very little difference in quality (with CDs probably edging the battle). However, what the two formats say about you is perhaps more important. CD says functional, it says convenience and instant playability. Vinyl, on the other hand, says serious collector. It points to a man who appreciates the art-form in his hand – from the seductive black grooves of the record, to the attention to detail in the cover artwork itself. And, though the CD may be easier to buy, nothing is better than the feeling of flicking, at speed, through a vinyl shop's stock and savouring that heavenly smell rising from the racks.

 EXPERT TIP The shape and contents of your room will make a difference to its sound. Bare surfaces cause harsh sound reflections. Prevent this with carpets and soft furnishings.

GET IT RIGHT: HOW TO BUY THE BEST AV SYSTEM

Work out what your system is for: for film buffs, picture quality will be just as important as sound but, if you listen to music more than you watch films, invest in a good two-channel stereo system. Digital technology is where the fastest sound developments are being made. But, if you're after a system you can tinker with, analogue may be better for you.

•

Develop a rapport with your supplier: find a retailer who will spend time talking to you and who will explain the pros and cons of different products. As with a tailor, you want something that will fit you perfectly – which isn't something you'll achieve in a couple of hours on a Saturday afternoon.

•

Don't be daunted: make sure you get what you want, rather than what the on-commission salesman wants to sell you.

•

Try before you buy: insist that your retailer sets up your complete system in-store for you to test before you part with your money. They should have a room available for this.

•

Spend as much as you can afford, then add a bit: you will be living with your system for several years. You get what you pay for, so see it as an investment rather than a cost.

•

Keep in touch with your supplier: they will hear about the best products with which to improve your system. Also, they love it when you compliment the system they sold you.

Wireless *vs* Cables

Currently, wireless systems cannot offer the same level of performance as cables. To get technical, it all comes down to bandwidth and, as things stand, it will be at least two years before wires will start to become obsolete.

Go Bespoke

Specialist companies can design and install bespoke audio systems that meet the needs of you and your home. This obviously costs more than buying a system from a normal retailer, but it allows you to integrate your audio system with your heating, lighting and security. Some manufacturers can make a range of products that can be installed discreetly in your home, without compromising on performance. A high-performance system may cost more, but it should still sound good 20 years down the line.

THE MONEY-NO-OBJECT HOME ENTERTAINMENT SYSTEM

Multi-room: both sound and vision can be sent to any room in your house from a central hub, while speakers no bigger than CDs can be hidden in the room's ceiling.

Central controller: install a server under the stairs and then control all your sound and vision needs from one simple wireless touch screen controller, pda or even your mobile phone. Your controller will be able to access the music and film library stored on your server and deliver it instantly to any TV or stereo in the house.

Remote access: choose a film from a catalogue of movies and, as you watch the first 15 minutes, the rest will download from a remote location at high-definition picture levels.

High quality disc player, processor and speakers: if top of the range, you may be using the same equipment as the film-maker whose film you're watching.

In-wall installation: hide your speakers and unsightly cables in the brickwork of your house.

Home cinema: a projector can be set up to provide the ultimate home cinema experience, alongside a 7.1 surround sound system. The projector screen can be hidden in the ceiling of your house and, at the touch of a button, can descend while the curtains automatically close and the lights dim. Should someone press your entry-phone buzzer while you are mid-film, the system can be programmed to pause before beaming the image from the door-camera to the screen.

Bath screen: waterproof flat-screens can be inserted into the tiles at the end of your bath to allow bathroom viewing.

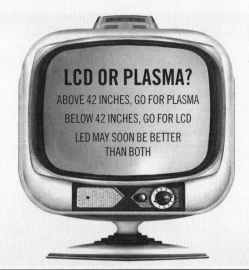

LCD OR PLASMA?
ABOVE 42 INCHES, GO FOR PLASMA
BELOW 42 INCHES, GO FOR LCD
LED MAY SOON BE BETTER
THAN BOTH

BEST BEGINNINGS
Memorable Openings of Novels

Adventures of Huckleberry Finn (1884)
by Mark Twain (1835–1910)

"You don't know about me without you have read a book
by the name of The Adventures of Tom Sawyer; but that ain't
no matter. That book was made by Mr. Mark Twain, and he
told the truth, mainly. There was things which he stretched,
but mainly he told the truth."

•

The Big Sleep (1939) by Raymond Chandler (1888–1959)

"It was about eleven o'clock in the morning, mid October,
with the sun not shining and a look of hard wet rain in
the clearness of the foothills. I was wearing my powder
blue suit, with dark blue shirt, tie and display handkerchief,
black brogues, black wool socks with dark blue clocks
on them. I was neat, clean, shaved and sober, and
I didn't care who knew it. I was everything the well
dressed private detective ought to be. I was calling
on four million dollars."

•

Catch 22 (1961) by Joseph Heller (1923–1999)

"It was love at first sight. The first time Yossarian saw the
chaplain he fell madly in love with him. Yossarian was in the
hospital with a pain in his liver that fell just short of being
jaundice. The doctors were puzzled by the fact that it wasn't
quite jaundice. If it became jaundice they could treat it.
If it didn't become jaundice and went away they could
discharge him. But this just being short of jaundice all
the time confused them."

•

A Farewell to Arms (1929)
by Ernest Hemingway (1899–1961)

"In the late summer of that year we lived in a house in
a village that looked across the river and the plain to the
mountains. In the bed of the river there were pebbles and
boulders, dry and white in the sun, and the water was
clear and swiftly moving blue in the channels."

•

The Great Gatsby (1925) by F. Scott Fitzgerald (1896–1940)

"In my younger and more vulnerable years my father gave me
some advice that I've been turning over in my mind ever since.
'Whenever you feel like criticising anyone,' he told me, 'just
remember that all the people in this world haven't had the
advantages that you've had.'"

Heart of Darkness (1902) by Joseph Conrad (1857–1924)

"The Nellie, a cruising yawl, swung to her anchor
without a flutter of the sails, and was at rest. The flood
had made, the wind was nearly calm, and being bound
down the river, the only thing for it was to come and
wait for the turn of the tide."

•

Lolita (1955) by Vladimir Nabokov (1899–1977)

"Lolita, light of my life, fire of my loins. My sin, my soul.
Lo-lee-ta: the tip of the tongue taking a trip of three steps
down the palate to tap, at three, on the teeth. Lo. Lee. Ta.
She was Lo, plain Lo, in the morning, standing four feet ten
in one sock. She was Lola in slacks. She was Dolly at school.
She was Dolores on the dotted line. But in my arms
she was always Lolita."

•

The Trial (1925) by Franz Kafka (1883–1924)

"Someone must have made a false accusation against
Joseph K., for he was arrested one morning without having
done anything wrong. The cook employed by his landlady
Frau Grubach who brought him his breakfast every morning
at about eight o'clock did not come this time. That had
never happened before."

•

One Hundred Years of Solitude (1967)
by Gabriel García Márquez (1927–)

"Many years later, as he faced the firing squad, Colonel
Aureliano Buendía was to remember that distant afternoon
when his father took him to discover ice. At that time
Macondo was a village of twenty adobe houses, built on
the bank of a river of clear water that ran along a bed
of polished stones, which were white and enormous,
like prehistoric eggs."

•

Underworld (1997) by Don DeLillo (1936–)

"He speaks in your voice, American, and there's a shine
in his eye that's halfway hopeful. It's a school day, sure, but
he's nowhere near the classroom. He wants to be here instead,
standing in the shadow of this old rust-hulk of a structure,
and it's hard to blame him – this metropolis of steel and
concrete and flaky paint and cropped grass and enormous
Chesterfield packs aslant on the scoreboards, a couple
of cigarettes jutting from each."

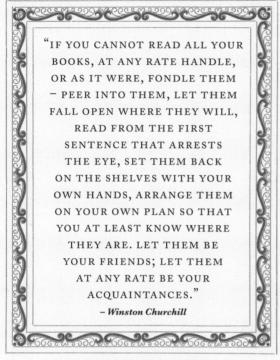

"IF YOU CANNOT READ ALL YOUR BOOKS, AT ANY RATE HANDLE, OR AS IT WERE, FONDLE THEM – PEER INTO THEM, LET THEM FALL OPEN WHERE THEY WILL, READ FROM THE FIRST SENTENCE THAT ARRESTS THE EYE, SET THEM BACK ON THE SHELVES WITH YOUR OWN HANDS, ARRANGE THEM ON YOUR OWN PLAN SO THAT YOU AT LEAST KNOW WHERE THEY ARE. LET THEM BE YOUR FRIENDS; LET THEM AT ANY RATE BE YOUR ACQUAINTANCES."

– Winston Churchill

CHECKLIST:
Ten Books to Impress

Bleak House (1852–53) Charles Dickens

The Catcher in the Rye (1951) J.D. Salinger

Crime and Punishment (1866) Fyodor Dostoevsky

The Crying of Lot 49 (1996) Thomas Pynchon

Naked Lunch (1959) William S. Burroughs

Nineteen Eighty-Four (1949) George Orwell

A Portrait of an Artist as a Young Man (1914–15) James Joyce

The Portrait of a Lady (1881) Henry James

Steppenwolf (1927) Hermann Hesse

Walden (1854) Henry David Thoreau

TEN CLASSIC PLAYS
YOU SHOULD READ/SEE

King Lear (1603–06)
William Shakespeare

•

Death of a Salesman (1949)
Arthur Miller

•

The Duchess of Malfi (1614)
John Webster

•

Glengarry Glen Ross (1983)
David Mamet

•

The Homecoming (1965)
Harold Pinter

•

The Importance of Being Earnest (1895)
Oscar Wilde

•

Look Back in Anger (1956)
John Osborne

•

Long Day's Journey into Night (1956)
Eugene O'Neill

•

Rosencrantz and Guildenstern are Dead (1966)
Tom Stoppard

•

Waiting for Godot (1953)
Samuel Beckett

ESSENTIAL MODERN POETRY

The Waste Land (1922) T.S. Eliot
Another Time (1940) W.H. Auden
Crow (1970) Ted Hughes
The Whitsun Weddings (1964) Philip Larkin
North (1975) Seamus Heaney
The Prodigal (2004) Derek Walcott
Self-Portrait in a Convex Mirror (1975) John Ashbery
Harmonium (1923) Wallace Stevens

HOW TO TILE A WALL

{1} Clear off any existing tiles using a hammer and bolster chisel.

{2} Sand walls then apply sealer.

{3} Using a spirit level as a guide – not the floor or ceiling – mark off a straight line across the floor that is one tile high. Pin a batten made from a strip of wood on that line.

{4} Drop a plumb-line from the top of the wall. Fix a vertical batten to that line. This creates a straight frame within which to tile.

{5} Apply adhesive firmly to the wall, then press tiles into it using a tile-spacer and spirit level. Use a wall scraper to remove any excess adhesive from the tile edges, then leave to dry for at least six hours.

{6} Remove the battens and then tile the uneven areas outside these. This may require a tile cutter.

{7} After 36 hours, apply water-proof and mould-resistant grouting between the tiles to seal them.

 EXPERT TIP Preparation is key. Before you start a job, make sure you have everything you need, and the time to complete the project. Good DIY takes commitment, planning and care – it is not something that can be rushed.

HOW TO SAND A WOODEN FLOOR

{1} Clear the room of everything, including furniture, carpets and anything else.

{2} Hammer down any protruding nails in the floor.

{3} Fill gaps between floorboards with thin strips of wood or papier-mâché treated with wood dye.

{4} Using a floor-sander (available from hire shops), fix coarse sandpaper to the machine's drum.

{5} With the window open to aid dust removal, and while wearing a mask and goggles, start at one end of the room and slowly walk forward in strips.

{6} Lift the sander carefully at the end of each strip. If using a handheld sander, sand with the grain.

{7} After sanding, vacuum thoroughly then wipe the floor with white spirit.

{8} When dry, apply two to three coats of varnish, allowing about three hours drying time in between each coat.

{9} Clean your varnished floor with solvent-based cleaners and polish. Never use water.

{10} Stiletto-wearing guests should take off their shoes or you risk their heels indenting the wood.

> "A DETERMINED SOUL WILL DO MORE WITH A RUSTY MONKEY WRENCH THAN A LOAFER WILL ACCOMPLISH WITH ALL THE TOOLS IN A MACHINE SHOP." – *Robert Hughes*

HOW TO WIRE A PLUG

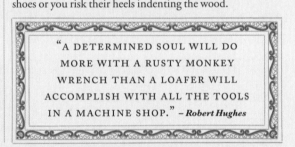

• STRIP 4CM OF CABLE SLEEVE.
Separate the wires inside and cut to length with wire cutters. Remove 5mm of insulation from the ends of the coloured wires and tightly twist the ends.

• CONNECT EACH WIRE TO THE CORRECT TERMINAL IN THE PLUG.
The live wire is brown, the neutral wire is blue and the earth wire is green with yellow stripes. Tighten the cable grip over the cable, ensuring it grips the cable's outer-sleeve – not the coloured wires.

• INSERT CORRECT FUSE.
As a rough guide, appliances up to 700 watts need a three amp fuse, appliances between 700 watts and 1000 watts require a five amp fuse, appliances over 1000 watts require a 13-amp fuse.

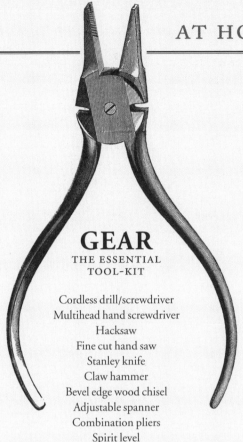

GEAR
THE ESSENTIAL TOOL-KIT

Cordless drill/screwdriver
Multihead hand screwdriver
Hacksaw
Fine cut hand saw
Stanley knife
Claw hammer
Bevel edge wood chisel
Adjustable spanner
Combination pliers
Spirit level
Power drill with hammer action and various drill bits
Mixed nails and screws
Radiator key
Tape measure
Safety goggles
Dust mask
Fold down workbench

Three things you need to be able to find in five seconds at home:

STOPCOCK
Controls the supply of water
into your home.

•

FUSEBOX
Controls the flow of electricity into your home.

•

GAS ISOLATION VALVE
Controls the supply of gas into your home,
often found next to the gas meter.

ECO-CONSCIOUS

LINGO: *carbon footprint / food miles /
renewable energy / sustainable sources*

EAT SEASONALLY

•

SAY NO TO PLASTIC BAGS

•

DRINK TAP (NOT BOTTLED) WATER

•

REDUCE, RECYCLE, REUSE

•

TURN YOUR THERMOSTAT DOWN A FEW DEGREES

•

DON'T LEAVE APPLIANCES ON STANDBY

•

ONLY RUN THE DISHWASHER WHEN FULL

•

DON'T OVERFILL THE KETTLE

•

USE ENERGY-SAVING LIGHT BULBS

Speak like a builder

BAG OF DUST: cement
BLOWN PLASTER: old, unstuck plaster
BONDIN: plaster undercoat
CHIPPIE: carpenter
FLUSH: either flat (as in a wall) or flat
against (as in shelves against a wall)
FROG: the dent in the top of a brick
JAMB: door or window frame
MDF: medium density fibreboard
NEWEL: post at top and bottom of stairs
POETS DAY: Friday
(P*ss Off Early, Tomorrow's Saturday)
PUG/MUCK: sand and cement mortar
SPARKIE: electrician
SQUARE: at right angles
THREE-BY-TWO: timber three inches
wide and two inches deep
TRAP: U-bend

"#$*@!"

Bed Basics

COMFORT IS ACHIEVED by support, not softness – it is a myth that a hard bed is better for you. The mattress should support your spine and mould to the shape of your body, without creating uncomfortable pressure points. Your weight is also a factor; the heavier your body weight, the firmer the mattress. To test your mattress, lie on your back and slide your hand into the small of your back – if you can't slide it in, then the mattress is too soft, but if there's a gap, it's too firm.

THE BEST MATTRESSES are pocket sprung, hand side-stitched, tufted and filled with natural materials. Divans or bedsteads should be sprung. Try to buy the biggest bed possible for your bedroom, especially if you are sharing with somebody. Even a standard double bed is not viewed by experts as big enough to allow two people to sleep comfortably without disturbing each other.

THREE BED-BUYING TIPS

{1} Lie on the bed for at least ten minutes before you decide if it's the right one for you.
{2} Always buy a new base and mattress – they are designed to work together.
{3} Invest – it is estimated that you will spend 120 days (3,000 hours) in bed a year.

THREE FAMOUS BED MOMENTS

{1} It is widely believed that Fred and Wilma Flintstone were the first couple to be seen sharing a double bed on American television.
{2} In *The Godfather* (1972), Jack Woltz wakes up in bed next to the head of his favourite horse, a stud named Khartoum.
{3} In 1969, during the Vietnam War and shortly after their marriage, John Lennon and Yoko Ono staged two week-long 'bed-ins', promoting world peace from their bed in the Amsterdam Hilton and later in the Queen Elizabeth Hotel in Montreal.

BEST BEDDING

DUVET: choose a duvet with a natural goose or duck down filling, baffle box construction (small, lined box-shaped sections) with a 100 per cent cotton ticking (fabric covering). A combination duvet consists of two duvets, of varying tog weight, that can be used separately or tied together to achieve the perfect duvet for each season.

IDEAL DUVET WEIGHT: SUMMER: 4.5 TOG; SPRING/AUTUMN: 9.0–10.5 TOG; WINTER: 12.0–13.5 TOG

LINEN: sheets and covers should be made of 100 per cent Egyptian cotton with a 200 thread count or higher. N.B. black or red satin sheets will send a potential *amour* running for the door.

PILLOW: a good pillow should hold your head and back in the same alignment as when you are standing up. Down and feather pillows are 'puffier' and softer than synthetic filled ones. Whether you opt for one pillow or two is a matter of personal choice, sleeping position and comfort.

Insomnia
n. *The inability to fall asleep or remain asleep.*

INDULGE: drink camomile tea, an age-old remedy for insomnia; studies claim that apigenin, a compound found in camomile, is an effective sedative.

AVOID: light. The body only produces sleep-inducing melatonin (also known as 'the hormone of darkness') in the dark. Invest in light-blocking curtains or blinds.

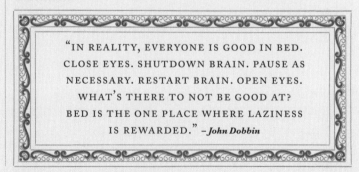

"IN REALITY, EVERYONE IS GOOD IN BED. CLOSE EYES. SHUTDOWN BRAIN. PAUSE AS NECESSARY. RESTART BRAIN. OPEN EYES. WHAT'S THERE TO NOT BE GOOD AT? BED IS THE ONE PLACE WHERE LAZINESS IS REWARDED." *– John Dobbin*

DUVETS *vs* SHEETS AND BLANKETS

DUVETS PROS:	DUVETS CONS:	SHEETS & BLANKETS PROS:	SHEETS & BLANKETS CONS:
Easy to make the bed.	Limited temperature control.	Satisfyingly crisp and clean.	Impossible to make well.
Adapt to your body temperature.	Potential for sleeping partner to steal.	Detailed temperature control through layering.	Potential to feel like a straitjacket.

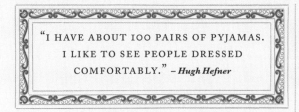

> "I HAVE ABOUT 100 PAIRS OF PYJAMAS.
> I LIKE TO SEE PEOPLE DRESSED
> COMFORTABLY." – *Hugh Hefner*

BATHROOM STYLE

For timeless sophistication, go sleek and minimal:

- Slate or limestone tiles.
- Concealed halogen lighting system.
- Extra large shower head.
- Body jet sprays.
- Chrome fittings.
- Marble or dark wood countertops.
- Storage to hide bottles and products.
- A well-lit mirror for shaving.

INSTANT EN-SUITE

Convert a box room or area of a large bedroom into an en-suite wet room. Indulge in easy open plan washing with a rainfall effect shower and body jet sprays. Choose one style/shade of tile to create a simple, sophisticated look. While you enjoy the convenience, you will also add value to your property.

PYJAMAS

DO Mind the gap.

DO Strictly cotton – brushed for winter, lightweight for summer.

DO Full length in both arm and trouser.

DON'T Never silk or satin.

DON'T No logos.

DON'T Never spots, always stripes.

SLIPPERS

DO Check beats plain.

DO Wool inside, suede or wool outside.

DO Go traditional, moccasins are for Native Americans.

DON'T Your feet don't need to be monogrammed.

DON'T Slip-ons aren't slippers.

DON'T Never novelty: tiger feet is a bad song, not a look.

UNDERFOOT

Choose flooring to create comfort and the right look

Corian *most suited to bathrooms*
Glass *use to create light and space*
Laminate *alternative to real wood*
Leather *black is the ultimate in modern-chic*
Loop Pile *hardwearing, natural fibre-looking carpet*
Rubber *different finishes and retro colours*
Seagrass *neutral, natural fibre, carpet-style matting*
Shag *retro bedroom classic*
Slate *ultimate natural colour and texture*
Tiles *varying styles for different looks*
Twist Pile *low-piled carpet; hardwearing*
Wood *solid or engineered; ages well*

THE ULTIMATE RECORD COLLECTION
From rock to rap, the albums you must own

Soul
Anthology Diana Ross
and The Supremes
The Birth of Soul:
The Complete Atlantic
Rhythm and Blues Recordings
1952–1959 Ray Charles
Call Me Al Green
I Never Loved A Man
The Way I Love You
Aretha Franklin
Innervisions Stevie Wonder
Live At The Apollo
James Brown
Otis Blue Otis Redding
Tell Mama Etta James
There's A Riot Goin' On
Sly and The Family Stone
What's Going On
Marvin Gaye

•

Folk
Anthology Of American Folk
Music Volumes 1–3 Various
Blue Joni Mitchell
Blood On The Tracks
Bob Dylan
Pink Moon Nick Drake
Astral Weeks Van Morrison
Unhalfbricking
Fairport Convention

Jazz
Blue Note Years Vols 1–7
Various
The Complete Hot Five
and Hot Seven Recordings
Louis Armstrong
The Definitive Charlie Parker
Charlie Parker
Ella and Louis
Ella Fitzgerald and
Louis Armstrong
A Love Supreme John Coltrane
It Could Happen To You
Chet Baker
Kind Of Blue Miles Davis
Lady In Satin Billie Holiday
Masterpieces Duke Ellington
Songs For Swinging Lovers
Frank Sinatra

•

Rock'n'Roll
The Chirping Crickets
Buddy Holly
Here's Little Richard
Little Richard
The Original Rumble
Link Wray
Rock, Rock, Rock
Chuck Berry
The Sun Sessions
Elvis Presley

Blues
Anthology Muddy Waters
Blues Breakers featuring
Eric Clapton John Mayall
Blues From The Gutter
Champion Jack Dupree
Born Under A Bad Sign
Albert King
Bumble Bee Memphis Minnie
The Complete Early Recordings
Skip James
The Complete Recordings
Robert Johnson
The Definitive Charley Patton
Charley Patton
Ice Pickin' Albert Collins
The Legendary Modern
Recordings 1948–54
John Lee Hooker
Statesboro Blues
Blind Willie McTell

•

Rock
Back In Black AC/DC
Bayou Country
Creedence Clearwater Revival
Born To Run Bruce Springsteen
Blonde On Blonde Bob Dylan
Dark Side Of The Moon
Pink Floyd
Definitely Maybe Oasis
Electric Ladyland
The Jimi Hendrix Experience
Exile On Main Street
The Rolling Stones
Grace Jeff Buckley
The Joshua Tree U2
Marquee Moon Television
Nevermind Nirvana
OK Computer Radiohead
Physical Graffiti Led Zeppelin
Remain in Light Talking Heads
Revolver The Beatles

The Rise And Fall of Ziggy
Stardust and The Spiders From
Mars David Bowie
Rumours Fleetwood Mac
Siamese Dream
Smashing Pumpkins
Spirit of Eden Talk Talk
Transformer Lou Reed
The Velvet Underground and
Nico The Velvet Underground
The Who Sell Out The Who

•

Indie
Modern Life Is Rubbish Blur
Daydream Nation Sonic Youth
Doolittle Pixies
Different Class Pulp
Loveless My Bloody Valentine
Stone Roses Stone Roses
Stories From the City, Stories
From the Sea P.J. Harvey
Screamadelica Primal Scream
The Queen Is Dead The Smiths
Unknown Pleasures
Joy Division
Up The Bracket The Libertines

Reggae
Dub from the Roots King Tubby
The Harder They Come OST
Various
Natty Dread Bob Marley
Night Nurse Gregory Isaacs
The Right Time
The Mighty Diamonds
Super Ape The Upsetters

•

Pop
A Night At The Opera Queen
Arrival Abba
Dare Human League
Goodbye Yellow Brick Road
Elton John

JAZZ *vs* BLUES
It's all about what you want to say. Jazz – whether it's
wild bebop, icy avant-garde, or romantic crooning –
says cool. It says sleek, smooth and in control. It says:
these are complicated sounds that I can master. What it
doesn't say, however, is heart. That's where blues comes
in, that's where love, loss and the pain therein are
explored with emotions never far from the surface.
Where the former is white collar, the latter is most
defiantly blue.

Graceland Paul Simon
High Land, Hard Rain
Aztec Camera
Like A Prayer Madonna
Rubber Soul The Beatles
The Original Soundtrack 10CC
Parallel Lines Blondie
Pet Sounds The Beach Boys
Please Pet Shop Boys
Rock'n' Soul Part One
Hall & Oates
Rio Duran Duran
Sign O' The Times Prince
Singles Collection The Kinks
101 Depeche Mode
Lexicon of Love ABC
Steve McQueen
Prefab Sprout
Saturday Night Fever
The Bee Gees
Thriller Michael Jackson
The Hounds Of Love
Kate Bush
*Welcome To The
Pleasuredome* Frankie
Goes To Hollywood
Wingspan Wings
Woodface Crowded House

Dance/Electronica

Black Cherry Goldfrapp
Blue Lines Massive Attack
Music for Airports Brian Eno
Dummy Portishead
Exit Planet Dust
The Chemical Brothers
Frequencies LFO
In Sides Orbital
Leftism Leftfield
*Second Toughest In
The Infants* Underworld
Trans-Europe Express
Kraftwerk

·

Punk

Armed Forces Elvis Costello
The First Four Years Black Flag
Horses Patti Smith
London Calling The Clash
*Never Mind The Bollocks Here's
The Sex Pistols* Sex Pistols
The Ramones The Ramones
Raw Power The Stooges
Singles Going Steady Buzzcocks
Sound Affects The Jam
The Undertones The Undertones
Chairs Missing Wire

Metal

Appetite For Destruction
Guns N'Roses
Master Of Puppets Metallica
The Number Of The Beast
Iron Maiden
Paranoid Black Sabbath
Reign In Blood Slayer

·

Country

40 Greatest Hits
Hank Williams
At Folsom Prison Johnny Cash
*The Essential Dolly Parton,
Volume Two* Dolly Parton
The Gilded Palace Of Sin
The Flying Burrito Brothers
Harvest Neil Young
Legends Of Old Time Country
The Carter Family
Live At The Old Quarter
Townes Van Zandt
Music From The Big Pink
The Band
Red Headed Stranger
Willie Nelson
Sweetheart Of The Rodeo
The Byrds

Rap

3 Feet High and Rising
De La Soul
Daily Operation Gang Starr
Enter The Wu-Tang Clan
The Wu-Tang Clan
Illmatic Nas
*It Takes A Nation Of
Millions To Hold Us Back*
Public Enemy
Straight Outta Compton NWA
Raising Hell Run DMC
Strictly Business EPMD
By All Means Neccesary
Boogie Down Productions

1960

WOODSTOCK 15–18 AUGUST, 1969

WHERE: Max Yasgur's farm, Bethel, New York
ATTENDANCE: approximately 400,000
PERFORMERS INCLUDED: The Band, Creedence Clearwater Revival,
Crosby, Stills, Nash and Young, Grateful Dead, Jimi Hendrix, Janis Joplin,
Santana, Sly And The Family Stone, The Who

1970

100 CLUB PUNK FESTIVAL 21–22 SEPTEMBER, 1976

WHERE: The 100 Club, Oxford Street, London
ATTENDANCE: 600 per night
PERFORMERS INCLUDED: Buzzcocks, The Clash, The Damned,
Sex Pistols, Siouxsie & The Banshees

1980

LIVE AID JULY 13, 1985

WHERE: Wembley Stadium, London; JFK Stadium, Philadelphia
PEOPLE: 82,000 in London, 99,000 in Philadelphia
PERFORMERS INCLUDED: Eric Clapton, David Bowie, Bob Dylan,
Elton John, Mick Jagger, Paul McCartney, Queen, Keith Richards,
U2, The Who

1990

GLASTONBURY JUNE 27–29, 1997

WHERE: Worthy Farm, Pilton, Somerset
ATTENDANCE: 95,000
PERFORMERS INCLUDED: Beck, The Chemical Brothers, Daft Punk, Primal
Scream, The Prodigy, Radiohead, Smashing Pumpkins, Supergrass, Van Morrison

Choosing the Right Dog

SELF-SUFFICIENT DOGS: spitz breeds, like Huskies, tend to be the best at looking after themselves. Initially they require a great deal of training, but they are fairly independent, so are ideal if the dog is likely to spend a lot of time alone. If this is likely, you should buy two – one younger than the other, and never from the same litter – so they will not get lonely.

FAMILY DOGS: Labradors, Retrievers, Irish Setters, King Charles Spaniels and Cocker Spaniels are bred to be family dogs and, consequently, are easy to handle. They tend to be good with children and are not over-territorial.

ENERGETIC DOGS: there are few dogs that won't enjoy long walks and runs, but tiny dogs are best avoided if you want an active animal.

STYLISH DOGS: Afghan Hounds are undoubtedly stylish, but they require a lot of work. However, English rare-breed dogs carry more prestige. Vulnerable breeds, like the Sussex Spaniel, Bedlington Terrier and Dandie Dinmont, are all wonderful dogs. Other gundogs, such as the German Longhaired Pointer, also make good-looking and rare pets.

HYPO-ALLERGENIC DOGS: dogs such as Poodles, the Finnish Spitz, Airedale Terriers and Labradoodles can be good for people with allergies – their coats grow, rather than shed.

DOGWALKING RULES

{1}
When walking, remember that your
dog's behaviour will reflect upon you.
{2}
Your dog should be under control
at all times when it is being walked.
{3}
Always carry small plastic bags in your
pocket to clear up after your dog.
{4}
Well-trained dogs should not need an
extendable lead; use a stout, leather lead
attached to a round, rolled collar.

TEN MEN AND THEIR DOGS

Humphrey Bogart Boxer
Marlon Brando Dachshund
Winston Churchill Pug
James Dean Dachshund
John F. Kennedy Dachshund
Pablo Picasso Afghan Hound
Elvis Presley Great Dane
Keith Richards Labrador
Frank Sinatra Cavalier King Charles Spaniel
John Wayne Airedale Terrier

KNOWLEDGE HOW TO BUY A PEDIGREE DOG

{1} Do your research and find a reputable breeder, preferably one approved by The Kennel Club.

{2} Never buy a mother-less puppy. Like humans, a dog passes on aspects of its character to its young. It is also the only way to guarantee your dog's origins and ensure that it has not been bred on a puppy farm.

{3} When choosing a dog, look for health and personality. A wet, damp nose, clear eyes, shiny coat and clean paws are the signs of good health. Inquisitive, curious dogs who approach you will have a good temperament. Avoid ones that cower in the corner.

{4} Check the dog's pedigree. You should be able to trace a pedigree puppy's family back several generations. Top breeders' dogs will have lots of champions in their lineage, though this will not always guarantee that your dog will become one too.

{5} As with buying a car, make sure you have the dog's paperwork – do not leave without The Kennel Club registration papers for the puppy.

{6} While a puppy needs a great deal of attention, it also needs to get used to being on its own. Get a cage and make sure your puppy spends time in it alone.

{7} Instil a routine as early as possible. Walk and feed your dog at the same time each day and put it to bed at the same time each night. Don't let your dog sleep around the house, make sure it goes to its own bed.

{8} To stop your puppy from mouthing your hand, squeeze the back of its neck firmly. This simulates the way its mother would normally restrain it, and also nips indiscipline in the bud.

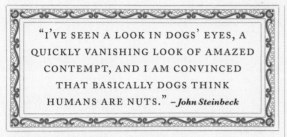

"I'VE SEEN A LOOK IN DOGS' EYES, A QUICKLY VANISHING LOOK OF AMAZED CONTEMPT, AND I AM CONVINCED THAT BASICALLY DOGS THINK HUMANS ARE NUTS." – *John Steinbeck*

FISH KEEPING TIPS

DON'T OVERFEED. It pollutes the water with toxins.

STOCK SLOWLY. Aquarium filters that process waste products need time to build up a population of bacteria.

CHOOSE CAREFULLY. Put the wrong types of fish together and there will be warfare and bullying until the loser dies.

RESEARCH YOUR FISH. They all have specific needs, so make sure you create a tank that matches the fish you intend to keep.

ALWAYS GO FOR THE BIGGER TANK. You will have more options, and they can be easier to look after – a large volume of water is more stable and, therefore, usually more successful.

KEEP WATER, NOT FISH. Apart from feeding, fish will look after themselves, but the water will need attention. Testing for pollutants and learning a little water chemistry is essential for long-term fish keeping.

WHAT FISH?

FOR SMALL SPACES: the Siamese Fighting Fish is a brightly coloured tropical fish with extensive finnage. They do well in small (30 centimetres) planted spaces – but keep two males together and they will fight until one is dead.

FOR BIG SPACES: some tropical fish – such as silver sharks, pacus (a piranha relative), arowanas and giant gouramies – can reach 60 centimetres or more. They're easy to care for, but need a tank at least six times their length (about 3.5 metres).

FOR REALLY BIG SPACES: the arapaima (a relative of the arowana) is one of the world's largest freshwater fish with a potential size of over 3 metres (most reach about 2 metres) – good specimens sell for a hefty price and need a specially built giant aquarium of over 6 metres.

FOR RELAXATION: a fully planted aquascape, stocked with angelfish and shoaling tetras, along with a few algae shrimps (to pick away at the plant leaves, cleaning as they go).

FOR IMPRESSING GUESTS: a large reef aquarium with corals and brightly coloured marine fish will impress, but it will take some serious equipment and dedicated care.

AQUARIUM FISH EXPLAINED

{1} COLDWATER FISH: the most well known coldwater fish is the common goldfish – frequently mistreated by being kept in unfiltered bowls. There are also selectively bred goldfish with rounder bodies and long flowing fins. A coldwater aquarium, preferably 1.5 metres or more, stocked with large goldfish makes a simple but impressive display.

{2} TROPICAL FRESHWATER FISH: the most popular aquarium fish. 'Tropicals' are easy to care for with proper fish-keeping practices. With research, it is possible to create aquariums with stunning fish and beautiful aquascapes. The current trend is moving towards aquarium biotopes combining selected species of fish and plant to create an underwater ecosystem.

{3} TROPICAL MARINE FISH: the ultimate aquarium, marine fish tend to be brightly coloured and make an impression in large tanks, especially species such as lionfish, triggerfish and pufferfish. A marine reef aquarium requires a lot of time, dedication and knowledge, as well as myriad high-tech pieces of equipment and a large budget.

Alternative Pets

POT-BELLIED PIGS: intelligent, easily trained and simple to domesticate, Vietnamese pot-bellied pigs make for a surprisingly sophisticated pet.

WALLABIES: playful and mischievous, these marsupials (like a small kangaroo) make good, if rambunctious, pets that can live both in and outside. The larger wallaroo can also be a good pet.

SUGAR GLIDERS: another marsupial native to Australia, these nocturnal possum-like creatures got their name from their ability to glide between tall trees. They require large amounts of care at home and often need the company of other gliders.

HEDGEHOGS: relatively simple to look after, hedgehogs make for undemanding yet striking pets that can also be house-trained.

DESERT FOX: energetic, curious and hard to catch, nonetheless desert foxes are quite similar to dogs once domesticated. They can be trained to walk on a lead and to live inside, but require plenty of attention.

CITY LIFE

GETTING ABOUT TOWN

{I} On Public Transport

Give up your seat for the elderly or pregnant (but be positive that she's expecting).

Curb your appetite: never eat smelly foods.

Temper loud talk with others/on your mobile.

Don't crowd. Be aware of people's personal space.

Don't laugh out loud at what you are reading.

Restrain excessive displays of affection.

{II} By Taxi

Hail a taxi by standing on the kerb and casually raising your arm – don't make dramatic gestures.

Know exactly where you are going; tell the driver the destination through the front window.

Hold the door open for those accompanying you and let them get into the cab first.

In London taxis, always sit on the fold-down seats and let women sit on the proper back seat.

When you arrive, get out first, leaving the door open behind you to let others out.

Pay the driver through the window from outside.

GET IT RIGHT: ENTRANCES AND EXITS

{I} Making an Entrance

You may want your arrival to be duly noted, but don't act like a drama queen.

Loitering near the entrance and waiting to be noticed won't create the desired effect – you will look lost and like a gatecrasher.

Walk in confidently, say hello to the host(ess).

Fit the mood – assess the event's ambience before launching into the social maelstrom.

Don't interrupt conversation or immediately buttonhole the guest of honour.

{II} Making an Exit

When the time has come to leave, be decisive.

Say your goodbyes, thank your host(ess), collect your coat and head for the door.

Choose your departure time carefully – make sure you're not exiting too early (or late).

If leaving mid-event, make your departure swift and discreet. Keep excuses believable and brief.

Don't be the party-bore. If you are the last man standing, make sure you're in keen company.

If your hosts are visibly wilting, you've outstayed your welcome. Make a swift exit.

VIP AREAS

Usually overrated and underwhelming, VIP areas rarely attract true VIPs and often lack the buzz and atmosphere of the rest of a venue. If, however, you're lucky enough to find yourself closeted with some recognisable faces, don't act overly impressed. Never try to take a photo, no matter how subtle you think you're being, and don't stare. If the bar is free, try to hide your enthusiasm – get stuck in but maintain an air of relaxed moderation.

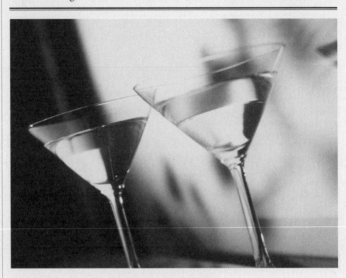

BASIC BAR BEHAVIOUR

AMBIENCE: avoid rowdy drinking games or embarrassing stag-do antics.
MANNERS: if you accidentally spill someone's drink, offer to replace it.
QUEUING: respect the 'first come, first served' rule at the bar.
ATTENTION-SEEKER: don't wave wads of notes or click your fingers.
MEMORY: remember what people want and what you're ordering.
PAY UP: have money or a card at the ready so you can pay promptly.
SETTLE UP: remember to settle the tab and not to forget your card.
ON THE PULL: play it cool and don't be sleazy.
STILL ON THE PULL: never hit on the bar/waiting staff.

Guest Lists

Those with friends in high places can avoid queuing and fast track themselves to the other side of the velvet rope – the power of the clipboard should never be underestimated. Those on the list should never shout their name or make a song and dance about their elevated status. If there's 'been a mistake', never beg or attempt the 'don't you know who I am' trick. Desperation is unlikely to get you VIP treatment.

URINAL RULES

{1}

Always leave an empty urinal between you and the
next man. If this is not possible, use the cubicle.

{2}

You are not crossing the road: don't look left and right.

{3}

Your arms should be involved in the business at hand,
not held up against the wall in front.

{4}

Conversation is for before or after, never during.

BOUNCER BASICS

TREAT THEM WITH RESPECT.

DON'T ARGUE.

THEY HAVE THE POWER TO REFUSE YOU ENTRY.

THEY CAN ALSO THROW YOU OUT.

ONLY THE BRAVE ATTEMPT BRIBERY.

 EXPERT TIP If you are in an unfamiliar, foreign
city and you don't speak the language, keep
a card from the hotel – with the address
on it – in your wallet so that you can easily
show a taxi driver where you want to go.

JUKE BOXES

Most important of all is to key your selection accurately.
There's nothing worse than returning to the table at which
you and your mates are sitting to find them staring agog as
the 'The Birdie Song' blares from the pub speakers. Which
brings up the second rule: judge your crowd. Your favourite
West End showstopper may not be an appropriate choice
for the biker bar within which you are drinking. Thirdly,
never hog the juke box. No-one wants to hear your music
all night long. If they did, they'd be round your house.

TIPPING IN TOWN

BAR TABLE STAFF: 10 per cent (check
that it's not already added to your bill).
BAR STAFF: 10 per cent (if it's that smart
and the cocktails were that exceptional).
PUBS: offer the barman/barmaid a drink
(they can always choose to keep the cash).
CLOAKROOM ATTENDANTS: a few coins
on departure (unless you had to pay).
LOO ATTENDANTS: a few small coins
on your last visit of the evening (if you're
feeling generous or are a regular).

HOW TO DO
THE HUSTLE

STYLE GUIDE DANCING

{1}

As the night progresses, you may think you're an
unbelievable mover but, sadly, the opposite is usually true.
Keep an eye on yourself. If you've turned into a sweaty,
uncoordinated, overambitious mess, then it is time to stop.
Equally, if you find yourself alone on the dance floor,
it may be wise to swiftly exit – unless your Travolta-esque
routine has drawn an admiring crowd.

{2}

If you are a reluctant dancer, there are certain occasions
when you should make an effort to participate. If you
are at a wedding or party and everyone else is dancing,
it would look antisocial to sit at the side. Keep it simple
and at least try to move in time.

{3}

If you are out with just one other person, don't leave
them sitting on the sidelines while you take to the dance
floor. They may well be bored by the spectacle of you
dancing or, worse still, secretly sniggering – you'll
probably end up going home alone.

IT'S YOUR ROUND

Getting your round in is fundamental to community
spirit and the essence of friendship. Freeloaders are quickly
recognised and lowly regarded. So, unless you're out with
your mate-who-has-the-expense-account, your boss or
someone who's just won the lottery, make sure you know
when it's your turn.

ON FOOT WALK HISTORIC PARIS

Les Halles: formerly the city's wholesale food market, now a network of shops beneath concrete and glass bubbles – it is currently undergoing an architectural re-vamp.

Pompidou Centre: designed by Richard Rogers, Renzo Piano and Gianfranco Franchini in 1977. This stunning exhibition space looks like a building turned inside out, with pipes, ducts, escalators and lifts all visible on the outside.

Musée National Picasso: a huge collection of Picasso's work is housed in the restored Hôtel Salé on Rue de Thorigny. Built in 1656, it is one of the loveliest buildings in the Marais district.

Place de Vosges: a beautifully symmetrical square at the heart of the Marais district, laid out in 1605 by Henri IV.

The Marais: a fashionable area for the wealthy in the 17th century who built many imposing mansions. It is rich with museums, galleries and quirky shops.

Ile St Louis: with many beautiful 17th–18th century mansions, this is a perfect place to admire some typically Parisian architecture.

Ile de la Cité: the cradle of Parisian civilisation, the Medieval centre of the city.

Notre-Dame: a Gothic masterpiece, begun in 1163, site of many of the great events of French history.

Pont Neuf: the oldest bridge in Paris, built 1578–1604.

Café de Flore, St Germain-des-Prés: favourite haunt of Jean-Paul Sartre and Simone de Beauvoir, with a classic Art Deco interior.

Boulevard St-Germain: a classic Parisian street lined with pavement cafés, shops and galleries – the heart of the Left Bank.

Jardin du Luxembourg: an island of peace surrounding the imposing 17th-century Palais du Luxembourg, home of the French Senate.

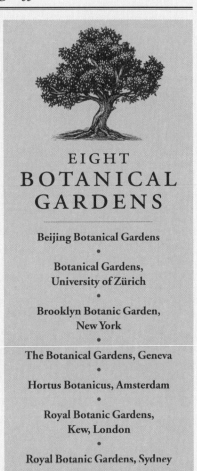

EIGHT BOTANICAL GARDENS

Beijing Botanical Gardens

•

Botanical Gardens, University of Zürich

•

Brooklyn Botanic Garden, New York

•

The Botanical Gardens, Geneva

•

Hortus Botanicus, Amsterdam

•

Royal Botanic Gardens, Kew, London

•

Royal Botanic Gardens, Sydney

•

Botanical Garden of the University of Vienna

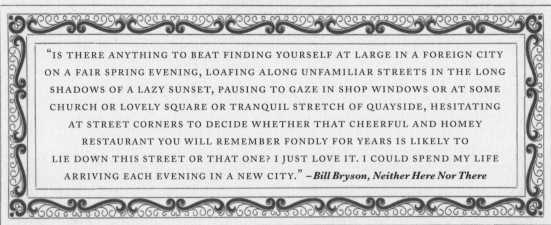

"IS THERE ANYTHING TO BEAT FINDING YOURSELF AT LARGE IN A FOREIGN CITY ON A FAIR SPRING EVENING, LOAFING ALONG UNFAMILIAR STREETS IN THE LONG SHADOWS OF A LAZY SUNSET, PAUSING TO GAZE IN SHOP WINDOWS OR AT SOME CHURCH OR LOVELY SQUARE OR TRANQUIL STRETCH OF QUAYSIDE, HESITATING AT STREET CORNERS TO DECIDE WHETHER THAT CHEERFUL AND HOMEY RESTAURANT YOU WILL REMEMBER FONDLY FOR YEARS IS LIKELY TO LIE DOWN THIS STREET OR THAT ONE? I JUST LOVE IT. I COULD SPEND MY LIFE ARRIVING EACH EVENING IN A NEW CITY." –*Bill Bryson, Neither Here Nor There*

SIX FOOD MARKETS

The Boqueria Market, Barcelona
Borough Market, London
Marché Richard-Lenoir, Paris
Rialto Markets, Venice
Tsukiji Fish Market, Tokyo
Union Square Greenmarket, New York

ON FOOT WALK HISTORIC MANHATTAN

Battery Park: from here you can see the Statue of Liberty and Ellis Island.

The Alexander Hamilton Custom House: now the National Museum of the American Indian.

Bowling Green Park: the first official park in New York, established in 1733.

Castle Clinton: a fort from the War of 1812.

Fraunces Tavern: built in 1719 for the old New York Delancey family.

The site of the Dutch Stadt Huys: the archaeological remains of early Manhattan.

Delmonico's Italian Steakhouse: an icon since 1837.

Wall Street: the heart of the financial district.

Federal Hall National Monument: George Washington was inaugurated here.

The New York Stock Exchange: a US National Historical Landmark, the building dates back to 1903.

Trinity Church: take a look at the historic graveyard.

City Hall Park: be sure to see the 1913 Woolworth building, 233 Broadway.

KNOWLEDGE THE A–Z OF SIGHTSEEING

AMSTERDAM hire a bike and explore
BEIJING wander down Yandai Xie Jie in Hou Hai
CHICAGO see the skyscrapers by boat
DUBAI visit Ski Dubai in The Mall of the Emirates
EDINBURGH walk up Calton Hill
FRANKFURT visit the famous zoo
GENEVA see the Flower Clock in the Jardin Anglais
HONG KONG take the Star Ferry from Central to Kowloon
ISTANBUL take a trip up the Bosphorus
JOHANNESBURG explore Constitution Hill
KIEV walk down St Andrew's Descent
LONDON look down on the city from the London Eye
MILAN shop in the Quadrilatero d'Oro
NEW YORK catch a baseball game
OSLO admire the sculptures in Vigeland Park
PARIS walk around the Cimetière de Montmartre
QUÉBEC CITY see the city from the Observatoire de la Capitale
RIO DE JANIERO watch football at the Maracaná Stadium
SYDNEY explore the Northern Beaches
TOKYO admire the Sony Building
UTRECHT dine in a canal-side restaurant
VIENNA see the Klimt at the Leopold Museum
WARSAW saunter along the wide-paved Nowy Świat
XIAN visit the nearby Terracotta Army
YEREVAN sample Armenian barbeque on Proshian Street
ZÜRICH admire Le Corbusier Pavilion

EIGHT CATHEDRALS WORTH A LOOK

Cologne Cathedral
·
Duomo, Milan
·
Notre-Dame, Paris
·
La Sagrada Familia, Barcelona
·
St. Basil's Cathedral, Moscow
·
St. John the Divine, New York
·
St. Paul's, London
·
St. Peter's Basilica, Rome

FREQUENT FAUX PAS

NO lateness. Arrive within ten minutes of your booking.

NO snapping of fingers to attract attention. Your waiter will, quite rightly, hate you.

NO "don't you know who I am" swagger, even if you dine there daily.

NO ordering off-menu, just for the sheer hell of it.

NO over-seasoning; don't doubt the chef's palate before you've even tasted.

NO shouting, bellowing or guffawing. Other diners aren't interested in you.

NO water snobbery; generally, tap water is fine.

NO sign of a mobile phone or pdas at the table.

DOGGY BAGS

The largely American habit of asking for a doggy bag – or, as they are more commonly called, a 'box', 'take-out box' or 'to-go box' – in a restaurant is not widely accepted this side of the Atlantic. While a 'waste-not-want-not' attitude is admirable, you should try to finish everything on your plate. Asking for a doggy bag is likely to be viewed as an unusual request and may raise eyebrows.

Money Matters

THE PERSON WHO REQUESTS THE PLEASURE, PAYS FOR THE PLEASURE: you should pick up the tab for a lunch or dinner – whether dating or business-entertaining – if you have invited the other person.

CHECK YOUR BILL: in the UK, tipping in restaurants is usually 'discretionary' but it is more discretionary in some places than others. 'Service not included' means just that, and it is usual to offer at least 10 per cent.

DON'T SEEM TOO SELF-INDULGENT: if you know that someone else will be picking up the bill, choose modestly.

BE GENEROUS: if you are footing the bill, let your guests choose what they want. Never order for other people.

GROUP DINING DIPLOMACY: split the bill equally between you; never start adding up what each person had.

DISCRETION: if you're picking up the tab, don't let your fellow diners know what it costs; equally don't huff and puff or act surprised when the bill arrives.

STYLE GUIDE NAPKINS

Unfold your napkin (never 'serviette') and place it in your lap before you start eating. It is not there to act as a catch-all solution to messy manners, so never tuck it into your shirt collar. It's okay to occasionally dab the corners of your mouth if necessary, but avoid grand side-to-side wiping gestures. When you have finished eating, place your napkin, unfolded, beside your plate.

THERE'S A FLY IN MY SOUP

If you are unlucky enough to find a foreign object in your food, don't cause a scene. If you unknowingly put it in your mouth, remove it discreetly and place the offending item on the side of your plate. Alert the waiter who should apologise profusely and replace the plate immediately. In a good restaurant, the dish should not appear on your bill. However, you may still think twice before returning.

Controlled Complaints

Don't lose your temper.

If dining in a group, don't upset the flow – only complain if there's a serious problem.

Remember that problems in a restaurant are rarely the fault of the serving staff.

If the problem doesn't get solved by the waiting staff, ask to speak to the manager.

Rudeness rarely works; politeness is positively disarming.

Remember the phrase "I'm sure we can resolve this".

As a last resort, subtly remind the manager of the restaurant's reputation.

WAITER & WAITRESS SUCCESS

A little charm goes a long way. Treating your waiter or waitress respectfully will enhance your experience no end, but keep it low-key. They have a job to do and other tables to serve, so allow them to get on. Help them know when you're ready to order by closing your menu. Gently attract attention by discreetly catching his/her eye. Most importantly, never try hitting on a waitress while she's on duty – she's not a hostess.

Principles of ordering wine

When dining in a group, defer to anyone more knowledgeable than you.

•

Remember, your companions' food orders should steer your choice of wine.

•

If you can't pronounce it, confidently point at the name on the list or tell the waiter the number.

•

Remember what you order so that you instantly recognise it when you are shown the bottle.

•

Ask the sommelier. It's their job to help and advise.

KNOWLEDGE MICHELIN STARS

The Michelin Red Guide originates from a 1900 book by The Michelin Tyre Company that listed motorist-friendly information, such as garages, hotels and restaurants. The restaurant recommendations proved so popular that soon anonymous inspectors were rating establishments. In 1926, the 'Michelin Star' was born; today's three star system was introduced in the 1930s. There is now *The Michelin Red Guide* for cities and countries across the globe, from London to Tokyo.

THE JUDGES' CRITERIA INCLUDE: quality of the produce; mastery of flavour and cooking; 'personality' of the cuisine; value for money; consistency between visits. Restaurants are judged only by 'what is on the plate', rather than on ambience, interior design or level of service.

WHAT A STAR MEANS:
★ A very good restaurant in its category
★★ Excellent cooking and worth a detour
★★★ Exceptional cuisine and worth the journey

Achieving a Michelin Star (or three) is the pinnacle of many chefs' careers. After being given this ultimate accolade, the establishment is firmly on the gastronomic map.

MENU JARGON DECODED

AU GRATIN (OR GRATINÉE): with a browned cheese or breadcrumb topping.

COULIS: smooth sauce of puréed fruit or vegetable.

JULIENNE: chopped into fine batons, like matchsticks.

JUS: a light sauce or gravy.

MEUNIÈRE: fish – floured and fried – served with butter and lemon.

PARMENTIER: includes potato.

QUENELLE: small, oval-shaped serving.

TARTARE: a preparation of minced raw steak, or raw fish.

VELOUTÉ: smooth, velvety liquid served as a sauce or soup.

FOUR
TOP TABLES

El Bulli, Girona, Spain

•

**Le Louis XV – Alain Ducasse
Hôtel de Paris, Monte-Carlo, Monaco**

•

Per Se, New York, USA

•

The Fat Duck, Berkshire, UK

CLUB MANNERS

{1}
If you are a member of a club, don't ever boast about it.

{2}
Meet your guests at the door or in the entrance
if you need to sign them in.

{3}
If you have more than one guest, tell reception
where you will be.

{4}
If you are a visitor, respect the club's codes of conduct.

{5}
Dress appropriately and respect the rules.

{6}
Don't talk about business.

{7}
Don't (obviously) network.

{8}
Be nice to the staff. Remember that you're
not in a regular hotel or a restaurant.

{9}
As a general rule, don't tip.

{10}
It's not the place to (actively) pull.

Nominations and Invitations

It is generally considered a bit desperate if you ask someone
to nominate you for membership of their club. It is best to
wait until you are 'invited' to join. Remember that you will
be a reflection of them if they put you forward – make sure
you 'fit in' to encourage that much coveted invitation.

Blofeld and Boodle's

It is rumoured that Ian Fleming drew inspiration for his
notorious baddie, Ernst Stavro Blofeld, at London club
Boodle's. Apparently Fleming spotted the surname of an
old school acquaintance, called Blofeld, on the membership
list and thought it perfect for his character. Incidentally, this
Blofeld was the father of cricket commentator Henry Blofeld.

BOND'S CLUB LIFE: BLADES

BLADES IS A FICTIONAL PRIVATE MEMBERS' CLUB IN
CENTRAL LONDON THAT FEATURES IN IAN FLEMING'S
BOND NOVELS. M IS A MEMBER AND JAMES BOND
OFTEN ACCOMPANIES HIM. IT IS WIDELY BELIEVED
THAT FLEMING BASED BLADES ON LONDON MEMBERS'
CLUB BOODLE'S, OF WHICH HE WAS A MEMBER.

"The amenities of Blades, apart from the gambling, are
so desirable that the Committee has had to rule that every
member is required to win or lose £500 a year on the club
premises, or pay an annual fine of £250. The food and wine
are the best in London and no bills are presented, the cost
of all meals being deducted at the end of each week pro rata
from the profits of the winners. Seeing that about £5,000
changes hands each week at the tables the impost is not
too painful and the losers have the satisfaction of saving
something from the wreck; and the custom explains the
fairness of the levy on infrequent gamblers." – *Moonraker*

"No newspaper comes to the reading room before it has
been ironed … There is a direct wire to Ladbroke's from the
porter's lodge; the club has the finest tents and boxes at the
principal race-meetings, at Lord's, Henley, and Wimbledon,
and members travelling abroad have automatic membership
of the leading club in every foreign capital." – *Moonraker*

"As usual he [M] paid, whatever the amount of the bill,
with a five-pound note for the pleasure of receiving in change
crisp new pound notes, new silver and gleaming copper
pennies, for it is the custom at Blades to give its members
only freshly minted money." – *The Man with the Golden Gun*

"Exactly one month before, it had been the eve of the
annual closing of Blades. On the next day, September 1st,
those members who were still unfashionably in London
would have to pig it for a month at White's or Boodle's.
White's they considered noisy and 'smart', Boodle's too
full of superannuated country squires who would be
talking of nothing but the opening of the partridge season.
For Blades, it was one month in the wilderness. But there
it was. The staff, one supposed, had to have their holiday."
– *You Only Live Twice*

ATHENÆUM   WHITE'S   REFORM   ST. JAMES'S   SAVILE   NATIONAL LIBERAL   GUARDS'   BROOKS'S   SAVAGE

> "I SENT THE CLUB
> A WIRE STATING:
> PLEASE ACCEPT
> MY RESIGNATION.
> I DON'T WANT TO
> BELONG TO ANY CLUB
> THAT WILL ACCEPT
> ME AS A MEMBER."
>
> – *Groucho Marx*

Definition: 'blackballed'

Being 'blackballed' is when an individual is refused membership of a club. Normally, an existing member will nominate someone for membership of the club.

The nomination process often requires the nominee to be 'seconded' by another member. It is then usually up to the membership committee to decide the fate of the prospective nominee.

The term 'blackballed' originates from a time when clubs held a secret ballot with a special ballot box to determine acceptance into the club. A white ball was put into the box to support the individual, or a black ball to reject them. Hence the term 'blackballed'. Sometimes, even just one black ball was enough to veto an individual.

Being 'blackballed' means you are deemed 'unsuitable' for the club – not something to brag about and an embarrassing situation for your nominator.

MISS DEBRETT *Charming vs Sleazy*

YOU MAY WANT to impress us with your man-about-town credentials, confident that we will be seduced by your *savoir-faire*, worldly finesse and exclusive haunts. But be warned: if you get it even slightly wrong, you will look like a sad *roué* – lecherous, needy, debauched – and we will be making a rapid exit, even if we're in the most exclusive club in town.

IF YOU TAKE US OUT, you'll find we're easily charmed. All it takes is a little attentiveness and focus on detail. Pay attention as the night progresses, and watch out for the first signs of irritability, fatigue or boredom. If you detect any of the symptoms, act swiftly: offer us a chair, a drink, a change of scene; ask us what we want to do; concentrate on our needs. Listen carefully to what we are saying, and respond accordingly. Be good-humoured, make us laugh and keep conversation light and discreet. Your good manners will instantly put us at our ease, and we will find you charming.

SLEAZINESS SHOULD BE AVOIDED at all costs; once you are saddled with this label, you will never be rehabilitated. Avoid overt sexual innuendoes, double-entendres and leering. Don't tell *risqué* jokes (until you know us very well). Never boast about past sexual conquests, Herculean drinking bouts or partying prowess.

MAINTAIN EYE CONTACT, but avoid any over-familiar touching until you know us better – we will be hyper-wary of lingering hands. Don't ever let us catch you eyeing up other women; we are sensitive to the tiniest flick of the eye in the direction of the competition, and will find your disloyalty both unforgivable and ominously sleazy.

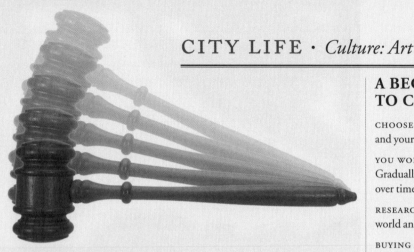

A BEGINNER'S GUIDE TO COLLECTING ART

CHOOSE ART that is suitable to your style and your life. Your home is not a museum.

YOU WON'T BECOME a 'collector' overnight. Gradually develop your tastes and confidence over time.

RESEARCH is crucial. Get a feel for the art world and visit as many galleries as you can.

BUYING ART can be intimidating. Ask questions and remember that the gallery dealers are there to talk about the artists' works – utilise their knowledge.

ASK ANY FRIENDS who already collect to help you; they may make an introduction to a gallery with which they have a relationship, or just accompany you on your research trips.

IT'S BETTER TO INVEST in fewer, better quality collectable pieces than lots of mediocre ones.

BE UPFRONT when it comes to money – most dealers don't appreciate people haggling. Build a relationship with a gallery and, over time, you may get favourable treatment.

ART FAIRS are the perfect place to start. You can see a good range of art, browse at your leisure and talk to the artists and dealers in a relaxed environment. Also, the exhibitors will have been vetoed, so you're guaranteed 'good quality' works from well-regarded artists.

LOOK INTO younger or lesser-known artists. You are gambling on the artist's profile increasing, but it may just be worth the risk if they make it.

DEGREE SHOWS offer very competitive prices, but it can be a risky investment as there's no guarantee the artist will continue their career.

NEVER BUY art off the web. A low-res screen shot is no substitute for seeing the real thing.

EMBRACE THE EMOTION of art; try to understand what it is trying to say. You're not buying a greetings card – as Aristotle explained: 'the aim of art is to represent not the outward appearance of things, but their inward significance'.

Auction Etiquette

{1} Usually, you have to register before the auction in order to bid. You may be asked for ID and a credit card number.

{2} When you register, you will be given a numbered 'paddle'; this is used to identify you in the saleroom.

{3} To make a bid, you raise your paddle (it's therefore unlikely you'll ever bid by mistake). If you aren't given a paddle, then it's customary to bid by raising your hand or nodding your head.

{4} Once the gavel (hammer) sounds, the item is won. The final price is called the hammer price.

{5} For lots worth a considerable amount, you can bid by phone. Someone will call you from the saleroom and bid for you; you are on the end of the phone line, listening in live.

{6} You can also make an absentee bid, where a maximum amount is set in advance, and someone bids on your behalf.

{7} Remember that you have to pay a buyer's premium in addition to the hammer price.

{8} Generally, you can take any lots won away with you after the auction.

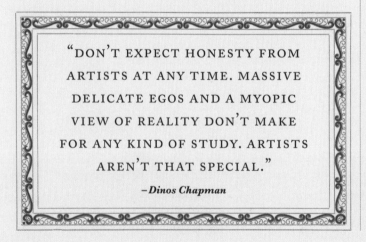

"DON'T EXPECT HONESTY FROM ARTISTS AT ANY TIME. MASSIVE DELICATE EGOS AND A MYOPIC VIEW OF REALITY DON'T MAKE FOR ANY KIND OF STUDY. ARTISTS AREN'T THAT SPECIAL."

– *Dinos Chapman*

FOUR ART FAIRS

Art Basel, Switzerland

Art Basel Miami Beach, USA

Frieze Art Fair, London, UK

Venice Biennale, Italy

IS IT ART? THE TURNER PRIZE

The controversial Turner Prize was set up in 1984 to 'celebrate new developments in contemporary art'. Despite being a prize for contemporary art, it is named after artist JMW Turner (1775–1851) because he had always wanted to set up a prize for young artists but never succeeded.

Entrants have to be British, under 50 years old, and must have notably exhibited or presented in the preceding twelve months. An independent jury that changes every year picks the winner. The provocative Prize always sparks debate and there have been many familiar names that have won, some with more memorable works than others…

1996 Damien Hirst *Mother and Child, Divided*
… the formaldehyde year.

1998 Chris Ofili *No Woman, No Cry*
… the one with the elephant dung.

1999 Tracey Emin *My Bed*
… yes, that dirty bed.

2001 Martin Creed *Work No. 277, The Lights Going On and Off*
… and it's exactly what they did.

FIVE SPECIALIST ART MUSEUMS

Musée National Picasso, Paris

Dalí Theatre-Museum, Figueres

The Munch Museum, Oslo

The Andy Warhol Museum, Pittsburgh

Van Gogh Museum, Amsterdam

TEN ART MUSEUMS

Fine Arts Museums of San Francisco
Don't miss: Claude Monet, Water Lilies

•

Musée du Louvre, Paris
Don't miss: Leonardo Da Vinci, Mona Lisa

•

Museo Nacional del Prado, Madrid
Don't miss: Peter Paul Reubens, The Three Graces

•

Museum of Modern Art (MoMA), New York
Don't miss: Jackson Pollock, One: Number 31

•

The National Gallery, London
Don't miss: Vincent Van Gogh, Sunflowers

•

Rijksmuseum, Amsterdam
Don't miss: Johannes Vermeer, Love Letter

•

Tate Modern, London
Don't miss: Mark Rothko, Murals

•

The Belvedere, Vienna
Don't miss: Gustav Klimt, The Kiss

•

The Pushkin Museum of Fine Arts, Moscow
Don't miss: Edgar Degas, Blue Dancers

•

Uffizi Gallery, Florence
Don't miss: Botticelli, The Birth of Venus

GOLDEN RULES OF GALLERIES

{1}
Respect the silence; avoid loud conversation.
{2}
Respect fellow visitors; don't intrude on personal space.
{3}
Appreciate the works, but don't lecture companion(s).
{4}
It's not necessary to like or understand everything.
{5}
Keep strong opinions to yourself ("Call that art!").
{6}
Don't 'hog' paintings or barge in front of other people.
{7}
Never, ever touch the exhibits.

TEN ESSENTIAL OPERAS
A BLUFFER'S GUIDE

{I} **Carmen** Bizet (Paris, 1875)
A sultry love triangle set in Seville. The opening scene in a cigarette factory is impossible to stage authentically these days following the ban on smoking in public places. Plot resumé: chinless mummy's boy falls in love with gypsy temptress, but she runs off with a butch toreador. Does she live happily ever after? Not a chance …

•

{II} **Don Giovanni** Mozart (Prague, 1787)
Also set in Seville, where a murderous lothario keeps a date with death. Famous for its 'Catalogue Aria', detailing Don Juan's cosmopolitan love life (including 1,003 women in Spain alone!). One of the very few operas in which the male lead, rather than the heroine, gets his come-uppance for bad behaviour. Mozart wrote the overture between five and seven in the morning, with a hangover.

•

{III} **Eugene Onegin** Tchaikovsky (Moscow, 1879)
Romantic wires are crossed in the Russian countryside when the impressionable young Tatiana writes a fateful love-letter to the aloof and worldly Eugene. In typical Russian fashion, duels are fought, balls are danced and the man doesn't get his girl in the end. In a strange twist of life mirroring art, Tchaikovsky received a letter from a besotted pupil whom he subsequently married with disastrous consequences.

•

{IV} **Julius Caesar** Handel (London, 1724)
A tale of derring-do set on the banks of the Nile. The opera has become all the rage ever since slinky soprano Danielle DeNiese, as Cleopatra, threw caution and clothing to the wind while singing with virtuosic gusto in a bath (of ass's milk no doubt) during a recent production at Glyndebourne. Handel, composer of the beloved oratorio 'Messiah', is considered a national treasure in Britain, although he was actually German.

•

{v} **La Bohème** Puccini (Turin, 1896)
Opera's finest tear-jerker set among a group of rowdy young artists (a poet, a painter, a philosopher and a musician) in shabby chic, Latin-Quarter Paris in the 1830s . In a typical 19th-century twist, tuberculosis brings an end to the fun and frolics. One of the most performed operas, *La Bohème* is good for getting back in touch with your inner rebel; the famous aria 'Che gelida manina' is a reminder of why paying the heating bills on time is a good idea …

{VI} **La Traviata** Verdi (Venice, 1853)
More romantic shenanigans in Paris: this time a tart with a heart teaches a stuffy old father and his priggish son a lesson in moral values. Great high-society party scenes, overflowing with drink and debauchery. Of course it all ends in tragedy, played shamelessly on the heart-strings for all its worth. The role of Violetta, the frail, consumptive heroine of the opera, was created by Fanny Salvini-Donatelli, who pitched in at what the critics described as a 'considerable' 20st 7lb.

•

{VII} **Rigoletto** Verdi (Venice, 1851)
The dashing Duke of Manuta, possibly one of the nastiest men in opera (and there are plenty of them) sings a string of sublime arias, among them 'La Donna è Mobile', a jaunty number, dripping with hypocrisy about the fickleness of women. Meanwhile Gilda, the innocent daughter of the vengeful, hump-backed court jester, is battered to death in a sack in a terrible case of mistaken identity (thankfully it doesn't stop her singing a long and deeply affecting farewell to the world before she breathes her last).

•

{VIII} **The Barber of Seville** Rossini (Rome, 1816)
Genuinely funny romp in which an old man is hoodwinked by a clever barber so that a loving couple are finally united. The prequel to Mozart's *The Marriage of Figaro* (see below) although written 30 years later. At the opera's famously accident-prone first night in 1816, one of the leads had a violent nosebleed during his aria and a cat caused mayhem when it dashed onto the stage during the finale.

•

{IX} **The Flying Dutchman** Wagner (Dresden, 1843)
Wagner with all the usual storm and fury but, running at just over two hours, it's relatively kind on the behind. A salty ghost story set at sea, so nothing to do with flying KLM. Lots of jaunty yo-ho-hos for the nautically inclined, but if you really want to impress, you'll have to sit through the *Ring Cycle*: all 16 hours of it …

•

{x} **The Marriage of Figaro** Mozart (Vienna, 1786)
Sublime music with revolutionary undertones. Use the Italian to sound like a true aficionado: *Le Nozze di Figaro*. A philandering count is forgiven by his long-suffering wife after she catches him making love to another woman. Meanwhile the servants comically get the upper hand on their masters. A warning to cads and bounders.

The première city and date appear in brackets after the composer

SIX SHAKESPEAREAN INSULTS

{1} THOU SPONGEY FAT-KIDNEYED CODPIECE!
{2} THOU TONGUELESS TOAD-SPOTTED STRUMPET!
{3} ACCURSED FULL-GORGED MINNOW!
{4} THOU ARTLESS MUDDY-MOTTLED HUGGER-MUGGER!
{5} THOU IMPERTINENT MUDDY-MOTTLED MALT-WORM!
{6} THOU SLANDEROUS BEEF-WITTED BAG OF GUTS!

STYLE GUIDE APPLAUSE

AT THE OPERA it is usual to applaud after the overture (before curtain-up), after an impressive aria (but never while someone is singing), at the end of a scene or act and, of course, at the end of the production. It is also the norm to clap the conductor when they take to the podium before the performance, after the interval and at the end (when the orchestra also take a bow).

AT SEATED MUSICAL CONCERTS you are expected to applaud between different compositions, but be cautious of clapping between movements within a piece.

AT THE THEATRE applause is expected at the end of each act, after a notable scene or moment and at the end of a production.

KNOWLEDGE THE BEST OF THE BARD
Shakespeare Plays Worth Seeing (and Quoting…)

HAMLET
"To be or not to be, that is the question…"

KING LEAR
*"How sharper than a serpent's tooth
it is to have a thankless child!"*

MACBETH
*"Is this a dagger which I see before me,
The handle toward my hand?"*

A MIDSUMMER NIGHT'S DREAM
"The course of true love never did run smooth."

MUCH ADO ABOUT NOTHING
"Everyone can master a grief but he that has it."

OTHELLO
"I will wear my heart upon my sleeve for daws to peck at."

ROMEO AND JULIET
*"What's in a name? That which we call a rose
by any other name would smell as sweet."*

THE TEMPEST
"We are such stuff as dreams are made on…"

TWELFTH NIGHT
*"Some are born great, some achieve greatness
and some have greatness thrust upon them."*

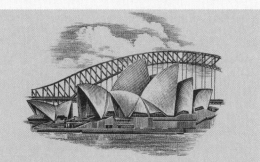

TEN TOP OPERA HOUSES

Bolshoi Theatre, Moscow
Hungarian State Opera House, Budapest
La Fenice, Venice
La Scala, Milan
Royal Opera House, London
Opera House, Sydney
Teatro Amazonas, Manaus
Teatro Colón, Buenos Aires
The Metropolitan Opera, New York
Vienna State Opera, Austria

TIME OFF

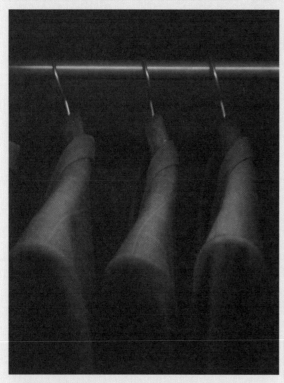

STYLE GUIDE BLAZERS VS JACKETS

JACKETS can look stylish in a variety of materials and patterns, from linen to seersucker, cashmere, houndstooth, Harris tweed and pinstripe.

WORN WITH A SHIRT AND TIE, blazers are smart and formal; pairing them with jeans looks classy and casual.

BLAZERS are coming back. Avoid the 'gin and Jag' formalities of a bygone generation by choosing a blazer with a modern silhouette, slender lapels and non-metallic buttons.

Blazer Trivia

The origins of the term 'blazer' are disputed. Some believe that it comes from the bright red jackets worn by the Lady Margaret Boat Club, the rowing club of St. John's College, Cambridge, whose jackets were 'ablaze' with colour. Others believe that it derives from the HMS Blazer, whose crew was decked out in short, blue-and-white striped jackets with brass buttons when Queen Victoria visited in 1837. Blazers continue to be linked with clubs, sporting associations, schools, colleges or regiments.

JUMPER RULES

IF WEARING A SHIRT, always wear a v-neck, not a round-neck, jumper. Keep your collars on the inside.

THE V SHOULD BE as high as possible. At most, it should break halfway down your chest.

MAKE SURE you invest in some good-quality cashmere for your wardrobe. Merino wool is about the only alternative worth considering for colder weather.

COTTON JUMPERS can be useful in the summer when it is warm, but they will not wear as well or as long as wool, and can lose their shape after a while.

WEAR PATTERNS WITH CARE – it's easy to look like a middle-aged golfer if you go wrong. Instead, wear plain, classic colours that suit you.

Short Style

CARGO SHORTS are probably the standard, but choose carefully to avoid looking like a frat-boy. Keep them on or above the knee – though never too high.

THREE-QUARTER LENGTH trousers are neither shorts nor trousers; leave them to women.

TRY TO AVOID HEAVY, enclosed shoes with shorts. Always wear flip-flops or sandals. If you must, wear plain deck shoes with no socks.

SHORTS SUIT T-SHIRTS, polo-shirts and short-sleeved shirts. If you combine your shorts with a long-sleeved shirt, always roll up your sleeves.

CUT-OFF DENIM SHORTS are never, ever right.

BELT RULES

{1}
Keep your buckle discreet. You're not a cowboy.
{2}
Vintage belts look better than new ones when worn casually.
{3}
Match the colour of the leather to your shoes/socks.
{4}
Match the metal to your cufflinks/jewellery.
{5}
Reversible belts are both practical and handy.
{6}
Store belts by coiling them or hanging them from a hanger.

GET IT RIGHT: CASUAL SHIRTS

ELEGANT AND CLASSIC, it is impossible to go wrong with a blue or white Oxford shirt. They can be worn with jeans, chinos, shorts or a suit, and should play a major role in the casual wardrobe.

A BUTTON-DOWN collar is a good casual look but, as the name suggests, it should always be buttoned.

CLASSIC STRIPES ARE BETTER than checks. They're more flattering and less brash. If you do wear checks, a pattern of small checks looks better then large.

TRY WEARING GINGHAM in red, blue or even brown as an alternative to checks. It's surprisingly wearable and creates a sharp but relaxed look.

BLACK SHIRTS should be as dark and true-black as possible. Worn with jeans they make a good contrast, but be wary of looking like a waiter.

NOT ONLY THE DOMAIN of the delivery guy, mechanic or fast-food restaurant worker, short-sleeved shirts are the perfect casual option for warmer days and mild evenings.

COMFORT-STRETCH SHIRTS are perfect for travelling as the stretch in the cotton means that any creases will fall out within a few minutes of wearing them.

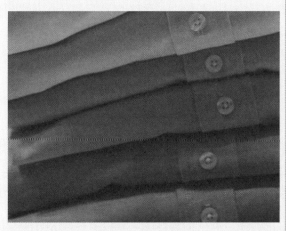

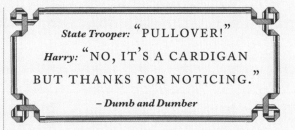

State Trooper: "PULLOVER!"

Harry: "NO, IT'S A CARDIGAN BUT THANKS FOR NOTICING."

– Dumb and Dumber

GEAR T-SHIRTS AND POLO SHIRTS

SIMPLE IS BEST – t-shirts in plain colours, without logos, stripes, overbearing patterns or designs. You're not an advert.

AVOID JOKES. You're not a stand-up comedian. Equally, band t-shirts are only acceptable if you were at that specific gig or if you own more than two of the band's records. If you can't name every member of The Ramones, don't wear the t-shirt.

WHITE T-SHIRTS always look good. The more broken in, the better, but make sure it stays white, and doesn't turn a washed-with-the-socks shade of grey. A worn-in t-shirt, paired with jeans and a jacket looks great in cool, casual circumstances.

BUY A VARIETY OF POLO SHIRTS. They are very versatile, so experiment and build up a varied collection. Logos and brand labels should be discreet, but it's smarter to opt for exclusive personalised designs.

Cardigans

NOT JUST FOR OLD MEN, a cardigan is perfect for layering. It can be worn with a jacket, on its own, casually or formally. Have them in a variety of colours and in a variety of knits – some chunky and some thin-knit. In many climates a jacket is too hot – the ideal time to wear a cardigan that will keep you warm, without being too heavy.

Polo Trivia

The origins of the polo shirt lie in the sport from which it gets its name. Polo players would wear these relaxed shirts in the colours of their teams. It is believed that the buttoned-down shirt also originates from days when polo players buttoned down their collars to stop them flapping about whilst riding.

CHINO STYLE

An ideal alternative to jeans, chinos are a slightly smarter option. They create a more relaxed look than jeans but, despite this, they should not be too baggy or too pleated. The slimmer the fit, the more flattering they will look. Versatile, casual and easy to dress up or down, they should be an essential item in the wardrobe. Wear them with white Jack Purcell Converse or, in more formal situations, deck shoes, and a blue cotton Oxford shirt or polo shirt.

FRAMES TO SUIT FACES: GLASSES AND SUNGLASSES

{1} GLASSES

HAIR, EYE AND SKIN colour are more important than face shape when it comes to choosing a pair of glasses.

FRAMES MUST NOT look too big or too small for your face.

ROUGHLY, YOUR EYES should be in the middle of the lens and the frame should be level with the side of your face.

MATCH BLONDE HAIR with light or rimless frames.

MATCH DARK HAIR with darker frames (so long as you have darker skin too).

GREY HAIR looks best with rimless, silver or grey frames.

REDHEADS can get away with both dark and rimless glasses.

ANYONE BALDING would be best to choose larger frames to divert attention from their (expanding) forehead.

{2} SUNGLASSES

SUNGLASSES should be exactly as wide as your face.

THE TOP OF YOUR FRAMES should bisect your eyebrows, meaning they cover part of them but not all of them.

SUNGLASSES should not ride up or slide down your nose.

THE BRIDGE ought to be a snug, but not too snug, fit.

ROUND frames tend to suit squarer faces.

RECTANGULAR frames are better for those with rounder faces.

BLACK, GREY OR AMBER lenses are always the safest bet.

SPORTS GLASSES are for playing sports in, not for casual wear.

MIRRORED SHADES work well … if you're a rock star.

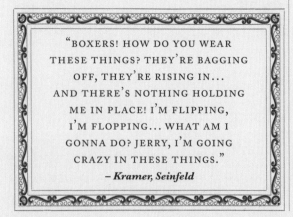

> "BOXERS! HOW DO YOU WEAR THESE THINGS? THEY'RE BAGGING OFF, THEY'RE RISING IN… AND THERE'S NOTHING HOLDING ME IN PLACE! I'M FLIPPING, I'M FLOPPING… WHAT AM I GONNA DO? JERRY, I'M GOING CRAZY IN THESE THINGS."
> – *Kramer, Seinfeld*

UNDERWEAR RULES

{1}
Tight underwear should be plain, not patterned.

{2}
White, navy, black or grey, nothing else, and never go novelty.

{3}
Never wear baggy boxers with a suit.
VPL affects men too – wear something tight instead.

{4}
The only person who should know who your underwear is made by is you. Keep your waistband to yourself.

{5}
You aren't a rapper; trousers should cover underwear.

{6}
Boxer shorts should never come below the mid-thigh.

{7}
If wearing just boxers, remove your socks immediately.

{8}
Keep them clean. Your mother was right about that bus.

{9}
Y-fronts are for your grandfather.

{10}
Going commando is for emergencies only.

{11}
There is no right or wrong type of underwear (except Y-fronts and thongs) – comfort is king.

{12}
For the ultimate luxury, have bespoke boxers made for you to match your bespoke shirt.

SANDALS *vs* FLIP-FLOPS

THOUGH IT SEEMS ridiculous to consider the formality of a pair of shoes that will leave your toes on display, the decision whether to wear either sandals or flip-flops is an important one.

SANDALS ARE THE SMARTER choice, but they should not be worn with everything – shorts tend to look better with flip-flops, for example.

SANDALS SHOULD BE MADE of leather – brown if possible. Avoid black as they will make your feet look pasty and over-exposed (not a good look when relaxing in the summer), and remember that ankle straps are never that flattering.

SANDALS CAN BE WORN in the evening in hot climes. They can be paired with lightweight, lighter-coloured trousers and even with jeans.

WEARING SANDALS WITH SOCKS, however, is the sartorial equivalent of wearing your trousers on your head and your underwear around your ankles.

FLIP-FLOPS ARE HARDER to get right. Essentially for day wear, they can look good in bright colours and neutral shades.

FLIP-FLOPS SHOULD BE KEPT simple – anything involving patterns or individual toe-holders should be shunned immediately.

GO FOR SOMETHING thin-soled, flat and with a single, V-shaped band for the toes.

THEY CAN BE WORN with shorts and, on occasion, jeans or chinos, but should be replaced with something else by the time the sun goes down.

WHILE IT IS FINE to wear sandals into town, flip-flops suggest a degree of casualness that might offend your fellow shoppers in smarter districts.

THE MOST IMPORTANT THING to remember when wearing either sandals or flip-flops is the hygiene of your feet. Keep your nails short and tidy, your toes lump-free and the smell never anything less fragrant than a field of summer daisies.

UNDERWEAR
THROUGH THE AGES

Ancient World: from slaves to Roman soldiers, loincloths were the norm – except for the Greeks, who didn't wear any underwear at all.

•

Middle Ages: large, baggy drawers called 'braies' replaced loincloths. They were linen, laced at the waist, and reached down to mid-calf.

•

Renaissance: braies became shorter to accommodate long leg-hugging hose called *chausses*. They were fitted with a front flap – the codpiece, shaped to emphasize, and exaggerate, the genitalia.

•

Victorian: drawers were knee-length, cotton, silk or linen with a simple button overlap in front and a drawstring waist.

•

1930s: with the innovation of elastic waistbands, buttonless drawers came into vogue – the first boxers.

GET IT RIGHT: CASUAL SHOES

THE PERFECT OUTFIT can be easily ruined by the wrong shoes. Some would argue that the right shoes can rescue even the worst fashion disaster – the reverse is hardly ever true.

WITH JEANS, a pair of tan brogues create a sleek look, especially when worn with a crisp blue shirt and Harris tweed jacket.

BLACK SHOES with jeans can look cold and stark; wear them with a white shirt, very dark jeans and a dark jacket.

SHOES SHOULD HAVE as rounded a toe as possible; pointy shoes have had their day for now. Square ended shoes should be regarded as a bizarre curiosity rather than a stylish look.

THE RIGHT PAIR OF TRAINERS can work with jeans. Worn with a suit jacket, jeans and t-shirt, a pair such as Jack Purcell Converse are a good way of dressing down and creating a relaxed look. Sporty trainers, meanwhile, should be reserved for the gym.

DECK SHOES or driving shoes can freshen up your look in the summer. In brown leather and paired with the right coloured jeans (white denim can work well) they can create a continental air that will lend a sense of style to even the dullest English summer day.

JEAN CARE

YOUR JEANS should be an old friend. They should be worn in to such an extent that they are essentially part of your body. If not, you're not wearing them properly.

JEANS SHOULD BE WORN for as long as possible before being washed (some say a year, if you can manage it). That will allow them to slowly become personalised to your body shape (which is what you want).

NEVER PUT JEANS through a tumble-dryer. It will make them horribly soft and fluffy.

WHEN WASHING JEANS, turn them inside out, choose a 30-degree cycle and then lay them flat to dry. Dry cleaning is better for them, though it can destroy any leather labels on the back of the jeans.

JAPANESE DENIM often has a better colour as it is darker and more authentically made. That means it will age well and will wear for longer, as the colour will not fade as quickly.

THE OUTSIDE LEG should have what's known as a 'busted seam'. This, basically, is the way the leg is sewn together and, over time, it will create a good fade on the jeans, helping them age properly.

JEANS AREN'T THAT EXPENSIVE so, when they stop looking good, replace them.

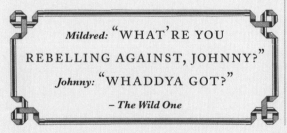

Mildred: "WHAT'RE YOU REBELLING AGAINST, JOHNNY?"
Johnny: "WHADDYA GOT?"
– *The Wild One*

STYLE GUIDE CUT

THERE ARE TWO ESSENTIAL FITS – classic and skinny. The classic fit will rise higher at the waist, while the skinny jean should sit lower and hug the leg more tightly. Baggy jeans are for teenagers, tapered jeans are for your dad.

GENERALLY, people with shorter legs should go for skinnier jeans – but not skin tight. They will elongate your legs and make you appear taller.

BIGGER PEOPLE can look better in less tight fitting jeans as they will not cling to the body and accentuate the wrong areas.

BOOTCUT JEANS only look good with boots, and sometimes not even then. While they may have looked fine in the early 1990s, they don't tend to look good now. If worn, they should be paired with a shirt rather than a t-shirt as they tend to look more formal.

Denim History

ORIGINALLY MADE of raw serge (twilled fabric) from Nîmes in southern France, denim got its name because it was known as *serge de Nîmes*.

THE SERGE WAS THEN made into trousers in Genoa (mainly for use by Genoese sailors) where it became known as *bleu de Genes* – or blue of Genoa – and then, eventually, just jeans.

MODERN, RIVETED JEANS were thought to have been invented by Levi Strauss in the 1850s in San Francisco. The rivets were added to jeans sold to gold miners to make their trousers more hard-wearing.

ORIGINALLY WORN as working trousers, jeans earned their place in mainstream popular culture when worn by teenagers as a statement of rebellion in the 1950s.

OVER THE FOLLOWING DECADES, jeans began to be mass-produced to keep up with demand. Projectile looms replaced shuttle looms as they could produce more material in less time. Many of the old shuttle looms ended up in Japan.

NOWADAYS, JAPANESE DENIM is seen by many as the finest in the world. The original method of fabric making, using shuttle looms, produces the highest quality selvedge denim woven from a single thread – the result is a stronger, tightly-woven fabric that is unlikely to fray.

JEANS MADE FROM SELVEDGE denim will always look and feel superior to other varieties. Jeans are an essential item in your wardrobe; make sure you buy the best quality and best fitting pair possible.

Colour Matters

THE DARKER THE BETTER. Dark blue jeans are the most versatile colour as they will go with almost anything – from a suit jacket to a t-shirt.

RINSED JEANS can be more practical. They are lighter and 'bluer' than raw jeans, and won't shrink so much if washed.

BLACK JEANS are another good choice and will match most things. They should always be fairly tight fitting.

WHITE JEANS require bravery but can look good on the few that pull it off. Success lies in wearing them when on holiday in hot countries, usually with a navy jacket and deck shoes.

HOW AND WHY TO WEAR A BIKER JACKET

Invented by Irving Schott in 1928 and first sold by Harley Davidson for the equivalent of £5.50, it wasn't until Marlon Brando wore a biker jacket in *The Wild One* that they became the true rebel's attire.

Rather than risk looking like Fonzie, opt for a James Dean-style café-racer jacket (which can be identified by its straight zip and tab collar). They should never look new. Second-hand shops are the ideal place to buy great looking, worn-in jackets, but it can often involve a long and fruitless search. Instead, look for a new jacket that has been made to look authentic and broken in.

Remember, if your jacket makes you look like you just got off a bike, then wear it. If it doesn't, don't.

DENIM RULES

{1}

There are few occasions now, in these more casual times, where jeans are an absolute no-no. There are plenty of occasions on which the wrong pair of jeans will mark you out for all the wrong reasons, so choose carefully – if your jeans are cut well and not looking too old and shabby, you will be suitably dressed in most situations.

{2}

Offices are becoming more casual and therefore jeans are more acceptable in the workplace. However, they should still be smart.

{3}

On dress-down Fridays you want to look casual but not too casual. A good pair of jeans, rather than the pair you slouch about in at the weekends, can be the key to this.

{4}

Jeans with a suit jacket will create a smart, dressed-down look but always ensure that you will be smart enough. A classic look that will serve you well on most occasions is dark blue jeans, a crisp white shirt and dark jacket.

TRADITIONAL DRESS CODES

WHITE TIE

Quick translation: tails.
Also called: 'full evening dress' or 'cravate blanche'.

BLACK TAIL COAT: single-breasted with silk lapels (always worn unbuttoned). Never confuse with a morning coat.

BLACK TROUSERS: matches the tail coat, with two lines of braid down each outside leg.

WHITE MARCELLA SHIRT: worn with a detachable wing collar, cufflinks and studs.

THIN WHITE MARCELLA BOW-TIE: always hand-tied.

WHITE MARCELLA EVENING WAISTCOAT: double or single-breasted.

BLACK PATENT LACE-UP SHOES: clean and shiny.

IN WINTER a black overcoat and white silk scarf can be worn.

Etiquette tip: nowadays it is not necessary to wear a top hat. Many see it as a pointless exercise as it is only worn en route to the event, and therefore goes unnoticed.

BLACK TIE

Quick translation: bow tie.
Also called: 'dinner jackets', 'tuxedo', 'dress for dinner' or 'cravate noir'.

BLACK WOOL DINNER JACKET: single-breasted with no vents. Silk (often grosgrain) peaked lapels (a shawl collar is also fine) and covered buttons.

BLACK TROUSERS: slightly tapered, single row of braid down the outside leg.

WHITE MARCELLA EVENING SHIRT: with a soft turn-down collar, worn with cufflinks and studs.

BLACK BOW TIE: always hand tied.

BLACK LACE-UP SHOES: highly polished or patent.

WHITE SILK SCARF: an optional but traditional accessory.

CUMMERBUNDS or low cut black evening waistcoats are rarely worn nowadays.

Etiquette tip: never wear a white dinner jacket (unless you are on a cruise).

MORNING DRESS

Quick translation: morning coat and top hat. Also called: 'formal day dress'.

MORNING COAT: black or grey, but black more usually worn. Single-breasted with peaked lapels, curved front edges sloping back at the sides into long tails.

TROUSERS: grey with a grey morning coat; grey and black striped with a black coat.

SHIRT: plain white with a stiff turned-down collar, double cuffs and cufflinks. Pale blue or pink is also acceptable.

TIE: in black or silver heavy woven silk. A cravat can be worn; a tie is slicker.

WAISTCOAT: grey under a black morning coat, buff under a grey coat. Coloured waistcoats can look garish. Never wear a backless waistcoat.

BLACK LACE-UP SHOES: highly polished.

HAT: grey felt or vintage black silk.

Etiquette tip: at weddings, hats should never be worn inside the church or in formal photographs.

DRESS CODES: OTHER OCCASIONS

BAR MITZVAHS AND BAT MITZVAHS
Men should wear a formal suit and skullcap.

•

HOLLYWOOD BLACK TIE
Originally meant a suit worn with a black tie, but has developed into a *laissez-faire* attitude of anything goes.

•

FUNERALS Men should wear a dark suit, a white shirt and a sombre tie.

•

LOUNGE SUIT This requires men to wear a suit and tie.

•

WEDDINGS Traditionally men wear morning dress, or a suit with a shirt and tie, unless an alternative is stated on the invitation (e.g. black tie).

HOW TO TIE A BOW TIE

Practice is everything, and soon you will get the knack…

•

Hang the tie around your neck, in place over the collar.

•

Adjust the tie so that one end is slightly longer than the other, crossing the long end over the short.

•

Bring the long end through the centre at the neck.

•

Form an angled loop with the short end of the tie crossing left. Drop the long end at the neck over this horizontal loop.

•

Form a similar angled loop with the loose long end of the tie and push this loop through the short loop.

•

Tighten knot by adjusting the ends of both loops.

 EXPERT TIP At official functions, traditionally the principal guest is seated on the host's right, the principal guest's wife on the host's left and the host's wife on the right of the principal guest.

Formal Dinners

Formal dinners – still common in the armed forces, at some universities and in the Inns of Court – are bound up in ritual and tradition. Follow the dress code on the invitation and arrive on time. Look to the 'top table' and your own companions for cues on when to sit down, start eating, etc. You must refrain from leaving the table during dinner. Don't drain your glass and find it empty for the toast. If the National Anthem is played you should be upstanding, leaving your glass on the table until the end. If the Loyal Toast is offered, simply stand and repeat 'The Queen' after the principal host. Speeches and port follow the toasts.

CORRECT FORM INVITATIONS

OFFICIAL AND FORMAL PRIVATE INVITATIONS: guests should use the reply card, if one is sent. Alternatively, reply on writing paper, showing your address. When an invitation includes 'and Guest' or 'and Partner', the reply should include name of who will attend.

> *Mr. William Debrett thanks the President of the Society of X for the kind invitation for Saturday, 12 February, which he accepts with much pleasure (or: which he much regrets being unable to accept).*

WEDDING INVITATIONS: replies should be handwritten, in the third person, on headed paper. The envelope is addressed to the hostess and the date should written at the bottom of the page.

> *Mr. William Debrett thanks Mr. and Mrs. James Smith for the kind invitation to the marriage of their daughter, Joanna, to Mr. Thomas Lucky at The Church, Barcombe, on Saturday 14th July at 3 o'clock and afterwards at The House, and is delighted to accept (or: regrets that he is unable to accept).*

ROYAL INVITATIONS: invitations from the Sovereign are commands; all replies must be addressed to the member of the Royal Household who issued the invitation. The reason for non-acceptance should be stated – a prior engagement is not considered to be a sufficient reason for failing to obey the Sovereign's command.

WEDDING LISTS

The circumstances of the bride and groom often influence the choice of wedding list. A couple setting up home have different priorities to those who have lived together for years. Lists are available through department stores, specialist wedding list companies, independent shops or charities. It is unusual to ask for money, but some couples request contributions or gift vouchers towards their honeymoon.

Guests should not think that they are being unoriginal by buying from the list – the couple has specifically requested those items. However, feel free to do something different if you would like to give a unique or more individual present. It is a gracious gesture to give a present even if you can't attend the wedding.

TWENTY THINGS TO DO BEFORE YOU DIE

{1}
Fly a MiG over Moscow
{2}
Visit the Rio carnival
{3}
See the Big Five: elephant, lion,
buffalo, rhino and leopard
{4}
Drive an F1 car
{5}
Visit Antarctica
{6}
Learn to fly a helicopter
{7}
Savour a bottle of Chateau d'Yquem 2001
{8}
Drive from Peking to Paris
{9}
Do the Cresta Run
{10}
Book your flight in space
{11}
Take a break in an ice hotel
{12}
Try sky-diving
{13}
Take a trip on the Trans-Siberian express
{14}
Buy an island
{15}
Take an American road trip
{16}
Take a girl to Paris and fail to leave your hotel room
{17}
Give the boll**king to end all boll**kings
{18}
Try eating fugue (pufferfish)
{19}
Do a wing walk
{20}
Book an entire floor of a hotel for a party

WHEN TO TREAT YOURSELF AND WHEN TO TREAT OTHERS

THERE ARE CERTAIN TIMES in your life, momentous occasions, when it is only right to reward yourself with a memento of your efforts. For instance, your first promotion may well be an occasion to splash out – perhaps on a quality watch or your first truly decent suit. Indulgence is easier when you are yet to acquire family responsibilities.

THERE ARE OTHER TIMES, too, when you'll want to do something solely for yourself – perhaps turning 40, being made a company partner, or retiring. Remember, this is about doing something which is entirely about your own pleasure. Go on, you've earned it.

SOMETIMES YOU NEED TO STEP BACK and let others do the celebrating. A major anniversary, for example, is not the time to go and look at the new car you've been considering. Instead, you should be splashing out on her – a balloon trip over the Serengeti, a stay on a remote tropical island or that diamond necklace she adores.

THE BIRTH OF A CHILD is another time to pamper your partner – and, of course, your new baby. Perhaps start a savings account with a healthy cash injection, or invest in something that will become a keepsake for your child in the future. Whatever it is, just make sure that you're not buying it for yourself.

Ostentatious?

If it can be in any way described as bling, it's ostentatious.

•

If people have to shield their eyes from it, it's ostentatious.

•

If your chief source of pleasure is from the look on others' faces when they see it, it's ostentatious.

•

If it is solely designed to display your fabulous wealth and taste, it's ostentatious. Oh, and you also have no taste.

•

If it cost unbelievable amounts, and you can't resist telling people as much, it's ostentatious.

Homer: "WELL, HE'S GOT ALL THE MONEY IN THE WORLD, BUT THERE'S ONE THING HE CAN'T BUY."
Marge: "WHAT'S THAT?"
Homer: (THINKS) "A DINOSAUR."
– *The Simpsons*

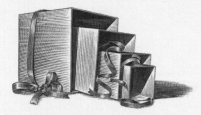

GET IT RIGHT: PRESENTS

PRESENTS SHOULD ALWAYS be given in good faith and with the sole intention of delighting the recipient. A thoughtful present should be appreciated regardless of cost. The time you have taken to select it will be apparent in your choice.

GENERALLY SPEAKING, the present should be appropriate to the depth of your relationship and to the reason behind the gesture. If possible, do some research to avoid making a basic error – the bottle of whisky to the teetotaller, or the chocolates to the dieter. Present-giving is not a competition, and there is no need to go over the top. A competitive spirit undermines the action and a disproportionate show of wealth could embarrass the recipient.

NEVER FALL INTO THE TRAP of buying a present that you really want for yourself, and that you fully intend to use, borrow or adopt. Remember what you have given in the past and never give a present with the aim of getting something of a similar value in return: giving and receiving are entirely separate activities.

RULES OF RE-GIFTING

THE FIRST RULE of re-gifting is no-one must ever know: not the original giver or the next-in-line receiver.

ENSURE THE RECEIVER is at least six degrees separated from the giver, and that the 're-gift' is shop-fresh (snagged threads or notes in the margin might just be a giveaway).

CHECK TO MAKE SURE that the present has not been personalised in any way by the original giver – i.e. an inscription inside a book, a date scribbled on a bottle of expensive wine.

NEVER TELL ANYONE about your penchant for re-gifting, they'll never give you anything again and will be perennially suspicious about the presents they receive from you.

DON'T PRESENT THE 'RE-GIFT' with too much fanfare. Just in case.

ALWAYS BE AWARE that the gift you are re-gifting may have been re-gifted to you too. Avoid handing it back to its original purchaser.

Blowing the Bonus

CASE STUDY 1: in 2002, it was reported that six London city bankers ran up a wine bill of more than £44,000 at Gordon Ramsay's Pétrus restaurant. They ordered a £1,400 1982 Montrachet, an £11,600 1945 Pétrus, a £9,400 1946 Pétrus, a £12,300 1947 Pétrus and a £9,200 1900 Chateau d'Yquem. They were not charged for the food – scant consolation for five of them who were subsequently sacked.

CASE STUDY 2: in 2005, it was reported that an investment banker spent £20,000 on bottles of vintage Cristal and Dom Perignon champagne at London's Mo*vida club. Rather than drink it, he sprayed it, grand prix-style, around the bar. The cleaning bill was a further £15,000.

BOYS' TOYS: FIVE RULES

{1}
The more gadgety, the better.
{2}
The less comprehensible to women, the better.
{3}
The more macho, the better.
{4}
The more expensive, the better.
{5}
The more green-eyed it makes others, the better.

POKER: ONLINE ETIQUETTE

Learn how to play on the free games that use virtual money.

Use the chat box only to make polite conversation or not at all. It is not there to aid you in doling out anonymous abuse.

Never reveal your hand if you are the winner.

Bluffing is easier online.

Online casinos may offer 24/7 gambling, but remember that there is a life away from your computer.

You don't need to dress smartly for online poker, but that doesn't mean you should play alone in your underwear.

RANKING OF POKER HANDS

{1} ROYAL FLUSH: a straight of ten to Ace with all the cards in the same suit.
{2} STRAIGHT FLUSH: five sequential cards of the same suit.
{3} FOUR OF A KIND: four equally ranking cards, with an odd fifth card.
{4} FULL HOUSE: three of a kind and a pair.
{5} FLUSH: five cards of the same suit but not in sequence.
{6} STRAIGHT: five sequential cards not of the same suit.
{7} THREE OF A KIND: three cards of the same rank with two unmatched, odd cards.
{8} TWO PAIRS: a hand in which there are two sets of two matching cards, alongside an odd card.
{9} ONE PAIR: two equally ranking cards and three odd cards.

WHAT TO CALL YOUR HAND

DEAD MAN'S HAND: two black Aces, two black eights.
THE DEVIL: three sixes.
FOUR HORSEMEN: four Kings.
JACKSON FIVE: a Jack and a five.
KING KONG: two Kings.
MAGNUM: two fours.
POCKET ROCKETS: a pair of Aces in the hole.
VILLAGE PEOPLE: four Queens.

KNOWLEDGE TEXAS HOLD 'EM

THERE ARE MYRIAD forms of poker and myriad different techniques and strategies for success, including seven-card stud, five-card stud and omaha, among others. By far the most popular form of the game, though, is Texas Hold 'em.

THE IDEA OF THE GAME is to make the very best, five-card poker hand from two cards in your hand (hole* cards) and five community cards on the table.

THE GAME STARTS when two blind bets are laid by the two players closest to the dealer; two cards are then dealt to each person at the table. The first round of betting then starts.

ONCE COMPLETED, the dealer lays three cards face up on the table. This is called the flop* and it heralds another round of betting. A fourth card is then dealt and, after a further round of betting, the final, fifth, card is dealt. The final round of betting takes place and, when all bets are equal, the winner is the player with the best hand still in the game.

IF YOU ARE A BEGINNER, keep it simple at first. The hole cards you are dealt are the most important – they are the only two cards that are not available to other players. Deciding to play and bet on your starting hand is the most crucial decision to make. A pair of Aces is the best you can expect (the chances are 220 to 1 against), followed by a pair, an Ace with a high kicker*, an Ace with a low kicker, unpaired high cards (Jack and above), then finally flushes and straights. Anything lower isn't worth risking unless your bluffing skills are monumental.

IF THE FLOP doesn't help your hand, it's best to fold*. If the flop only leaves you with an outside chance of a good hand, again, it's best to fold. If the flop helps considerably, bet big as your hand is over 70 per cent complete at this point. Remember that, if the flop turns up a good hand, it is a good hand shared by everyone at the table.

THE TURN* card often does little to change hands, so betting is minimal here and, by the fifth card (the river*), you will know if you have a good hand and you should bet accordingly. Beware the lucky player, or backdoor player as they are known, who has inexplicably stuck with a bad hand only to have it transformed by the river card.

*HOLE: the first two cards dealt to each player.
*FLOP: the first three community cards dealt.
*KICKER: a card used to decide between two players who both have, for example, a pair of Aces. If one player also has a ten and the other a nine, then the player with the ten wins.
*FOLD: withdrawing from the round.
*THE TURN: the fourth community card to be dealt.
*RIVER: the final community card to be dealt.

Blackjack

{1} In Blackjack you are attempting to beat the dealer, not your fellow players.

{2} You are aiming to achieve a hand as close as possible to, but not more than, 21.

{3} You are dealt two initial cards and can either hit (take more cards to reach 21) or stand.

{4} The dealer will then leave one of their two cards facing upwards after it has been dealt. You must not show your cards to anyone.

{5} If your initial two-card hand totals between 13 and 16 (the worst hand to get), you should only hit if the dealer's upcard is a six or less. They will need to improve their hand, meaning there is a good chance they will go bust.

{6} If they have a seven or better showing, there is a high chance that they have a ten underneath. This means that they will probably stand, so you need to better their score of 17, and you must hit.

{7} Always hit if your cards total eight or less. Always stand if they amount to 17 or better.

{8} Individual hands won't earn you big money – this is a game about accumulation rather than big payouts.

{9} Blackjack is also known as Twenty-one, Vingt-et-un and Pontoon.

COMMON CHIP VALUES

WHITE	RED	BLUE	YELLOW
1	2	5	10
1	5	10	25
1	5	25	100

 EXPERT TIP Keep your eyes open and watch other players carefully at the poker table as everyone has a tell – taking a drink, tapping their feet, or something very subtle.

CASINO RULES

{1}
Check what the table minimum and maximum bets are.

{2}
Look smart – a shirt, tie and jacket should be *de rigueur*.

{3}
UK casinos also require that you become a member to be able to gamble there; bring ID with you on your first visit.

{4}
Don't engage dealers in chat (they're not allowed to), nor will they accept tips (for the same reason) or shake your hand (in case chips are being exchanged).

{5}
Dealers will alert the management if your behaviour is out of line.

{6}
Let the dealer go about their business. Don't get in their way or try to help them. They know what they're doing. Or should.

{7}
Make sure your cards stay in view (the backs, not the face).

{8}
Phones, pdas, cameras and most other electronic equipment is banned at the table.

{9}
Never, ever touch another player's chips. You wouldn't like them putting their hand in your wallet.

{10}
Never touch any card dealt face up; only handle cards that are dealt face down.

{11}
Be a good winner and a good loser. No gloating or crying.

 EXPERT TIP If you have never gambled before – either at home or on the internet – simply observe at first. Only join in if you think there is a table whose experience matches your own.

Roulette

ROULETTE is the most popular game at most British casinos.
YOU CAN BET on individual colours, odd numbers or even, individual numbers, sequences, groupings and more.
ON A UK roulette wheel there is only one zero, on American and some European wheels there are two.
ON A UK wheel, there is a 35 to one chance of a payout. Betting on four numbers increases the chances to eight to one.
BETTING ON 24 numbers gives you a 63 per cent chance of winning but you will only be able to double your money.
REMEMBER THAT it is a game of complete luck.

HOW TO BET

BET TO WIN: backing one or two horses to place will, in the long run, not offer you the same returns as betting on three or four horses to win.

AVOID OUTSIDERS: those 100/1 odds may appear attractive but there's a reason your horse isn't fancied. Shy even further away from long shots if the going is soft or better. If the going is heavy, though, form generally means nothing – an outsider can be worth a punt.

LOOK FOR FORM: study the form guides and look for a horse that has improved gradually. If you're betting on a big race, there's a good chance that it has been trained especially for the event.

KEEP YOUR EARS OPEN: listen to betting shop chatter and keep an eye on any horse that is being well-backed.

STACK YOUR BETS: accumulator bets will often net the biggest rewards – if you have the nerve to stay with them.

LAY YOUR BETS: laying a bet is the process of betting on something not happening; for example, betting on a horse not to win a race. It can offer rewards and is often a good method to recoup some money if you sense a bet could be going awry.

SPREAD BET: with occasionally massive rewards (and big losses) on offer, spread betting can be very attractive. Similar to market trading in the City, essentially you are betting on the extent to which you think the outcome of a race, match or event will be different to a bookie's prediction. While you earn money the more often you are proved correct, you lose more money the more often you are proved wrong.

EXCHANGE YOUR BETS: rather than betting against a bookie, you bet against another punter who has the opposite view to you. Normally internet-based, you should come up with a bet you want to make, and then find out whether someone is willing to take that on.

IF ALL ELSE FAILS, LOOK FOR THE SIGNS: if you fancy backing a horse because it reminds you of your mother-in-law, at least you've got a better indication than none at all.

For similar reasons, bookies fear good horses with human names. In 1999, Bobbyjo was massively backed at the Grand National by people who had friends called either Bobby or Jo, even though the horse had not shown much in the way of form. It won at 10 to 1 costing bookmakers a fortune.

USE YOUR HEAD: if you don't think a bet is worth it, don't bet. If you can't afford to lose the money, don't bet.

KEEP AN EYE ON YOURSELF: if you are becoming obsessed with betting, look for advice or help.

HOW TO BUY A HORSE

{1} Unless you have plenty of money to burn or want to be hands-on, join a syndicate.

{2} The average yearling will cost around 120,000 guineas (one guinea is approximately £1.05) and will cost roughly £20,000 a year to train, stable, vet and transport. Jockey fees will be added on top of that. However, shares in a syndicate generally cost between £10,000 and £30,000 a year.

{3} Syndicates are often run by experts who understand what they are doing, making your life easier. They should make sure that the trainers are top quality, too. That should mean (but won't guarantee) higher returns when the horse is sold on – generally after three years.

{4} Decide on your horse. Do you want a flat racehorse, a jumps horse or one that can do both? Horses can be bought at auction (two of the best bloodstock auctioneers are Tattersalls, based in Newmarket, and Doncaster Blood Sales) or privately.

{5} If outside a syndicate, find a trainer. Decide between one with an established reputation – who may be more expensive – or an up-and-coming trainer who could be cheaper. Also, think about how often you want to visit the stables and choose one conveniently located for you.

{6} Whether in a syndicate or not, choose your silks and then name your horse. The name must be registered with horse racing's administrators, Weatherbys.

{7} Enter your horse into a race. For a standard race, this is normally done by your trainer five days in advance. For a major race, plan ahead as entry can be required months or years beforehand.

SPEAK LIKE A BOOKIE

BEESWAX: tax
GRAND: £1000
JOLLY: a favourite
KITE: cheque
KNOCK/WELSH: to owe money and not pay up
MONKEY: £500
PONY: £25
ROCK CAKE: small bet
SCORE: £20
TON: £100

ROYAL ASCOT

THE DRESS CODE for racegoers varies depending on the area of the course you will be frequenting. For general admission, smart attire is expected. For men, it goes without saying that jeans, sportswear and shorts are not permitted.

IN THE ROYAL ENCLOSURE, men must wear black or grey morning dress. A top hat must also be worn, except when in a private box.

TO GAIN ENTRY to the Royal Enclosure, racegoers must be recommended by someone who is already on the list. Convicted criminals and undischarged bankrupts are barred; divorcées have been allowed in since 1955.

EACH YEAR, racegoers consume approximately: 2.4 tonnes of smoked salmon, 6,000 lobsters, 4.5 tonnes of strawberries, 120,000 bottles of champagne, 12,000 bottles of Pimm's and 75,000 bottles of wine.

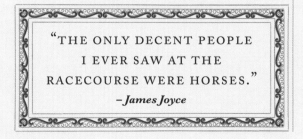

"THE ONLY DECENT PEOPLE
I EVER SAW AT THE
RACECOURSE WERE HORSES."
– James Joyce

POLO THE BASICS

TWO QUARTETS, or teams, thunder around the field (five times the size of a football pitch) on horseback, hitting a small white ball with long handled mallets.

TEAMS CONSIST of a forward (goal striker), two midfielders and a back. Players wear knee-pads, hard-helmets and team shirts with a number on the back; two mounted umpires usually wear striped shirts.

THE GAME is divided up into seven-minute periods called chukkas. Each game might be four, six or eight chukkas in length; a bell or hooter is sounded to indicate that the seven minutes of the chukka has elapsed. At the end of a chukka, there can be up to 30 seconds extra time followed by a three-minute break. The ponies (never called horses) are swapped for fresh ones (a bit like new balls in tennis).

HALF-TIME is just five minutes; this is when spectators tread-in the divots (the turf kicked up by the ponies).

THERE ARE GOALS at either end of the field and the teams change ends after each goal. Goals are scored by the ball crossing the line between the goal posts, regardless of who knocks it in, even if it's a pony. The team with the most goals wins.

PLAYERS HAVE a rating called a handicap that indicates their ability. A handicap can range from minus two (the worst) up to a maximum best of ten.

GAMES ARE PLAYED where both teams' sum handicaps are weighed up against each other and the team with the lower handicap is given a few goals which will be calculated according to the number of chukkas being played.

GREYHOUND RACING RULES

{1}
It's better to bet onsite than offsite.
Atmosphere is everything.
{2}
Virtual greyhound racing is not
real greyhound racing. Avoid it.
{3}
This is not a classy night out.
It is fun, though – treat it as such.
{4}
Don't look at the form too hard.
Allegedly nobbling is still rife.
{5}
Don't bet the house.
There'll be another race in a minute.

WHAT TO SHOOT

CLAY PIGEON: most game is out of season during the British summer months, so clay pigeon shooting will help you stay sharp. It is also the best way to learn.

DOVE: the best dove shooting in the world can be found in Argentina, where the Córdoba Province boasts literally millions of birds, making them something of a pest for local farmers. The season is open all year round and there are no bag limits. Closer to home, good dove shooting can be found in Morocco between June and mid-August.

DUCKS AND GEESE: often flying rapidly overhead without warning, duck and goose shooting presents both a unique challenge and a chance to explore a more unusual wetland landscape. If there are likely to be coots and moorhens, ask your host whether he wants them shot.
SEASON: 1 September–31 January (inland).

GROUSE: the Glorious 12th means one thing for grouse: danger. They are one of the most difficult birds to shoot and are therefore one of the most alluring to the sportsman, representing the pinnacle of shooting.
SEASON: 12 August–10 December.

PARTRIDGE: shoots are frequently both spectacular and demanding and, as such, partridge shooting presents the best alternative to grouse shooting in England. Out of season, travel to Spain for more shooting opportunities.
SEASON: 1 September–1 February.

PHEASANT: with indigenous numbers unreliable, most shoots mix wild with reared birds to ensure a good bag. Many believe pheasant shooting to be the most challenging, while certainly there's little argument that it's the most British.
SEASON: 1 October–1 February.

PIGEON: pigeon shooting in the UK takes considerable skill and much use of fieldcraft as these birds can be elusive to find and hit; the best time to hunt them is often shortly before dusk when they return from feeding. As an agricultural pest, it is legal to shoot most types of pigeon all year round, and it is not so season-based.

PTARMIGAN: found in Scotland, these plump, partridge-like gamebirds often live in the mountains above the snow line, meaning shooting them requires both stamina and skill.
SEASON: 12 August–10 December.

DEER: once royally protected to ensure both the animal's survival and to provide an exclusive sport for the aristocracy alone, stalking deer provides one of hunting's greatest challenges. There are various different seasons for each type of deer (and they are different in Scotland) but, very broadly, hinds and does can be shot during the winter months (starting in November), whereas some stags and bucks can be shot over the summer season.

COMMON SNIPE AND WOODCOCK: both are wading birds found in thick cover so present something of a challenge for the huntsman. They do provide excellent shooting when driven or, more commonly, in rough shooting. N.B. Jack snipe is fully protected in England, Wales and Scotland.
SEASON: Common Snipe 12 August–31 January, Woodcock 1 October–31 January.

TARGET: often incorporating pistols, rifles and air-rifles, target shooting – both indoors and outdoors – is a much-maligned sport in the UK, despite Britain's Olympic success. For anyone wishing to shoot without having to tramp across acres of muddy moorland, club shooting is often a more accessible and attractive option.

PHEASANT   PARTRIDGE   GROUSE

SHOOT RULES

{1}

Never point your gun at anyone or anything but the sky or ground – even if it is unloaded.

{2}

It is essential for beginners to take lessons at a shooting school; safe gun handling will then become instinctive.

{3}

Ask your shoot's host if you can bring a mentor, such as a shooting instructor.

{4}

If invited on a shoot, it is perfectly acceptable to borrow a gun.

{5}

Always keep your phone off.

{6}

Know the local rules and obey them.

{7}

Always carry the gun broken over your arm; always break your gun before handing it to someone else or crossing a stile; bring the stock to meet the barrels after loading, not vice versa.

{8}

If you ever accidentally drop your gun on the ground barrel first, ensure it is completely clean before shooting it.

{9}

Keep your gun in a sleeve when you are not on your peg.

{10}

Never shoot low birds unless you are on a grouse moor.

{11}

It is deeply unsporting to shoot anything at close range.

{12}

High birds are for experts only. Birds over 100 feet are hard to shoot and you risk injuring, rather than killing, them.

{13}

Always make sure there is sky behind a bird when you shoot.

{14}

Never shoot a quarry that is nearer your neighbour.

{15}

Always have enough cartridges, never run out.

{16}

Never be anything less than friendly with the beaters.

{17}

Remember where your birds fall to help the pickers find them. Tip your gamekeeper well – ask about the going rate.

{18}

Don't brag about your bag.

EXPERT TIP A 12-bore is the closest thing to a standard gun, used for pheasant, partridge and grouse; a 16-bore is lighter and is also a good all-round gun.

WHAT TO WEAR

Nothing quite beats the feel of the traditional tweed, russet-coloured, four-piece shooting suit: a jacket that allows you to free your arms and contains plenty of pockets for pipes, hip-flask and cartridges, and a waistcoat, trousers or plus-fours. Stout boots or wellingtons are also a must. A leather shoulder-bag is useful for storing essentials like car keys and a mobile phone. Shooters' socks are conventionally garish; as they are covered up, they can't scare away any birds.

If you must go modern, make sure your clothes are waterproof, breathable and warm, such as a wax or quilted jacket. Shooting glasses that increase visibility are also available, while binoculars – some include built in range finders – are an essential. Above all, wear greens and browns as they afford you the most camouflage.

HOW TO SPEAK GUN

ALL OUT!: what the beaters call at the end of a drive.

BANGERS: cartridges – also known as squabs.

BULLSHOT: a warming, spicy, vodka-infused soup.

BUM-BELLY-BEAK-BANG: a mantra to repeat while aiming at a bird to ensure you swing correctly.

COVER CROPS: fields of maize, mustard and kale (among others) that provide both food and cover for birds.

COVEY: a group of grouse or partridge.

FLUSH: an explosion of birds overhead.

GUN: both the weapon and the person shooting it.

OVER: quarry is coming towards you.

OVER-AND-UNDER: a gun with one barrel over the other, easier to use than a side-by-side, and becoming the norm.

PRICKING: shooting a bird but not killing it. Often the result of aiming for a too high bird.

PULL: the instruction allowing a clay pigeon to be released.

QUARRY: an animal being hunted.

ROUGH SHOOTING: when the shooter flushes the quarry as he walks, also known as walked-up.

SIDE-BY-SIDE: a traditional gun with both barrels next to each other. Harder to use than an over-and-under.

SLOEGASM: a cocktail of champagne poured over sloe-gin.

WISP: a group of snipe.

> "THERE IS A PASSION FOR HUNTING SOMETHING DEEPLY IMPLANTED IN THE HUMAN BREAST."
> – *Charles Dickens, Oliver Twist*

HOW TO BE A COUNTRY HOUSE GUEST

CONFIRM TIMES of arrival and departure in advance and turn up on time (not late, not early).

TAKE A PRESENT with you: some wine, flowers, something seasonally gastronomic.

LET YOUR HOST KNOW of any genuine food intolerances in advance.

COME EQUIPPED: bring appropriate shoes; if it looks wet, bring wellies and waterproofs.

MAKE YOUR OWN BED and at least attempt to wash-up after yourself.

YOU'RE NOT IN THE CITY anymore: don't spend hours leaning out of windows trying to get a phone signal.

DRESS ACCORDING to the grandeur of the house. A country cottage won't require black tie, but a stately home just might.

TELL GOOD STORIES but don't bang on about yourself and your marvellous city life.

EMBRACE THE PETS. The countryside is all about animals, you've just got to accept it. If bringing your own dog, ask permission first.

KNOW WHEN TO LEAVE. As the expression goes, 'visitors, like fish, stink in three days'.

KNOW THE CODE: 'stay for lunch on Sunday' means 'leave soon afterwards'.

IF YOU'VE LEFT something behind, be careful how soon you turn back. You don't want to catch your host celebrating your departure.

NEVER CALL ANYTHING quaint, backwards or inefficient. Remember that you aren't in the big smoke.

WRITE A NOTE of thanks within a day.

COUNTRYSIDE RULES

{1}
Greet strangers – things are different in the country.
{2}
Stick to designated paths, especially in crop fields. Angry farmers are best avoided.
{3}
When walking on a rural road, face the oncoming traffic.
{4}
When rounding a bend or blind corner, move to the other side of the road to avoid head-on collisions.
{5}
Leave gates as you find them – they will be open or closed for a reason.
{6}
Use stiles or gates rather than clambering over walls.
{7}
Take your litter home with you if you can't find a bin.
{8}
Wild or farmland animals shouldn't be approached, even if in distress (at which point inform the farmer).
{9}
Even friendly-looking dogs on leads should be given a wide berth, unless the owner invites you to pet them.
{10}
Your dog, meanwhile, should be kept under control at all times.

CITY SLICKER

Not a fan of the countryside? Here's how not to be invited back:

RSVP and then arrive late bearing petrol station flowers or, better, nothing.

•

Announce that you are a vegetarian. Time your revelation to coincide with the carving of Sunday lunch.

•

Complain about the cold. Country house inhabitants pride themselves on their hardiness. You, on the other hand, should moan about the lack of central heating and double-glazing.

•

Make loud comments about the one-toothed local in the village pub. Then order a martini.

•

Refuse to walk anywhere, insist on using the car.

•

Criticise your host's wine, then finish his whisky.

•

Talk about nothing other than yourself, preferably down your mobile phone to someone back in town.

•

Hit on your host's wife or, if legal, their daughter.

•

Praise the hunting ban.

Croquet

CROQUET IS THE QUINTESSENTIAL British summer sport. It is one of the rare games that can be enjoyed, and enhanced, by having a drink in hand. Played on a flat lawn, the game also provides excellent opportunities for cruelty towards your competitors as you send their ball hurtling towards a flower bed. Even better, this sort of mischief is positively encouraged by the rules. While the UK Croquet Association recommends wearing white shorts and shirts for play, pale trousers, a blazer, striped club tie and a Pimm's in hand is a far more stylish look.

FISHING

FISHING IS A TIME for reflection and solitude. It can only be done with friends who are content to sit with you in silence for long periods. There are obviously practical reasons for this – fish won't bite when there's lots of noise – but it's the spirit that will benefit most from time spent gazing contemplatively out at a stretch of river, lake or sea.

THERE ARE THREE broad types of fish that can be caught in Britain – coarse, game and sea fish – and each category has its own rules and traditions. Game fish like salmon and trout tend to be the most prized as they may require the most skill to catch – and they're often the best to eat. Ensure, though, that you fish in season.

COARSE FISH (pike, chub, perch, bream, eel, roach or rudd, for example) make up most of the other types of freshwater fish that can be caught in this country. The coarse fishing season runs from 15 March–15 June in the UK and applies to all rivers, streams and drains but not to most still waters. You must have a licence to fish in the UK.

SEA-FISHING is entirely different to freshwater fishing. Different rods, baits and techniques are required as, more often than not, is a boat. Best done, at first, in the company of an expert, there is often less peace to be found when fishing for the likes of cod, Dover sole, plaice or even shark; however, there is also considerably more excitement.

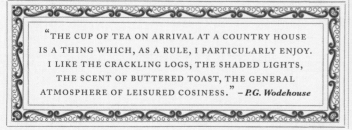

"THE CUP OF TEA ON ARRIVAL AT A COUNTRY HOUSE IS A THING WHICH, AS A RULE, I PARTICULARLY ENJOY. I LIKE THE CRACKLING LOGS, THE SHADED LIGHTS, THE SCENT OF BUTTERED TOAST, THE GENERAL ATMOSPHERE OF LEISURED COSINESS." – *P.G. Wodehouse*

HOW TO MAKE A ROARING FIRE

{1}
Never use firelighters. They denote an amateur. Use dry, seasoned wood if possible.

{2}
Build a small pyramid of kindling and newspaper in the centre of the hearth. This is your base.

{3}
Roll up a handful of newspaper, light it, then hold it under the chimney. This will warm the flue and improve the draw.

{4}
Light your kindling pyramid and, slowly, add twigs and very small logs.

{5}
At first, the heat will only remove the water from the wood by evaporation and won't flame. The fire needs to get to 500°F to release its volatile gases, which need to be heated to 1,100°F to catch fire – this is when you're in business.

{6}
When you have some decent flames, add bigger logs carefully. Don't stack them closely, instead leave room for the oxygen required for a great fire to circulate.

{7}
Stand back, shift the dog, raise your outstretched palms towards the fire, and admire.

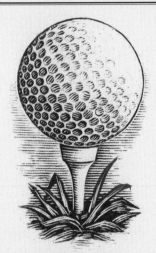

FANTASY GOLF COURSE

OUT	PAR	YARDS
{1} Prestwick, 1st hole	4	346
{2} Royal Liverpool, 2nd hole	4	371
{3} Durban Country Club, 3rd hole	5	468
{4} Royal County Down, 4th hole	3	213
{5} Royal Portrush, 5th hole	4	384
{6} Royal Melbourne, 6th hole	4	428
{7} Pebble Beach, 7th hole	3	106
{8} Royal Troon, 8th hole	3	123
{9} Royal County Down, 9th hole	4	486
OUT	34	2,925

IN	PAR	YARDS
{10} Augusta National, 10th hole	4	495
{11} Ballybunion, 11th hole	4	451
{12} Muirfield, 12th hole	4	381
{13} Augusta National, 13th hole	5	510
{14} Carnoustie, 14th hole	5	483
{15} Pine Valley, 15th hole	5	591
{16} Cypress Point, 16th hole	3	231
{17} St Andrews, 17th hole	4	461
{18} Carnoustie, 18th hole	4	499
IN	38	4,102
OUT	34	2,925
TOTAL	72	7,027

STYLE GUIDE CLOTHING

MANY LEAVE STYLE at the door when striding out for a round. Perhaps it's the claustrophobia of a dress code or the effects of being in close proximity to nature, but there are many errors made on the course that would not be made elsewhere.

LAYERING IS THE MOST IMPORTANT aspect of golfing clothing. It is performance wear and must be adaptable and breathable, while still water- and wind-proof. Jackets should be lightweight but warm – a cashmere-lined windbreaker is ideal. Jumpers should be comfortable but durable, and trousers need to be strong and hardy (you should also have a waterproof pair). Polo shirts should be worn that are made, ideally, of a material that wicks sweat away from the body while also keeping you warm.

ENOUGH OF THE PRACTICALITY, though. Golf is a sport to be enjoyed and you should be attired in such a way as to enhance that enjoyment. This means that, though useful, your clothes must have a touch of luxury too. They should fit in such a way as to never impede your swing – while also not letting you down once back inside the club house.

SHOES NOW TEND to come in two types – those that are trying to look like trainers and those that still look like golf shoes. The rule is simple: even if you normally wear trainers, never wear golf shoes that look like trainers on the golf course.

HOW TO BOOST YOUR DRIVE

{1} For really powerful drives, work on your glute muscles in the gym. These are the power source for all your movements and so are essential for big driving. You should be using your right glute muscles on the backswing and your left as you start the downswing.

{2} Swing a weighted club with speed on a regular basis. It will develop explosive power, engage your core muscles and train your wrists to be lively and flexible.

{3} Work on your wrist speed. Swing your club with just your right hand, then just your left hand so that you develop whip-crack energy with your wrists. Imagine that you are pulling your club back with your big muscles and throwing it forward with your wrists. Wrist-wise, think of a chip shot like a drop-shot in tennis, and a drive like a squash shot along the wall from the back corner.

{4} Before teeing off at the first, if possible, spend 20 minutes hitting balls in a driving range. If your golf club has no range then grab two clubs, hold them together, and perform practice swings with just your right hand and then just your left hand. This will loosen you up, get your wrists working and help your timing.

Five Ways To Lower Your Handicap

{1} Use a driving range. Golf is a time-consuming activity and most people can't afford to be permanently on the golf course. Instead, visit the driving range at least once a week to work on your long game.

{2} Buy a weighted training club. Swing it regularly at home and it will keep your muscles both loose and trained while also synchronising the elements of your swing. When you hit the course, you will be supple and your timing will improve. Plus, if it's good enough for Vijay Singh and Gary Player, it's good enough for you.

{3} Video your swing. What you think you're doing and what you're actually doing is very different. At home, practise your swing in front of the mirror – it will improve exponentially.

{4} Make sure you learn how to chip, pitch and get out of bunkers. According to top golf professionals, this is even more important than learning to how to putt. Poor pitching is the fastest way to an ugly score, whereas if you can chip the ball to within 20 feet of the hole, you should always be able to get down in two.

{5} Get lessons. Speak to a golf professional every now and again – they will keep you on the right lines and will iron out any bad habits before they become too disastrous.

GET IT RIGHT: GRIP

YOUR GRIP is the interface between your body and the club and, as such, is absolutely crucial. It will also define the angle at which the club hits the ball, making grip more crucial still. An incorrect grip will disrupt the path of the club, meaning you will not be able to put the ball where you want it.

TO GET YOUR GRIP RIGHT, buy a good teaching book, speak to a professional, or buy a moulded training grip. Put the training grip on a 6-iron and play with it for six months. It should get your hand used to holding the club correctly. To get really good, you should practise your grip in front of a mirror regularly (every day).

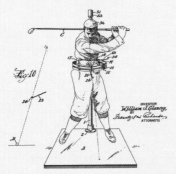

TEN CLASSIC COURSES

St. Andrews Links Old Course,
St. Andrews, Fife, Scotland

•

Augusta National Golf Club
Augusta, Georgia, USA

•

Carnoustie Golf Links Carnoustie, Scotland

•

Hirono Golf Club Kobe, Japan

•

Kingston Heath Golf Club Melbourne, Australia

•

Pine Valley Golf Club Pine Valley,
New Jersey, United States

•

Pebble Beach Golf Links Pebble Beach,
California, United States

•

Royal Birkdale Golf Club Southport, England

•

Royal County Down Golf Club
Newcastle, Northern Ireland

•

Shinnecock Hills Long Island, USA

BALL RULES

GO FOR THE BIG NAME BRANDS as they have often invested the most money into their ball technology; if they're endorsed by a big-name player, so much the better.

IF YOU ARE AN AMATEUR, buy the amateur ball in the range. The pros may use the softest balls, but they are not very durable and are far more responsive, so errors are exacerbated.

Golf Bag Essentials

For those new to the game, use a lofted driver, 3-wood, 5-wood and utility/rescue club, irons from 5- through to pitching wedge (leaving the 2-, 3- and 4-iron; a 1-iron is famously hard to use), one 60 degree lob wedge, one 56 degree sand wedge and a putter you feel comfortable with (this is the club you use the most). Avoid gadgets and 'miracle' clubs; the only thing worth considering is a weighted club.

HOW TO CLIMB MOUNT EVEREST

{1} ESSENTIAL EQUIPMENT REQUIRED

Seven 3-litre bottles of oxygen.

Sack to collect ice and snow for melting into water.

Satellite phone, two-way radio.

Foot powder.

Boil in the bag food – your body burns 6,000 calories a day on the mountain.

Non-insulated mug, to allow your hands to keep warm while drinking.

Harness, ice-axe, jumar, head-lamp, karabiners, climbing harness, rappel, ski-poles, altimeter, crampons, mask.

Boots, thermals, socks (two pairs, one for day, one for night), thin fleece trousers and sweater, thick fleece jacket and trousers, headscarf, balaclava, fleece hat, sun hat, thin inner gloves, thick mountain mittens.

Waterproof, breathable climbing jacket and trousers.

Insurance.

{2} ROUTES: SOUTH COL *vs* NORTH RIDGE

There is a greater chance of success on the South Col route as you will spend less time over 8,000 metres (an altitude known as the 'death zone').

Top camp on the North ridge is at 8,400 metres and it will take longer to reach the summit from there – along a narrowing ridge and in extreme conditions – than the equivalent route on the South Col.

The North ridge, however, is a cheaper route as it starts in Tibet, where climbing permits are cheaper than in Nepal (where the South Col route starts).

Technically, the climbing is harder on the North Ridge than on the South Col – it is also more dangerous.

On the South Col route, however, climbers must face the Khumbu ice-fall, regarded by many as the most dangerous stage of climbing Everest as crevasses open frequently and without warning.

{3} BEFORE CLIMBING EVEREST

Seek professional advice: you are undertaking an enormous physical and mental challenge.

Fitness is paramount. Start your regime 12 months in advance and be aiming to run eight miles in an hour in hilly terrain at a regularity of four days on, one day off.

You will also need upper body strength, so work hard on this in the gym.

You could lose up to 20 per cent of your body weight on Everest, so put on weight before you go.

You will need to have high altitude experience of at least 6,000 metres.

You need considerable Alpine mountaineering experience and should have taken part in at least one 8,000-metre expedition.

You should be able to climb Alpine routes graded AD or harder.

You must be prepared to survive in a tent at 8,000 metres in a storm for up to five days.

Age matters. Climbers over 60 are three times more likely to fail or die, according to research.

{4} RISKS

ALTITUDE SICKNESS: with reduced oxygen at altitude, you breath faster leading to blood vessels leaking in the brain or lungs.

COUGH: dry mountain air can lead to a cough so bad you'll rip out throat tissue.

CUTS: at altitude, these won't heal.

DEATH: it has been estimated that there is one death for every ten successful attempts.

DIGESTION PROBLEMS: your body will stop any processes it deems inessential to survival at altitude. Digestion is one of these affected.

FROSTBITE: once a part of your body has turned black, get used to the idea of losing it.

HYPOTHERMIA: your body temperature can drop to such an extent that all you want to do is sleep, the likely outcome of which is death.

SUNBURN: perhaps the most inevitable and likely hazard on Everest. Sunburn on the roof of the mouth, as people pant for air, is alarmingly common.

THROMBOSIS: your blood can be thickened at altitude, leading to blood flow problems.

TRENCH FOOT: wet feet are common and it can lead to trench foot.

HOW TO CROSS THE POLES

MAN HAULING: pulling your own sled.

KITING: being pulled along by a sail, while skiing and dragging your own sled.

DOG SLEDDING: following a dog team, who drag your sled.

KAYAKING: in summer at the North Pole, open water can be traversed.

ARCTIC *vs* ANTARCTIC

"The South Pole is mentally tougher than the North Pole," says Tom Avery, a polar explorer who has traversed both poles. Essentially, this is because the landscape of the North Pole is interesting, meaning it is easier to keep alert.

THE SOUTH POLE is 10,000 feet above sea level, so it poses even greater physical challenges. Crevasses are a real danger and, unless they are open, are hard to spot. Often explorers have only realised they are standing right on a crevasse when, answering nature's call, their urine has melted straight through the snow to reveal a perilous drop below.

A TRIP ACROSS the poles will take approximately two years worth of planning and will cost at least £50,000. You will also need cold-weather training in Norway or Greenland, as well as wind-tunnel training. You can also visit an industrial freezer, set the temperature to -40°C, and get used to the freezing conditions.

CLOTHING YOU WILL NEED includes thermals, fleeces, wristlets, seal-skin mittens, Eskimo dog-fur hoods, snow boots, goggles and a microfibre jacket. Your clothes must be breathable and it's important not to be too hot as, if you sweat, it can turn to ice underneath your clothes.

ARCTIC DANGERS: polar bears, thin ice, crevasses, open water, tumbling ice blocks, bitterly cold temperatures, running out of food, drowning, hypothermia, frostbite.

ANTARCTIC DANGERS: killer storms, sastrugi ridges (wind-blown ridges of snow), crevasses, hypothermia, frostbite.

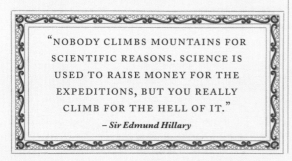

"NOBODY CLIMBS MOUNTAINS FOR SCIENTIFIC REASONS. SCIENCE IS USED TO RAISE MONEY FOR THE EXPEDITIONS, BUT YOU REALLY CLIMB FOR THE HELL OF IT."

– Sir Edmund Hillary

EXTREME CHALLENGES

SEVEN SUMMITS
Climb the highest peaks on each continent, Kilimanjaro (Africa), Elbrus (Europe), Carstensz Pyramid (Australasia), Aconcagua (South America), Denali (North America), Vinson Massif (Antarctica) and Everest (Asia). Plan on the expedition taking a minimum of four years.

MARATHON DES SABLES
A six day, 151-mile (243-km) endurance race across the Sahara Desert in Morocco. Equivalent to five and a half regular marathons, the longest stage is 52 miles (83.6km) in the blistering North African sun. The race is considered one of the toughest ultramarathons in the world.

THREE PEAKS CHALLENGE
Far less extreme than the seven summits challenge, but made all the harder by the time constraints. Aim to scale each of Britain's highest peaks – Scafell (978m), Ben Nevis (1,344m) and Snowdon (1,085m) – within 24 hours. Better still, run it.

IDITAROD
A dog sled race across 1,161 miles (1,868.4km) of Alaskan mountains, tundra, frozen rivers, forest and coastline, with blizzards, treacherous winds and sub-zero temperatures. The record time is an hour and 14 minutes short of nine days.

THE POLAR CHALLENGE
A 400-mile (643.7-km) team race from Polaris Mine on Little Cornwallis Island to the magnetic North Pole that takes place from mid-April to mid-May each year. Facing temperatures around -50°C, polar bears and extreme conditions, teams of two or three people take four weeks to finish the race.

IMPORTANT Before undertaking any kind of training or extreme challenge you should consult a medical professional and seek expert guidance.

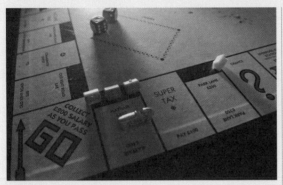

Monopoly

Monopoly is produced in 37 languages in 103 countries.

Approximately 500 million people around the world have played the game.

Monopoly was first sold in America in 1933.

In 1998, the car was announced as the most popular token.

Over five billion little green houses have been produced since 1935.

The man on the board and box is called Mr Monopoly.

Edgar Mallory sends you to jail; Jake the Jailbird is the man behind bars.

Count your opponent's properties and divide by seven – the result is how many rents you can expect to pay out on your next lap of the board.

Nine of the Community Chest cards give you money, but only two of the Chance Cards.

On average, the stations and the orange properties, closely followed by the reds, are the most landed on.

The dark purples – Mayfair and Park Lane in England – are the least frequented.

Gaming Trivia

Cluedo's Miss Scarlett is called Fraulein Ming in Germany; Colonel Mustard is called Madam Curry in Switzerland.

Jenga was invented by a British woman who grew up in Africa; the name is based on the Swahili word for 'to build'.

Twister shot to fame after Johnny Carson and Eva Gabor played it on *The Tonight Show* in 1966. That year, three million sets were sold.

TIDDLYWINKS: *Are You Serious?*

The English Tiddlywinks Association advises that it is a game of strategy. Four players, each playing one colour, play in two pairs on a felt mat with a pot placed in the centre (in singles matches, each player operates two colours).

There are six winks – small plastic discs, two larger than the others – each, of blue, green, red and yellow. A 'squidger' (larger disc) is used to move any wink of the player's colour not covered by another wink, potentially also moving winks underneath it in the same shot. Different squidgers are used for different shots (like selecting a golf club).

The aim of the game is to secure the highest number of table points ('tiddlies'). At the end of a game, three tiddlies are scored for each wink in the pot and one for each wink on the mat not covered by another.

RISK: *A Game of World Domination*

Laid out on a stylised world map from the Napoleonic era, players control armies. Their aim is to gain territory from other players and, ultimately, conquer the world. Risk cards, representing territories, forces and weaponry are awarded throughout the game. Deploy these useful strategies:

GAIN CONTROL OF AUSTRALIA. It's the easiest continent to defend by fortifying just Siam or Indonesia.

SOUTH AMERICA is a good offensive base for gaining control of North America and Africa.

ELIMINATE WEAK PLAYERS who hold a large number of risk cards. You will acquire their cards.

GENTLEMAN'S AGREEMENTS. Form unofficial alliances or truces for mutually beneficial defence or attacks.

SCRABBLE TIPS

The modern-day Scrabble we play is based upon a game called Criss-Cross, developed by American architect Alfred Butt in the 1930s.

Approximately 120 two-lettered words are allowed.

The most useful letter-tiles for creating high scoring words are J, Q, S, X and Z.

The most useful tile is the blank.

Try and finish before your opponents to maximise your score.

Utilise the double and triple letter squares.

CHESS THE ULTIMATE BATTLE

TECHNICAL, ANALYTICAL and undeniably aggressive, chess is a game that has led to wars, to peace, to spy scandals and has even been used as Cold War propaganda.

SAID TO HAVE BEEN INVENTED in India in the 6th century – as a game called *chatarunga* – it was modified in Europe from 1200 onwards, when it began to resemble today's game.

IT BECAME A SPORT in 1851 when London hosted the first modern chess tournament, won by German Adolf Anderssen. In the 20th century, the game was dominated by Russians. From 1948 until the break up of the Soviet Union, the only non-Soviet World Champion was American Bobby Fischer.

PLAYERS ARE RANKED according to a system devised by Arpad Elo (known as the Elo rating). A rating of 2,500 is required to become a chess grandmaster and the highest ever Elo rating was 2,851, held by Garry Kasparov in July 1999.

> "I LEARNED THAT FIGHTING ON THE CHESSBOARD COULD ALSO HAVE AN IMPACT ON THE POLITICAL CLIMATE IN THE COUNTRY." – *Garry Kasparov*

HOW TO CHECKMATE IN TWO MOVES

{1} FOOL'S MATE
The quickest checkmate is what's known as Fool's Mate and is a classic trap with which to trick amateur opponents. Your opponent, however, would have to be particularly bad to fall for Fool's Mate – the tactic relies on a weak opening by them.

There are variations but, essentially, it runs like this. You play as black and, as your opponent is white, they move first.

WHITE: pawn to f3.
BLACK: pawn to e5.
WHITE: pawn to g4.
BLACK: pawn to h4. Checkmate.

{2} SCHOLAR'S MATE
An alternative tactic is Scholar's Mate. It is more common and almost as quick, relying instead on your opening. This time, play as white.

WHITE: pawn to e4.
BLACK: pawn to e5.
WHITE: queen to h5.
BLACK: knight to c6.
WHITE: bishop to c4.
BLACK: other knight to f6.
WHITE: queen to f7. Checkmate.

MISS DEBRETT *Gamesmanship*

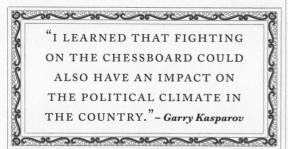

WHILE WE MAY ENJOY SPORT, it isn't in our blood. We don't bond with each other over it, and we don't talk about it with each other. We understand the visceral excitement of sport, and tolerate manifestations of it in men, but we do have to draw the line somewhere. We are bemused, and frequently dismayed, by the antics of men in the sporting arena. Gamesmanship – the art of winning unfairly at sport without actually cheating – is simply embarrassing, especially when amateur enthusiasts ape the less attractive attitudes of professionals. The histrionic questioning of line calls, the hectoring and haranguing of the referees, the taunting and goading of opponents … Is winning really *that* important?

SPORTSMANSHIP, on the other hand, elicits our admiration. We know how much you want to win, so we cannot fail to be impressed when you are gracious in defeat.

We enjoy your good manners as you congratulate your opponents on effective play and accept the decisions of the referee with good grace. We are touched by your ability to face defeat with a brave face. We applaud your refusal to whine, argue or sulk.

SPORTING PROWESS is impressive, but our heads will be turned by good sportsmanship. We will conclude that in life, as in sport, you are a good loser, a gracious victor and a civilised human being, who has learnt to control their baser, more primitive – and less than attractive – instincts.

BMX

IDENTIFY IT: low-slung and lightweight, with small wheels and a seat surplus to requirements.

PROS: easy to perform tricks, easy to transport when not in use and versatile.

CONS: no good for long-distances, gear-less, and it will make you look like a 13-year-old.

FOR: teenagers.

CLASSIC

IDENTIFY IT: upright, often with chain guard, mud-flaps, and with U-shaped handle bars bent towards the rider.

PROS: an elegant and traditional bicycle that distinguishes you from the street-racer, cycle courier and BMX bandits.

CONS: unless you get a modern remake, they can be heavy, lacking in gears and prone to malfunction.

FOR: city gents.

FOLD-UP BIKE

IDENTIFY IT: normally with small wheels, an upright frame and single bar on which the pedals are mounted.

PROS: excellent for commuting, easy to store away, a design that is classic and robust.

CONS: not the most elegant of bikes, heavy and, thanks to its small wheels, not the fastest (unless it's a Moulton).

FOR: commuters.

HYBRID BIKE

IDENTIFY IT: basically a cross between a touring bike and a mountain bike, it is sturdy, with flat-handle bars and an off-road style frame.

PROS: a good town bike, it combines the better elements of both off-road and on-road bikes, making it the most common and versatile bike on our streets.

CONS: as a compromise between two different styles of bike, it is neither as good off-road as a mountain bike, nor as good on-road as a tourer. Instead it is a happy medium.

FOR: the occasional cyclist.

MOUNTAIN BIKE

IDENTIFY IT: chunky, lightweight, with multi-gears and fat, wide-tread tyres. Often with suspension too.

PROS: nothing will get you up, or down, a mountain better. The wide, grippy tyres will give you extra stick on mountain paths and the suspension will make the ride easier.

CONS: bad for on-road use as the wide tyres slow you down, and the suspension is a useless, bulky accessory in town.

FOR: the extreme sportsman.

ROAD BIKE

IDENTIFY IT: ultra-lightweight, with dropped handle bars, narrow tyres and slick streamlining.

PROS: built for speed, these are the pinnacle of high-performance bikes. They are sleek, fast and honed for racing.

CONS: often uncomfortable and built solely to carry a rider, they are useless for transporting anything other than the person pedalling.

FOR: cycle couriers.

TOURING BIKE

IDENTIFY IT: often with drop handle bars, a touring bike is strong, comfortable yet svelte, and often pannier racks are available on the back.

PROS: ideal for long-range cycling, they can carry plenty of weight without losing stability, while also providing speed. Also useful for commuting, they are versatile bikes.

CONS: if equipped with panniers, mudguards and the works, they can become heavy and, therefore, slow.

FOR: weekenders.

TRACK BIKE

IDENTIFY IT: frequently space-age, with a single gear, and made of super-light but tough material.

PROS: extremely fast, they are built to go round a track at high speed. That means, with only one purpose to fulfil, their simplicity is often their strongest selling point.

CONS: as these are cycling's super-car equivalents, they can often be every bit as twitchy as their petrol-driven counterparts. Like supercars, they are great at speed or round a track, but not so useful at any other time.

FOR: professionals.

TRICYCLE

IDENTIFY IT: three-wheeled, and often with storage space handy for transporting larger items.

PROS: stable, sturdy and capable of carrying big loads and towing trailers.

CONS: heavy, bulky and wide in the road.

FOR: parents.

TANDEM

IDENTIFY IT: the bicycle built for two.

PROS: powerful, pacey and excellent for touring.

CONS: you need someone else to ride it with you.

FOR: friends.

HELMETS

ROAD HELMETS

These should be lightweight and streamlined without sacrificing comfort, safety or strength. The most effective in terms of ventilation tend to be those built using a lattice-work structure. However, though style is important, this is perhaps the one area where form follows function – a helmet's most important duty is to protect your skull from tarmac, concrete or a car's front bumper.

MOUNTAIN BIKING

There are two main types of specialist helmets available – both, however, should be strong as falling off at speed down a mountain is a serious business. The first is similar to a road helmet, and should be light, with holes scooped throughout for ventilation. The second is more military in style – think of a World War II GI helmet – and will not provide the same level of ventilation, but it will give a less sporty look.

BMX

Similar to a motorbike helmet, this should have a visor and chin guard (both of which can be removed) as the amount of stunts performed on the bike means that, if you fall, you are likely to come down at odd angles.

HOW TO CHANGE A BICYCLE TYRE

YOU WILL NEED: tyre levers, pump, tyre chalk, patch kit, and possibly a new inner tube.

{1} Attempt to locate the source of the puncture – if it is a thorn, for example, remove it from the tyre.

{2} Remove all the air from the tyre.

{3} Unscrew the nut on the air valve.

{4} Insert the tyre levers under the tyre's lip – start on the opposite side of the wheel to the air valve – then work your way around the tyre, prising the tyre over the rim.

{5} With one side of the tyre over the rim, remove the inner tube, making sure not to damage the air valve.

{6} Inflate the removed inner tube with air and squeeze it. You are listening for the escaping air that will denote where the hole is. If you are at home, submerge the inflated inner tube in water and look for the bubbles that the air escaping from the puncture will cause.

{7} Mark the puncture with the chalk.

{8} Scuff up the area around the puncture, making sure the surface is rough to the touch. This will help the glue and rubber repair patch grip.

{9} Spread glue around the hole and stick a patch over the hole.

{10} Quarter-inflate the tube, then slip it back under the tyre that is still half-on the wheel.

{11} Once in, slip the tyre back into position.

{12} Re-inflate your tyre to its correct pressure and then cycle away.

TOUR DE FRANCE JERSEYS

YELLOW JERSEY (*maillot jaune*): overall race leader
GREEN JERSEY (*maillot vert*): sprint leader
POLKA DOT JERSEY (*maillot à pois rouges*): king of the mountains
WHITE JERSEY (*maillot blanc*): under-25 leader

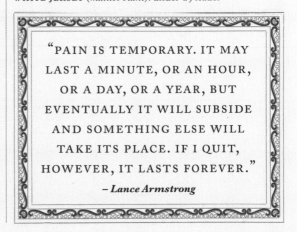

"PAIN IS TEMPORARY. IT MAY LAST A MINUTE, OR AN HOUR, OR A DAY, OR A YEAR, BUT EVENTUALLY IT WILL SUBSIDE AND SOMETHING ELSE WILL TAKE ITS PLACE. IF I QUIT, HOWEVER, IT LASTS FOREVER."
– *Lance Armstrong*

MOTORING

HOW TO DRIVE FAST

{1} Smoothness is key. Learning how to get on and off your brakes evenly will gain you more speed than simply hitting the accelerator hard.

{2} Plan ahead. Work out your braking point, and ease into the corner. Knowing how to come off your brakes is just as important as knowing when to accelerate.

{3} Find the right line. The racing line varies from corner to corner and car to car. Hitting an apex midway round a bend will give you constant speed, but it will not suit every car.

{4} Know your car. If cornering in a heavy car like a Bentley Continental GT, you need to go into a corner more slowly, but should be able to power away. That will mean hitting a later apex in the bend. If driving a lighter, very responsive sports car, go into the corner early then leave at speed.

{5} Understand the physics and dynamics of the car you are in. Each car has its own idiosyncrasies and behaviour; the better you understand these, the faster you will drive.

{6} Don't feed the wheel. Though this is a staple of the driving test, at speed it destabilises the car and breaks down the contact between you and the vehicle. Instead fix your hands onto a set point on the wheel at even spaces, meaning your hands are always on the steering wheel, allowing greater precision. To quell any further doubts: it's the technique used by Michael Schumacher.

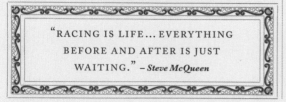

"RACING IS LIFE... EVERYTHING BEFORE AND AFTER IS JUST WAITING." – *Steve McQueen*

HOW TO DRIVE AROUND THE NÜRBURGRING

Perhaps one of the world's most challenging race tracks, the Nürburgring in Germany is considered the most dangerous, tough and treacherous circuit around. At nearly 21km (13 miles) long, it has extreme height changes and contains some of the world's most difficult bends. And it's open to the public.

{1} Given its length, learning all the corners is next to impossible. This makes it tricky for technically minded drivers who like to know what each bend will throw at them, but favours more instinctive drivers who take each corner on its merits.

{2} The track covers such a large area that it can be raining heavily on one part of the course and be bone-dry on another, providing different challenges as you progress. Versatility is key.

{3} There are big elevation changes, meaning you should have a powerful car rather than a quick, lightweight one.

{4} Break the track down into manageable sections and don't make the mistake of getting too over-confident. Many corners look similar to others on entry, but will only reveal their true identity half way round.

{5} As the track is open to the public, you will be sharing the tarmac with other vehicles – and you will be encountering the full range of driving competence. It's not unusual to be battling with motorcycles, vans, lorry cabs and even buses. The worst danger, potentially, is the driver in the hire car he cares little about.

{6} Beware of the locals. Many of the circuit's neighbours have been driving round here for years and so know it like the back of their hands. They like nothing better than to bait those in fast cars, before leaving them standing.

Track vs Road

AS BENTLEY'S MANAGER of Driver Training says, "There are some people who can drive fast on the road and some people who can drive fast on the track. Crossing over is the big skill."

BOTH SKILLS REQUIRE very different techniques. On the track, you know that nothing will be coming in the opposite direction. You have the entire road to play with, but there are more places you can make mistakes. A good track driver will prepare in advance, working out the fastest route around bends before repeating the trick almost mechanically.

SAFETY IS PARAMOUNT. The first sign of a good driver on the road is one who does not put himself or others at risk. He must think on his feet, working out each corner as it arrives. On the road, there are more variables in play and, therefore, greater risks.

HOW TO DRIVE IN THE DESERT

Sand is similar to snow in that it's incredibly slippery, meaning braking and cornering performance is reduced.

Normally, in a desert, you will have summer tyres, which will not have the grip of winter tyres.

Sand drifts are common, meaning that roads are often covered in deep sand – especially in dips – to the point where the road can entirely disappear.

You should be prepared for skidding, slides and even to be dramatically slowed if you hit a deep sand drift.

What to do if you aquaplane

AQUAPLANING is more likely on a concrete road than a tarmac road as water drains better through tarmac.

SOME CARS have aquaplane detection systems that prevent you from over-steering, over-braking and over-accelerating while on water.

IF YOUR CAR does not have this, back off the throttle easily and slowly, don't brake and hold the steering straight.

IF YOU DO STEER, the tyres will grip and, when you reach the other side of the water, the car will go in the direction you are steering – almost certainly no longer the direction you want to go. Instead, keep going straight if possible.

HOW TO DRIVE IN SNOW

AN ICY ROAD is twice as slippery as a snowy one, four times as slippery as a wet one, and eight times as slippery as a dry one.

IF POSSIBLE, drive a four-wheel drive car fitted with winter tyres. This should provide you with as good a grip as possible.

SNOW NATURALLY ADHERES to itself, so the best winter tyres pick up small amounts of snow and use that to bind to the snow on the road.

WATCH OUT for wildlife. Moose, reindeers and elk will do serious damage to your car and possibly you.

DON'T FOLLOW the car in front too closely, as spray from that car can impede your visibility.

BEWARE OF OVERTAKING. Cars tend to follow a similar path, meaning two grooves will appear on the road. The displaced snow from those grooves accumulates in the middle of the road, meaning your car must cross those snow deposits both when pulling out, and again when pulling back in.

IF YOU SEE SOMEONE who has broken down, be a good citizen and stop and help.

WHAT TO DO WHEN YOU HAVE A BLOW-OUT

After a puncture, a car will try and pull you in one direction. Counter this as smoothly and easily as possible.

You are 30 per cent more likely to get a puncture when it is raining. Once rubber is wet, it is far easier to penetrate.

A puncture at 200mph is safer than a puncture at 80mph. At high speed, the centrifugal force of a tyre spinning around holds the tyre in position to a degree. Between 60 and 80mph, the car becomes unbalanced and difficult to control.

The heavier the car, the more difficult it is to control after a blow-out. A lighter car will support itself better.

Help to avoid the problem by making sure your tyres are in good condition and correctly inflated. Also, keep your eye on the road surface and avoid anything that could cause damage.

HOW TO DO A HANDBRAKE TURN

The trick to a good handbrake turn is balance, steering and timing. You should steer just enough to unbalance the car and, the moment you reach that point, pull on the brake. As the inertia of the car builds, release the brake and steer away from the skid to ensure a perfect 180 degrees. Top drivers say, however, that a handbrake turn is never necessary on the road.

 EXPERT TIP Invest in your tyres; they are the sole link between the car and the road, and are therefore vitally important.

IN-CAR ENTERTAINMENT

{1} To get the best out of your in-car entertainment system, get it put in when the car is built. If done this way round, the system can be integrated into the car. If not, the car will have to be rebuilt around the system which could damage performance.
{2} Top-end manufacturers will design in-car entertainment systems to enhance the driving experience while fitting in with the car's surroundings. Hence, it's often better to go with their recommendations than your own. Often it will be perfectly tuned to the car.
{3} Sound is always more important than looks. Flashing lights and fancy add-ons mean nothing if the noise from the speakers is no good.
{4} Get the system sounding how you like it, rather than how the person installing it likes it – you'll be the one driving it, not them. Bentley Mulliner, for example, will offer you a consultation on the type of music you like, before tailoring the system towards those needs.
{5} A car is, fundamentally, a bad environment for listening to music. Accept that you will not be able to get a system installed in a vehicle that sounds as good as the one at home. Also, the difference between something like top of the range and mid-range cables will not be so obvious in a car.
{6} Rear seat television screens are great for keeping children entertained or if you regularly have passengers in your back seat. They're not a worthwhile investment if you're the only person who uses your car.
{7} There's very little that can't be built into a car – provided you have the right car – from state of the art DVD players to computer game consoles and HD screens. Home cinema, surround sound systems, modems, wireless internet, computers, fridges and drinks cabinets can all be accommodated.
{8} Older and vintage cars can be equipped with stereos but it should be done sympathetically, using systems that blend with the car's looks, rather than those that stick out like sore thumbs.

ROAD RAGE

ONCE IN A CAR, normal manners may fly out of the window. Perhaps it's because, with all that metal in which you are encased, you feel more invincible; perhaps it's because you know another driver may not hear you through the glass windows and engine noise. Perhaps it's because other road users are simply so enraging…

A CAR is a potentially lethal weapon, and a good driver will always remember this before using it as a way of expressing irritation, frustration or red-blooded rage.

IT GOES WITHOUT saying, therefore, that aggressive driving should be avoided at all costs. Tailgating, with or without flashing headlights, and pointless horn-blowing are not the signs of alpha superiority, merely a dangerous inability to control emotions while in charge of a very powerful, and dangerous, machine.

DAMAGE LIMITATION: CRASHES

SIT IN THE CAR correctly, making sure that you are the appropriate distance from the airbag and steering wheel, with the seat belt correctly fitted. Cars' safety features are designed to work at their optimum when the driver is sitting in the proper position.

KEEP YOUR FEET on the brakes for as long as possible. Every mile an hour you can shave off your speed helps. If you are sitting properly, your knee should be bent and, when you crash, your leg will fold towards you. If you are sitting incorrectly, with a fixed, straight leg, you are in trouble.

KEEP YOUR HANDS on the wheel. Last-minute steering can be crucial in avoiding a crash. If, however, you can't avoid a collision, the airbag will blow your arms away from the danger zone anyway.

DON'T WEAR a thick coat in the car. Seat belts are designed to rest closely against your body and thick coats can distort their effectiveness.

DON'T WEAR a big watch. If you are holding the steering wheel at the top, when the airbag goes off, you will hit yourself in the face with your watch. The bigger it is, the more damage it will do to your skull.

DON'T KEEP pens or glasses in your top pocket. If you crash, the seat belt that is resting over that pocket will suddenly tighten and snap anything within, meaning you can be stabbed in the chest.

DON'T HAVE A BIG BELT BUCKLE. When the seat belt contracts, the buckle can penetrate your stomach.

Chauffeur Rules

The era in which people had their own, dedicated chauffeurs has nearly died out, but basic rules are still the same.

•

Most chauffeurs now tend to work for a chauffeuring company, rather than an individual.

•

If you like a driver from the chauffeur company, you can request that he does all your driving.

•

Trust is the most important aspect of the relationship between driver and passenger.

•

You must make sure that your driver is discreet – you may be discussing deals or intimate details of your life that you do not want repeated elsewhere.

•

Your driver also needs to trust you. If you are out for the evening then tell your chauffeur roughly how long you expect to be. It is unfair on your chauffeur to regularly keep him waiting for hours on end without prior warning.

•

Remember that chauffeurs are professional drivers and, if they're good, they should have an encyclopaedic knowledge of shortcuts, back routes and little-known roads, and exceptional map-reading skills.

•

They should not be questioned unless you utterly object to the route they have chosen – what's the point in having a driver if you keep giving him directions?

•

It is important to remember that a chauffeur is an employee, and should be treated as such. He should be given respect, warmth and friendliness, but should not be treated as a friend. If someone considers you a mate, it makes it difficult to raise the glass partition.

•

A chauffeur should be appropriately attired; he is part of your image too.

•

When driving, a chauffeur should steer with exceptional smoothness. As Sir Paul McCartney once commented: "You get a chauffeur and you find yourself thrown around the back of this car and you think, I was happier when I had my own little car! I could drive myself!"

•

A good test is to close your eyes when drawing near to a junction: if you can't tell when you've stopped, he's a good driver.

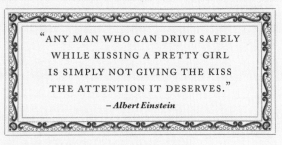

"ANY MAN WHO CAN DRIVE SAFELY WHILE KISSING A PRETTY GIRL IS SIMPLY NOT GIVING THE KISS THE ATTENTION IT DESERVES."
– *Albert Einstein*

DRIVING MANNERS

LET OTHER CARS into the queue in front of you with a friendly wave or flash of the headlights – a graceful gesture that will only cost you seconds.

IF CARS ARE PARKED on your side of a narrow road, give way to oncoming traffic. Indicate when overtaking. Always acknowledge other motorists' gestures – it will make crowded, frustrating roads seem infinitely more civilised.

BREAKING THE SPEED LIMIT is dangerous, and can be costly in terms of penalty points on your licence, but you should also bear in mind that hesitant kerb-crawling can be very annoying for drivers caught behind you. If you are lost, pull over and consult a map or a passing pedestrian.

NEVER TURN into a back-seat driver: you may be ashen-faced with fear, but stamping on imaginary brakes and barking commands are not going to improve anyone's driving.

BE AWARE of other road-users. Always give cyclists plenty of leeway and slow down when approaching pedestrian crossings – make plenty of allowances for unpredictable behaviour, and you will help to make the roads a safer place.

HOW TO RESTORE A CLASSIC CAR

FIND AN EXPERT. An advisor will not share your romantic attachment to a particular car and will be able to tell you whether the car you have fallen in love with is a heap of junk.

FIND A GOOD RESTORER, develop a relationship with them, and use their expertise.

RESTORE SYMPATHETICALLY. A 1960s car with brand new chrome, leather and wood will just not look right.

CONVERT YOUR CAR to unleaded fuel – leaded fuel is becoming increasingly unavailable.

ADJUST YOUR EXPECTATIONS. The car is doing less for you as it contains less technology, so brakes, handling, balance and much else besides are very different than in new cars.

SERVICE YOUR CAR every six months, and look after it well. Old cars need pampering.

HOW TO CHANGE THE OIL

You will need: new oil, new oil filter, spanner, jack, large empty container.

{1} Ensure your car has a cold engine, then run it for two to three minutes before turning off the engine to aid the oil draining process.

{2} Remove the oil filler cap under the bonnet. Check it is clean, if not either clean it or replace it.

{3} Underneath the engine, find the sump plug and oil filter. The sump plug is normally hexagonal and slightly behind the engine. Jack up the front of the car if the sump plug and oil filler are otherwise inaccessible.

{4} Unscrew the sump plug, making sure that you have a large empty container ready to catch the draining oil. Oil should be disposed of at a garage or dedicated disposal site.

{5} Check the tip of the sump plug. It is magnetic so, if it is covered in small metal filings, it is a sign that your engine is wearing – possibly because the oil has not been changed regularly enough.

{6} Unscrew the old oil filter, bearing in mind there may still be some old oil still in place. Then wipe a thin layer of oil around the rubber seal of the new filter to ensure a good seal. Screw the new oil filter in place to hand tightness only.

{7} When the oil has finished draining, replace the sump plug.

{8} Lower the car from the jack, pull out the dipstick, clean it, then replace it.

{9} Pour the new oil into the oil filler hole pint by pint, checking the dipstick regularly, until it is at the correct level. When it is, replace the oil filler cap.

{10} Start your engine and check that the oil light does not come on. If it doesn't, drive away.

HOW TO CHANGE A TYRE

You will need: jack, spare tyre, screwdriver.

{1} Take the spare tyre, jack and any tools from where they are stored in the car. Make sure your spare tyre is properly inflated before starting.

{2} Prise off the wheel's hubcap using a screwdriver, then loosen the wheel nuts but don't completely remove them.

{3} Jack up the car underneath the wheel you want to replace. It should be several inches off the ground.

{4} Fully remove the loosened wheel nuts, then pull the tyre off the car.

{5} Put on the new tyre, tighten the wheel nuts and lower the jack. When on the ground, check that the wheel nuts are fully tightened, then drive away.

HOW TO JUMP-START A CAR

You will need: jumper cables, another car.

{1} Bring the working car close to the dead car, so that the jumper cables will reach from one car's battery to the other. Then switch off the engine of the working car.

{2} Attach the red jump lead or crocodile clips to the positive terminal on each battery. Then attach the black lead or clips to the negative terminal. You should attach the clips to the working car first.

{3} Switch on the working car's engine and allow it to tick over for several minutes.

{4} Try the dead car's motor. It should now start.

HOW TO DEAL WITH MECHANICS

{1} Know enough not to be scammed, but don't tell the mechanic his job.

{2} Describe the problem as specifically as possible. Stick to symptoms; don't tell the mechanic what you think is wrong.

{3} Trust your mechanic. He knows more than you do.

{4} Give him time. He won't be able to fix your car in under two hours.

BULLETPROOFING YOUR CAR

{1} Armouring should be added to your car as it is built, so that the car's chassis will be strong enough to take it. The car's engine can be designed to propel the extra weight.

{2} Decide how armoured you want your car to be – from anti smash-and-grab to full bullet and bomb proofing.

{3} The fuel tank, battery, tyres and windows are often the most important parts to protect.

{4} Ease of escape and a fire-extinguishing system should also be considered.

HOW TO CHANGE YOUR SPARK PLUGS

You will need: spanner, new spark plugs.

{1} Ensuring the engine is cold, locate the spark plugs then remove the wire from their rubber end. Only do one at a time to prevent mixing wires up.

{2} Wipe the exposed spark plug with a rag, then remove it by twisting it anticlockwise with the spanner.

{3} Twist in the new spark plug, after making sure the surfaces are clean. When finger pressure stops working, use the spanner to make sure it is firmly in place. Don't over-tighten, or you will risk breaking the spark plug.

{4} Replace the spark plug wire, then repeat the exercise for each new plug.

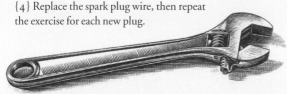

"THE BEST SAFETY DEVICE IS A REAR-VIEW MIRROR WITH A COP IN IT" – *Dudley Moore*

HOW TO ORDER A BESPOKE CAR

{1} Coachbuilders, like Bentley Mulliner, who will build a car from scratch are few and far between. As a result, those that exist tend to be the best.

{2} In the same way that bespoke tailors have a general style that is personalised to you, a car builder will have a certain approach that will be tailored to your specifications. It would be unwise, therefore, to look for an Italian-style sports car from a traditionally English company.

{3} Everything is open for discussion – from petrol caps to pedals. When building a bespoke car, you start with the chassis and move up from there, discussing every detail of the car as you go.

{4} Work out what you want to use your car for. If you rarely have back seat passengers, you probably don't need four doors. If you spend a lot of time doing business in your car, the back needs to be equipped for that – the front should be designed for your chauffeur. If you want to block out the outside world, soundproof the car, add darkened windows and curtains.

{5} Be prepared to wait – it will take time for your car to be built. Also, if you rush the consultation process, you won't end up with the car you want.

{6} A bespoke car will have its balance, brakes and handling tested. Simply customising an existing car may give you the look you want, but it won't necessarily guarantee you the performance of a bespoke car.

MISS DEBRETT *Driving*

FORGET THE JOKES ABOUT women drivers: we do like to drive, we own our own cars, we're good at it. We don't drive like testosterone-fuelled furies, and we don't treat our car as a lethal weapon. We have a great safety record – so why not sit back and enjoy the ride?

DON'T HARANGUE US for driving slowly (i.e. within the speed limit), or drum your fingers on the dashboard when we don't accelerate away fast enough from the lights. Don't hector us into overtaking when we're sitting comfortably behind that articulated lorry. If we are the victim of some high-octane road antics, don't encourage us to blow our horn, or – even worse – lean over and do it for us. Women, especially when they are on their own, feel more vulnerable than men, and are understandably anxious about inciting psychotic road rage.

WHEN WE'RE STRUGGLING to parallel park, do the decent thing and look the other way – rude remarks about our defective spatial awareness will induce panic, rendering us humiliatingly incapable. Refrain from any huffing and puffing about dodgy hill starts and stalled engines. It's just not good manners to criticise.

IF BEING A PASSENGER is far too much for your *amour propre*, remember that we like to feel safe when we're being driven. You don't have to putter along like a geriatric grandfather, but you need to drive steadily, calmly and competently. Outbreaks of irritability, aggressive tailgating, headlight-flashing, bullying of transgressing drivers, shouting, swearing and apoplexy are all causes for alarm.

WE WILL CONCLUDE that in life – as well as in the driving seat – you are volatile, intemperate, and intolerant.

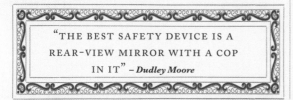

THE KNOWLEDGE

Since 1851, London taxi drivers have been required to know, intricately, the 25,000 or so streets and 1,400 landmarks of London and they should be able to tell you the shortest, fastest and cheapest way between two points.

The test that grills them on this is famously known as The Knowledge, and they must pass it before being granted a licence to drive a cab.

The Knowledge takes between two and four years to complete – normally by mastering the 320 routes prescribed in the Public Carriage Office's infamous *Blue Book*. Once these city runs have been learned, there are further suburban runs to study.

Prospective cabbies say the simplest way to pass the test is to think of a route as being made up of as few straight lines as possible.

Studies on cab drivers who have passed The Knowledge discovered that they had a larger right hippocampus than the control subjects, meaning they have greater navigational ability than others. The longer they've been in the job, the bigger the hippocampus gets.

Cabbies call the period after Christmas 'the kipper season' as, traditionally, that is when their takings are at their lowest. It's so called because cabbies' families were often forced to eat cheap kippers in lieu of more expensive food.

STOPPING DISTANCES

20mph: 12 metres (3 car lengths)

30mph: 23 metres (6 car lengths)

40mph: 35 metres (9 car lengths)

50mph: 53 metres (13 car lengths)

60mph: 73 metres (18 car lengths)

70mph: 96 metres (24 car lengths)

FIVE ARCANE LAWS

{1}

Taxis in the City Of London are not allowed, by law, to carry rabid dogs or corpses.

{2}

It is illegal to flag down a cab if you have the plague or small pox, and the cabbie has a right to ask you if you are suffering from either.

{3}

It is legal for a man to urinate in public, as long as he does so on the rear wheel of his own car while keeping his right hand on the vehicle.

{4}

Until 1976, London taxi drivers were required to keep oats and a bale of hay on top of their cabs in order to feed their horses.

{5}

Being drunk in charge of a steam engine on the road could cost you a £200 fine.

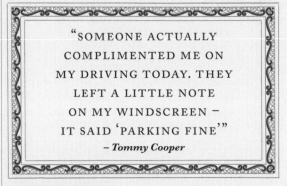

> "SOMEONE ACTUALLY COMPLIMENTED ME ON MY DRIVING TODAY. THEY LEFT A LITTLE NOTE ON MY WINDSCREEN – IT SAID 'PARKING FINE'"
> – *Tommy Cooper*

BOND'S CARS

Among others, James Bond has driven an Aston Martin DB5, Aston Martin DBS, Aston Martin V8 Volante, Aston Martin V12 Vanquish, Bentley Mark II Continental, Bentley Mark IV, BMW 750iL, BMW R1200 motorbike, BMW Z3, BMW Z8, Citroen 2CV, Ford Mondeo, Ford Mustang Mach 1, Lincoln Continental, Lotus Esprit S1, Lotus Esprit Turbo and a T-55 Russian tank.

Driving Trivia

GPS – or Sat Nav – was invented by the US Department Of Defense. The man responsible was Ivan Getting, who also developed the Tomahawk missile. GPS cost the US tax payer £6.32bn to develop.

TEN FAMOUS
ON SCREEN CARS

1955 Ford Lincoln Futura Batmobile from the TV series

•

1963 Aston Martin DB5 *Goldfinger*

•

1963 Model 117 Volkswagen Type 1
Deluxe Sunroof *Herbie*

•

1967 Shelby GT 500 Mustang *Gone In 60 Seconds*

•

1968 390 CID V8 Ford Mustang *Bullitt*

•

1968 Mini Cooper S *The Italian Job*

•

1969 Dodge Charger *The Dukes of Hazzard*

•

1982 Pontiac Trans Am *Knightrider*

•

1983 De Lorean DMC 12 *Back To The Future*

•

6-wheeled, custom made, pink Rolls Royce FAB1
Thunderbirds

Helpful advice from the Highway Code

DO NOT TREAT speed limits as a target. It is often not appropriate or safe to drive at the maximum speed limit.

DO NOT ALLOW yourself to become agitated or involved if someone is behaving badly on the road. This will only make the situation worse. Pull over, calm down and, when you feel relaxed, continue your journey.

SLOW DOWN and hold back if a road user pulls out into your path at a junction. Allow them to get clear. Do not over-react by driving too close behind to intimidate them.

AVOID ARGUING with your passengers or other road users.

BE AWARE OF OLDER DRIVERS: their reactions may be slower than other drivers. Make allowance for this.

POINTS FOR SPEEDING IN THE UK (VARIABLE)

Exceeding the limit between 5 and 14mph: 3 points

Exceeding the limit between 15 and 19mph: 4 points

Exceeding the limit between 20 and 24mph: 5 points

Exceeding the limit between 25 and 29mph: 6 points

Exceeding the limit by 30mph or more: instant ban

Driving Trivia
British motorists will spend an average of nearly three and a half years in the driving seat in their lifetime.

Maximum Speed Limits from Around the World

AUSTRALIA: 130km/h

CHINA: 120km/h

CZECH REPUBLIC: 130km/h

DENMARK: 130km/h

FINLAND: 120km/h (110km/h in winter or in bad weather)

FRANCE: 130km/h (dry), 110km/h (wet)

GERMANY: no limit (130km/h recommended)

ITALY: 130km/h

INDIA: variable, from unlimited (Uttar Pradesh) to 60 km/h (New Delhi)

JAPAN: 100km/h

NETHERLANDS: 120km/h

NEW ZEALAND: 100km/h

NORWAY: 110km/h

PAKISTAN: 120km/h

REPUBLIC OF IRELAND: 120km/h

SINGAPORE: 90km/h

SOUTH AFRICA: 120km/h

SWEDEN: 110km/h

SWITZERLAND: 120km/h

UK: 70mph (112 km/h)

USA: variable by state; 65–80mph (105–129km/h) on interstate highways.

Some others who drive on the left

AUSTRALIA	JAPAN
BANGLADESH	KENYA
BHUTAN	MAURITIUS
BOTSWANA	MOST CARIBBEAN ISLANDS
BRUNEI	NEPAL
COOK ISLANDS	NEW ZEALAND
CYPRUS	PAKISTAN
FALKLAND ISLANDS	SEYCHELLES
FIJI	SOUTH AFRICA
INDIA	SRI LANKA
HONG KONG	UGANDA

ESSENTIAL
CAR FILMS
Bullitt, Ronin, C'était un Rendezvous,
Vanishing Point, Le Mans

CLASSIC

IDENTIFY IT: not just retro-styled, but retro…full stop. These are the bikes that made motorcycling cool, with raw sounding engines, romantic looks and a spirit of speed and adventure.
WHO ARE THEY FOR? anyone wanting to ride across deserts, countries or down long highways.

CRUISER

IDENTIFY IT: often long, low-slung and retro in styling, these are big machines built for long rides in style as much as short, sharp bursts of speed. A classic bike in modern clothing.
WHO ARE THEY FOR? easy riders.

MUSCLE

IDENTIFY IT: throaty, rumbling exhaust, beefy, fat engines and wide back wheels, these are the nightclub bouncers of the road. Often converted from their original state – with long, cow-horn handle-bars, for example – it's not compulsory to have a long beard when riding one, but it helps.
WHO ARE THEY FOR? Hell's Angels.

SPORT

IDENTIFY IT: the biking world's supercar equivalent, these are ultra-fast, sleek and built for speed. They are light, nimble, responsive and modern – a slick combination of sharp angles and aerodynamic design.
WHO ARE THEY FOR? boy racers.

OFF-ROAD

IDENTIFY IT: lightweight, powerful and built for extreme conditions, these bikes are masses of fun when bombing down dirt tracks, but their noise and suspension become somewhat superfluous in the city.
WHO ARE THEY FOR? country boys.

TOURING

IDENTIFY IT: with comfort and storage space paramount, these are armchairs on wheels. Big, heavy bikes – some almost as wide as cars – on which the miles can be eaten up.
WHO ARE THEY FOR? the biking equivalent of caravanners.

STYLE GUIDE HELMETS

First, a choice must be made as to which helmet suits you. When picking between full-face, open-face, flip-up and moto-cross, think about what sort of bike you have and when you will be using your helmet. A moto-cross helmet, for example, will look ridiculous on anything but a moto-cross bike; a classic motorcycle will suit a classic, open-face helmet far more than the more modern full-face or flip-up helmet.

Think about safety, since that is the helmet's most important function. While an open-face helmet certainly has more style appeal, it clearly can't offer the same all round protection that a full-face helmet offers.

Finally, consider styling. Though the likes of Valentino Rossi can get away with garish helmets (his 2008 season lid featured a picture of himself screaming on its dome), you will not look so hot when dawdling along the high street in something similar. Instead, pair your helmet to your bike. Sportier bikes mean you can get away with jazzier helmets, more traditional bikes allow for more conventional, plain coloured helmets. Think, too, about customising – motorbikes are very individualistic, so there's no harm in introducing a touch of unique style into your helmet. And remember too that, even if it all goes wrong and you do pick the absolute worst helmet going, no-one will be able to see your face.

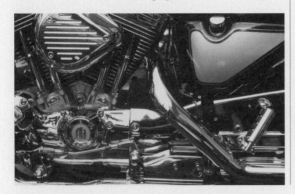

THREE ESSENTIAL
MOTORCYCLE BOOKS

Hell's Angels Hunter S. Thompson

•

Jupiter's Travels Ted Simon

•

Zen and the Art of Motorcycle Maintenance
Robert M. Pirsig

HOW TO CHANGE A MOTORBIKE TYRE

You will need: tyre-marking chalk, valve tool, tyre remover, soapy water, rim protectors, tyre irons, new tyre, air pump.

{1} While the tyre is still attached, draw an arrow on the wheel to show which way it rotates.

{2} Release the air from the tyre.

{3} Separate the edge of the tyre from the wheel's metal rim using the tyre remover. Do the same on both sides of the wheel.

{4} Position the rim protectors near to each other on the wheel. Grip the tyre's lip with a tyre iron, then lift it over the wheel's rim. Leaving that iron in place, repeat the process around the tyre with the other two irons. You should then be able to remove the tyre.

{5} Ensuring both the arrow on the new tyre and the arrow you drew on the wheel point in the same way, push one side of the new tyre over the wheel rim.

{6} Use the three tyre irons to prise the rest of the tyre into position on the wheel. Two tyre irons should be used to grip the tyre, keeping it in place, while the third is used to work the tyre into position.

{7} Inflate the tyre until it sits into the correct place.

SCOOTERS *Sports vs Classic*

There are basic personality differences between those who choose classic and those who choose sports scooters. New, modern scooters are for people who want to nip around town with ease, who want to beat congestion charges or pop down to the shops. They are efficient, functional, and carry none of the romance of a classic scooter – though they are, of course, less prone to breakdowns, mechanic's fees and brake failure.

A classic scooter says so much more. These are the machines that can imbue the rider with either that indefinably Italian sense of style, or evoke vivid memories of English mods on Brighton seafront. They have history, they emanate decades of sophistication, and ooze chic. If you look the part when riding one, you will too.

THREE CLASSIC SCOOTER FILMS

Quadrophenia (1979)

•

Roman Holiday (1953)

•

La Dolce Vita (1960)

Europe's Best Motorcycle Roads

A537, Buxton to Macclesfield, England, 7 miles.

A2, the Antrim Coast Road, Northern Ireland, 60 miles.

The Amalfi Coast Road, Naples to Salerno, Italy, 31 miles.

The Transfagarasan Highway, Sibiu to Curtea de Arges, Transylvania, Romania, 22 miles.

Cabo de Gata to Granada, Spain, 130 miles.

FIVE ICONIC MOTORBIKE FILMS

The Wild One (1953) *Marlon Brando*

•

Easy Rider (1969) *Peter Fonda and Dennis Hopper*

•

The Motorcycle Diaries (2004) *memories of Che Guevara...*

•

Girl on a Motorcycle (1968) *Marianne Faithfull*

•

The Great Escape (1963) *Steve McQueen*

Leathers

Classic beats contemporary every time.

Strength and function beats beauty, too.

Black or brown beat any other colour.

All-in-ones should only be worn if on a serious ride. You'll look odd wearing them in the post office.

Garish leathers look wrong on classic bikes; traditional leathers look wrong on sports bikes.

SCOOTER RIDERS

Marlon Brando

Gary Cooper

Salavador Dali

Robert De Niro

Cary Grant

Dean Martin

Paul Newman

Tiger Woods

THE TRAVELLER

FOUR PIECES OF ESSENTIAL LUGGAGE

{1} **SUIT BAG:** for short trips, a suit bag with added pockets and storage is the ideal carry-on luggage. It allows room for all your packing needs, without forcing you to stow anything in the hold. You'll also be able to hang it up in the Business or First Class wardrobe.

{2} **TROLLEY-BAG:** long gone are the days when a trolley-bag made you look like an air-stewardess. They now represent a useful and convenient option – especially as large airports may demand that you walk vast distances. Even better, small trolley-bags can be carried on board, avoiding the necessity of checking-in your luggage. Functionality is key, so buy one with a separate sleeve for your laptop, a top pocket for passport and tickets, inside pockets for safe-keeping of important items and wheels that actually decide to run in the same direction as each other. Three, in varying sizes, ought to mean that you are covered for anything from a short-haul business trip to a long-haul holiday.

{3} **LEATHER HOLD-ALL:** a weekend away in the country should not require anything other than a bag that can be slung over the shoulder, and perhaps an evening suit. A hold-all should be big enough for clothes and shoes to fit comfortably inside, but also small enough to be chucked into the boot of a sports car.

{4} **MESSENGER BAG:** useful for when you arrive at your destination. Can be folded down to fit inside your main luggage and then unfolded for use as a day-bag. While a backpack tends only to look good on hikers, a cross-body messenger bag is a practical and stylish casual option.

BAG RULES

{1} IF YOU HAVE LUGGAGE that will need to be checked into an aeroplane hold, there is a case for substituting style for practicality. Airport baggage handlers are trying to load fast; they are not connoisseurs of soft leather, ergonomic styling or sleek lines. It is likely that your beautiful cow-skin suitcase will not survive too much air travel.

{2} INSTEAD, TRAVEL ABROAD with durable, functional, nylon suitcases or tough, plastic ones. They may not look as good, but at least they will survive for more than one flight. Also, the more anonymous and less luxurious your bag, the less chance it has of being stolen, though personalising your luggage is useful when trying to identify it on the baggage carousel.

{3} IF YOU WANT TO AVOID stowing your luggage, buy a bag that fits most airlines' overhead luggage restrictions. The allowance in Business and First Class should be enough to keep you in clean clothes for at least a week, and toiletries can always be bought at your destination.

Capsule Wardrobes

What to pack if you don't want to check-in your luggage:

SUIT: stay looking sharp by wearing a crease-free suit. Smooth your passage through the airport metal detectors by packing your cufflinks and belt in your luggage. Shoes without laces can also ease the security process.

CABIN BAG: carry a bag you can fit in the overhead lockers or a suit bag to contain your laptop, clean shirt, spare tie, underwear, socks, slim novel, toothbrush and adaptor kit.

What to pack for the 48-hour business trip:

THREE SHIRTS: you never know when you might need that spare one.
THREE TIES: one for each day and another in case you need one in the evening.
ONE SUIT: the one you're already wearing, preferably.
TWO PAIRS OF SHOES: you never know what might happen to the first.
TRAINING CLOTHES: on a two-day trip, there's still time to hit the gym.
SWIMMING SHORTS: there's also still time for a quick dip.
BOOK: to kill time in the airport, enjoy at the hotel and ward off strangers who want to chat.

What to pack for the weekend away:

THREE SHIRTS: one for the day, one for the evening, one spare.
T-SHIRT OR POLO SHIRT: you're supposed to be relaxing.
ONE JUMPER: it's two days away, you can cope with one jumper.
JEANS: you're not in the office now.
FORMAL JACKET: for evening wear, alongside your jeans.
SHOES: something casual for the day, something more formal for the evening.

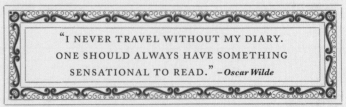

"I NEVER TRAVEL WITHOUT MY DIARY. ONE SHOULD ALWAYS HAVE SOMETHING SENSATIONAL TO READ." *– Oscar Wilde*

A WEEK IN THE SUN

SANDALS: leather sandals can be worn almost anywhere in the sun, though flip-flops can work too. Socks, when worn with sandals, are strictly off-limits.

CANVAS SHOES: deck shoes or light-coloured fabric trainers are essential, but running shoes will make you look cheap.

LEATHER SHOES: more formal leather shoes, for evening wear, are a must.

SHORTS: one pair of cargo-style shorts should see you through as you will be wearing swimming gear the rest of the time.

SWIMMING SHORTS: at least two pairs, so that when one is drying, the other can be worn.

HAT: a Panama is the classic choice and will always travel well. A straw hat – preferably a Trilby, but never a cowboy hat – is also acceptable, but may not have the panache of a Panama.

SHIRTS: light-coloured and made of cotton, you should have day shirts for lounging by the pool and evening shirts for dining. Short-sleeved shirts are also a good option for warmer climates.

TROUSERS: jeans will be uncomfortable in most hot climates, though lightweight ones are preferable if they are essential wear for you. Chinos, linen-trousers and lightweight cotton trousers – as long as they can be worn smartly for evening-wear – are probably a better, and more comfortable, bet.

JUMPERS: in light wool or cotton for evenings.

SMART JACKET: you never know when a jacket – that can be paired with jeans or chinos – might come in handy.

SUIT: for evening meals or smart bars, a light-coloured suit may be essential. Linen suits can be risky as they can rapidly become shapeless and crumpled, so one in a tan cotton or seersucker may be more appropriate.

HOW TO PACK A SUITCASE

SHOES: place them in a bag in the bottom of your suitcase. This area of your bag will potentially get the most knocks, so something hard-wearing should be put there. Shoes should be in shoe bags to protect other items from polish and dirt.

SOCKS: roll them up and put them in your shoes. One, it will save space and, two, it will help your shoes keep their shape.

TIES: roll these up tightly – never, ever fold them – and, if there is room, put them in your shoes. Alternatively, you can slot them, like belts, in your bag.

WASHBAG: as a heavy item, this should go towards the bottom of your suitcase (and at the wheels-end of a wheelie suitcase) so that it doesn't press down on everything else when the suitcase is upright. Be careful if it contains glass aftershave bottles, as these may need to be protected so that they don't shatter if a baggage-handler takes a particular dislike to your luggage. Also, make your washbag easily available. When you arrive, the first thing you will want to do is freshen up.

TROUSERS: lay your trousers flat against the bottom of the case and leave the legs hanging over the sides. Place a layer of tissue paper over the top to prevent buttons or zips rubbing against other items of clothing. The legs will be folded back over at the end.

SHIRTS/JUMPERS: the key is to get everything as flat as possible, so fold shirts well before placing them in your bag. If you don't need to travel with many shirts but need them in pristine condition, place them button side down and then fold the arms and tails around a thick magazine for shape. Jumpers can be rolled, if necessary, to save room and eliminate creases. Creased shirts can be pressed on arrival or hung in a steamy bathroom.

JACKETS: lay your jacket, full-length, over your case. Fold the sleeves in, to form an X, then put tissue paper over the top to prevent rubbing and hence creasing. If you don't have tissue paper, turn your jacket inside out and fold it in the same way. It may still crease but there's no risk of the outside getting dirty if something breaks in your washbag.

TO FINISH: wrap your overhanging trouser legs around everything. This will ensure there are only soft folds, rather than unsightly creases, in your trousers.

 EXPERT TIP When flying with hand luggage only, use an expandable bag that can be zipped up for passing security, but unzipped once on board to allow more room inside.

WHAT FLYING DOES TO YOUR BODY

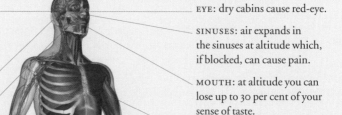

BRAIN: stress and fatigue can mean judgement and decision making drop by 50 per cent; communication drops by 30 per cent; attention is reduced by up to 75 per cent; memory is reduced by 20 per cent.

EAR: air in the middle ear expands during take-off, leading to popping or worse.

NOSE: recycled air contains less oxygen and more bacteria, causing light-headedness and infection.

BEHIND: trapped wind expands which can lead to gas.

CIRCULATION: increased air pressure and dehydration causes blood to thicken.

LEGS: deep vein thrombosis. Cramped conditions, low cabin pressure, dehydration and low humidity increase the risk of DVT.

EYE: dry cabins cause red-eye.

SINUSES: air expands in the sinuses at altitude which, if blocked, can cause pain.

MOUTH: at altitude you can lose up to 30 per cent of your sense of taste.

HEART: lower oxygen levels can cause blood vessels to expand in an attempt to supply more oxygen.

STOMACH: slower digestion and bloating.

FINGERS, ANKLES AND FEET: pressure can cause swelling.

BODY: dehydration can lead to dry skin, light-headedness and lethargy.

AIRPORT PROCEDURE

IF, OF COURSE, you aren't in the market for an upgrade, the best way to check in is in advance, online, and from the comfort of your computer. Spare yourself the tedium of queuing behind holidaymakers, those who haven't flown before, and those whose first language differs from the people behind the desk. However, for an upgrade, first person contact is essential.

TO ENSURE you turn left, not right, as you board the plane, you will need charm, smart clothes and, as a last resort, money. You will also, ideally, be travelling alone and clutching only carry-on luggage.

KNOWING SOMEONE of importance at the airline is the first step – a jumbo pilot is ideal – and this can best be achieved with a Frequent Flyer card of the right colour (i.e. platinum, gold or silver at a push) which will allow access to the lounges and then, with luck, to seat 1A.
FAILING THAT, arrive late to check in. Flights are frequently overbooked and, should you find that there is no more room in your class, then a bump up in to the next cabin will no doubt ease the situation. This can never be achieved by screaming, shouting or throwing your weight around. A more successful tactic is to smile, joke and never be

pushy with the person behind the desk. Charm works. Letting them know that you are in a genuine position to put much more business their way is also of considerable appeal to those with the power to grant flat-beds.
FEIGNING AN AILMENT is beneath you and, anyway, is seldom successful. Far better to simply try your luck, grin warmly, and ask. Never sup the complimentary champagne should you succeed: it always denotes an amateur.
AND, IF ALL the above should still leave you without the magic *Suitable For Upgrade* stamped across your ticket? Get out your wallet and pay for it.

SEATING PLAN

British Airways Boeing 737

RESERVE: 11 C, D, E; 12 A, B, C, D, E, F – all have extra legroom.
REFUSE: 1 A, C, D, E, F – restricted legroom.
10 A, F; 18 A, B, C – do not recline.
19E, F – near the toilet.

British Airways Boeing 747

RESERVE: 2 A, 2K – more secluded than 1A and 1K.
28 B, J; 29 A, K; 33 A-K – all are bulkhead seats.
62 A, K – private and spacious, the best upper deck seats.
REFUSE: any central seats (E, F) in Business Class
(unless travelling with a partner).
31 D, E, F, G – all are narrower than normal.
36 C, H, 53B-J– next to the toilet / limited recline.

British Airways Boeing 777

RESERVE: 2 A, E, F, K – further from the toilet than row 1.
REFUSE: 1 A, K – near the toilet.
10 A, B, J, K – near the galley so may be disturbed.
40 D, E, F – don't recline; usually crew seats.

Singapore Airlines, Qantas and Emirates Airbus A380

RESERVE: 1–4 A, F – the best seats on the lower deck.
12–15 A, K – the best seats on the upper deck.
REFUSE: 11 A, K – narrow seats.
3 C, D – unless travelling with a partner.
42 A–K, 63 D–G, 82 A, C, H, K, 82–83 E, F – limited recline.

ON BOARD RULES

Tracksuits are for the gym, not the plane.
•
Shorts are for the beach.
•
Never go barefoot.
•
Feign sleep to silence the bore next door.

HOW TO BEAT JET LAG

DO drink plenty of water before, during and after flying.

DO set your watch to the same time as your destination
as you board and sleep accordingly.

DO try to sleep as much as possible.

DO book unpopular early morning flights that land at night.
They will be empty and will aid your sleep when you arrive.

DON'T drink caffeine before the flight.

DON'T drink alcohol on board.

DON'T go to bed earlier than 10pm at your destination.

DON'T eat during the flight – it will leave you bloated
and unable to drop off.

STEWARDESS ETIQUETTE

{1} When the doors close, you are on their turf.
{2} Always be polite, and do what you are asked.
The seatbelt rule applies to you too.
{3} Cabin crew are working. Treat them as you would
want to be treated professionally.
{4} Cabin crew are there for your safety, not to act as
waiters or servants.
{5} If you can carry your bag aboard, then you can lift
it into the overhead locker yourself.
{6} If you really want cabin crew to like you, buy duty free
on board – they get commission.
{7} Never say 'trolley-dolly' (loud enough to be heard).
{8} Never try to chat them up. They've heard it all before.

HOW TO SURVIVE A PLANE CRASH

Get your seatbelt off quickly: many people panic and
forget how to release their buckle.

•

Adopt the brace position: it stops you flying forward,
hitting the seat in front, and prevents jack-knifing.

•

Wrap a scarf around your face: in a post-crash fire, you're
more likely to be killed by toxic fumes than the flames.

•

Plan your escape: count the number of seats in front of you,
behind you and across from you to the exit. If the lights fail
on crashing, you can still find the emergency escape.

•

Sit over the wing: a guaranteed safe-seat does not exist
but the area around the wing is reinforced with the
most metal. It also has an exit.

three of the world's
MOST EXPENSIVE HOTEL SUITES

{1} **City Slicker** *Ty Warner Penthouse, Four Seasons Hotel, New York*

4,300 square feet with 360-degree views of Manhattan – cantilevered glass balconies, floor-to-ceiling windows and 25-foot cathedral ceilings. Gold and platinum threaded fabrics, infinity-edge bathtub and library with grand piano. Access to every TV channel in the world; personal butler; personal trainer and therapist; private chauffeur with Rolls Royce Phantom or Mercedes Maybach. {2008: $30,000/NIGHT}

{2} **Culture Vulture** *Villa La Cupola, Westin Excelsior, Rome*

7,909 square feet of Roman opulence above Via Veneto, including a 39ft-high, hand-frescoed cupola, hand-carved wood panelling, hung tapestries and antique tiling. Bang and Olufsen surround sound system and private cinema; personal fine wine and cigar selection. The private spa offers a sauna and Jacuzzi; 1,808 square feet of terraces and balconies and an outdoor bar. {2008: 20,000 EURO/NIGHT}

{3} **Playboy** *Hugh Hefner Sky Villa, Palms Fantasy Tower, Las Vegas*

10,000 square feet of Playboy Mansion style and glamour in Vegas, featuring a cantilevered bunny-branded pool with a glass wall suspended right out over The Strip. It includes an 8-foot rotating bed, mirrored ceiling, extra large 'show-tub', indoor waterfall, pop up plasma television screens, private spa facilities, gym, poker table and art on the walls chosen by Hef himself. {2008: REPORTEDLY $40,000/NIGHT}

TEN HOTELS
TO EXPERIENCE

Amanjena Marrakesh, Morocco
·
Château de Bagnols
Beaujolais, France
·
COMO Shambhala Estate Bali
·
Ellerman House
Cape Town, South Africa
·
Gôra Kadan Hakone, Japan
·
Le Taha'a French Polynesia
·
San Ysidro Ranch Santa Barbara, USA
·
Singita Grumeti Reserves Tanzania
·
The Lowell New York, USA
·
Villa Feltrinelli Lake Garda, Italy

HOTEL TIPS
N.B. unit = one dollar, euro or pound

BELLBOYS OR PORTERS: one or two units per case, given as they leave the room (if overlooked in the USA, the staff will talk).

DOORMEN: one or two units if a cab is called for you (but not if ordered from the desk). As you leave for home, hand them a handsome tip and your next visit will be a very happy one.

HOUSEKEEPING: leave a banknote and a thank you note in your room (five units for short stays, more for longer). Never give it to reception – it is unlikely to reach the correct pocket.

ROOM SERVICE: two units for supper, one unit for drinks. (the exception is in the USA where they will have added 15 per cent or 17.5 per cent delivery charge already – unless the messenger is exceptional, don't bother).

MANAGERS: shouldn't be patronised by tipping.

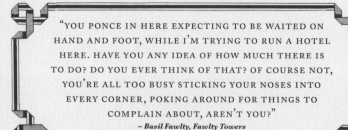

"YOU PONCE IN HERE EXPECTING TO BE WAITED ON HAND AND FOOT, WHILE I'M TRYING TO RUN A HOTEL HERE. HAVE YOU ANY IDEA OF HOW MUCH THERE IS TO DO? DO YOU EVER THINK OF THAT? OF COURSE NOT, YOU'RE ALL TOO BUSY STICKING YOUR NOSES INTO EVERY CORNER, POKING AROUND FOR THINGS TO COMPLAIN ABOUT, AREN'T YOU?"
– *Basil Fawlty, Fawlty Towers*

Nine Celebrity-Inspired Suites

BUFFALO BILL CELEBRITY SUITE The Cliff House at Pike's Peak, Colorado

CHURCHILL SUITE La Mamounia, Marrakech, Morocco

EDWARD VIII ROOM Pera Palas, Istanbul

JOHN WAYNE SUITE Raffles Hotel, Singapore

MARILYN MONROE SUITE Hollywood Roosevelt, Los Angeles

NELSON MANDELA PLATINUM SUITE Saxon Boutique Hotel and Spa, Johannesburg

PAVAROTTI SUITE Pangkor Laut Resort, Malaysia

THE BLACK MAGIC BEDROOM BY CARLOS SANTANA Hotel Triton, San Francisco

THE GEORGE BUSH PRESIDENTIAL RETREAT Cheeca Lodge, Islamorada, Florida Keys

RESIDENT RULES

Be charming to staff, with a touch of formality.

•

Dress appropriately in public areas.

•

Never leave the room excessively messy.

•

No bare feet, bare backs or football shirts.

•

Remember what you've drunk from the mini bar.

•

Call reception if running late when checking-out.

FOUR CELEBRITY-OWNED HOTELS

Bono and The Edge (U2) Clarence Hotel, Dublin

Clint Eastwood Mission Ranch, California

Francis Ford Coppola Blancaneau and Turtle Inn, Belize; La Lancha, Guatemala

Robert Redford Sundance Resort, Utah

FOUR HOTELS FROM THE MOVIES

Bellagio, Las Vegas, USA [*Ocean's Eleven*]

Park Hyatt, Tokyo, Japan [*Lost in Translation*]

Taj Lake Palace Hotel, Udaipur, India [*Octopussy*]

The St. Regis Hotel, New York [*The Godfather*]

FIVE FAMOUS HOTEL ROOM DEATHS

1900: Hotel D'Alsace, Paris (Room 16) Oscar Wilde died from cerebral meningitis; shortly before his death he said "I am dying beyond my means" *(now called L'Hôtel)*.

1970: Hollywood Landmark Hotel, California (Room 105) Janis Joplin was found dead from a heroin overdose in her room *(now called Highland Gardens Hotel)*.

1978: Chelsea Hotel, New York (Room 100) Sid Vicious's girlfriend, Nancy Spungen, died from a stab wound. He was arrested and charged, but died shortly afterwards from a heroin overdose.

1982: Chateau Marmont, Los Angeles (reportedly in Bungalow 3) John Belushi died from a speedball (heroin and cocaine mix).

1997: Sydney Ritz-Carlton, Sydney (Room 524) Michael Hutchence committed suicide, and was found hanging in his room *(now called Stamford Plaza Double Bay)*.

TRAVEL WITH BOND

{1}

Ian Fleming Suite, Hilton Seychelles Northolme Resort, Seychelles *Fleming's stays here inspired 'For Your Eyes Only' – this overwater villa boasts a library of Bond DVDs and a Bond-esque circular bed.*

{2}

Goldeneye Resort, Jamaica *A luxury resort – stay in Fleming House where Fleming wrote 17 of his books.*

{3}

James Bond Beach, Jamaica *Near to the Goldeneye Resort, this beach was where Ian Fleming used to swim.*

{4}

James Bond Island, Thailand *Officially called Ko Tapu, this island, just off Phang Nga Bay, was 'renamed' after featuring in 'The Man with the Golden Gun'.*

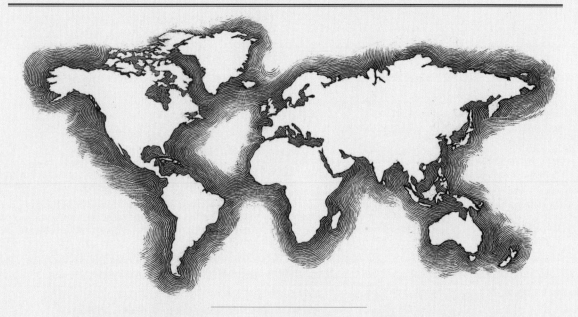

AROUND THE WORLD

10 SANDY BEACHES

Anse Source d'Argent [La Digue, Seychelles]

Devil's Bay [Virgin Gorda, British Virgin Islands]

Hanalei Beach [Kauai, Hawaii]

Myrtos Beach [Kefalonia, Greece]

Nungwi [Zanzibar, Tanzania]

One Foot Island [Aitutaki, Cook Islands]

Honda Bay, Palawan [Philippines]

Pink Sands Beach [Harbour Island, Bermuda]

Varadero [Cuba]

Whitehaven [Whitsunday Islands, Australia]

•

9 SURFING DESTINATIONS

Backdoor Pipeline [Oahu, Hawaii]

Corralejo [Fuerteventura, Canary Islands]

Croyde Bay [Devon, UK]

Essaouira [Central Morocco]

Hossegor [Les Landes, France]

Playa Santa Teresa [Mal Pais, Costa Rica]

Puerto Escondido [Oaxaca, Mexico]

The Soup Bowls [Bathsheba, Barbados]

The Superbank [Queensland, Australia]

8 URBAN BEACHES

Bondi Beach [Sydney, Australia]

Barcelona Beach [Spain]

Cannes [French Riviera]

Clifton Beach [Cape Town, South Africa]

Ipanema [Brazil]

South Beach [Miami]

Venice Beach [Los Angeles, USA]

Venice Lido [Venice, Italy]

•

7 ESSENTIAL WONDERS

Grand Canyon [Arizona, USA]

Valley of the Kings [Egypt]

Uluru [Australia]

Angkor Wat [Cambodia]

Petra [Jordan]

Great Wall of China [China]

Victoria Falls [Zambezi River]

6 ROBINSON CRUSOE GETAWAYS

Le Taha'a Private Island and Spa [French Polynesia]

Mnemba Island [Zanzibar]

North Island [Seychelles]

Petit St. Vincent [St. Vincent and the Grenadines]

Peter Island [British Virgin Islands]

Soneva Gili [Maldives]

•

5 AMAZING TRAIN JOURNEYS

Blue Train South Africa [Pretoria–Cape Town]

The Canadian [Toronto–Vancouver]

The Ghan, Australia [Adelaide–Darwin]

Trans-Siberian Express [Moscow–Vladivostok]

Venice Simplon-Orient-Express [London–Paris–Venice]

•

4 SKY HIGH BUILDINGS

Empire State Building [New York]

Petronas Towers [Kuala Lumpur, Malaysia]

Taipei 101 [Taipei, Taiwan]

Two International Finance Centre [Hong Kong]

•

3 AMAZING TREKS

Inca Tail to Machu Picchu [Peru]

Milford Track [New Zealand]

Way of St. James [Spain]

•

2 PLACES TO WATCH THE SUN SET

Oia [Santorini, Greece]

Serengeti National Park [Tanzania]

•

1 THING TO SEE BEFORE YOU DIE

Aurora Borealis [Arctic]

TEN BOOKS
ABOUT JOURNEYS

Old Glory: A Voyage Down the Mississippi
Jonathan Raban

•

**The Old Patagonian Express:
by Train through the Americas**
Paul Theroux

•

Roughing It Mark Twain

•

The Road to Oxiana Robert Byron

•

A Short Walk in the Hindu Kush
Eric Newby

•

Shadow of the Silk Road
Colin Thubron

•

On the Road Jack Kerouac

•

A Time of Gifts Patrick Leigh Fermor

•

**The Valleys of the Assassins:
and Other Persian Travels** Freya Stark

•

Way of the World Nicolas Bouvier

FIVE BOOKS
ABOUT COUNTRIES/REGIONS

Arabian Sands
Wilfred Thesiger

•

**Black Lambs and Grey Falcon:
A Journey Through Yugoslavia**
Rebecca West

•

In Patagonia Bruce Chatwin

•

Homage to Catalonia George Orwell

•

Sea and Sardinia D.H. Lawrence

GUIDE TO KNOTS

REEF KNOT   SHEEP SHANK

MAKING FAST
TO A
LARGE RING

ROUND TURN AND
TWO HALF-HITCHES

MAKING FAST
TO A
SMALL RING
OR
TO THE BIGHT
OF ANOTHER
ROPE

SINGLE SHEET BEND

CLOVE HITCH

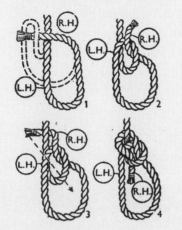

BOWLINE
(Useful knots for various purposes)

Beach Behaviour

WHILE YOU MAY BE HALF NAKED on the beach, that's no excuse to let standards drop – particularly when it comes to both style and manners. The most important thing to remember is that people have come to the beach to relax. Never park too close to the people next door and maintain at least a towel's length between you and your neighbours. Never play music except through headphones and if you must throw a ball, Frisbee or anything else around, do it as far away from anyone else as possible.

IN TERMS OF STYLE, there are a surprising number of *faux pas* for an environment in which so few clothes are worn. If you are large, don't wear skimpy swimming trunks. In fact, no matter what size you are, don't wear skimpy trunks. Not even ironically. Board shorts and tight shorts are the most acceptable form of beachwear. Micro-briefs have their place only if their wearer can pull them off. These men are few and far between.

COVER UP WHEN YOU LEAVE the beach to go in to a restaurant or shop and never, ever go naked unless you are on a nudist beach. Always wear sun cream and, whenever possible, wear a hat, particularly a straw fedora or Panama.

YACHT RULES & ETIQUETTE

- There will be limited storage on a yacht, so pack light and use soft luggage. Always bring a spare set of everything. There's more than a chance you'll get wet.
- Never wear black, leather-soled or hard shoes; always wear plimsolls, trainers or, ideally, deck shoes.
- Ask for permission to board before stepping from the shore.
- Noise travels on water, keep your opinions about your neighbours' attire to yourself.
- Port and starboard, never left and right.
- Fore and aft, never front or behind.
- Actually owning a yacht carries more kudos than dressing in such a way as to make everyone think you do.
- Never throw anything overboard.
- Never argue with the captain.
- Champagne tastes better on the high seas.

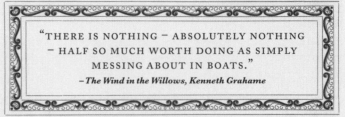

"THERE IS NOTHING – ABSOLUTELY NOTHING – HALF SO MUCH WORTH DOING AS SIMPLY MESSING ABOUT IN BOATS."
– *The Wind in the Willows, Kenneth Grahame*

HOW TO SPEAK SURF

BAIL OUT: to jump or dive off the board to avoid a wipeout.
BEACH BUNNY: a girl who watches surfers.
BITCHIN: excellent, brilliant.
BOMB: an unusually large wave.
CARVE: making a smooth turn on a wave.
COOKING: excellent conditions.
DECK: the top of the board on which the surfer stands.
FRUBE: someone who doesn't catch a wave in a session.
KOOK: an idiotic, bad surfer.
RAIL SANDWICH: the board hitting between the legs.
SAND FACIAL: being dragged, face first, along the bottom.
SOUP: the white foam of the wave or the whitewater.
SURF BUNNY: the girlfriend of a surfer.
TUBE: the hollow, tunnel-like hole in a wave.
WIPE OUT: to fall or be knocked off the board.

STYLE GUIDE SWIMMING TRUNKS

MICRO-BRIEFS

WHAT IT SAYS ABOUT YOU: extrovert, body-confident and European.
WHAT YOU NEED TO PULL IT OFF: athletic build, washboard stomach, intimate wax, nerve.
WHAT YOU'RE AIMING FOR: Ian Thorpe.
WHAT TO AVOID: Ben Stiller in *Meet The Parents*.

THONG

WHAT IT SAYS ABOUT YOU: tan-conscious, style-free and rich enough not to care.
WHAT YOU NEED TO PULL IT OFF: money, a private yacht, a lack of taste.
WHAT YOU'RE AIMING FOR: Rod Stewart.
WHAT TO AVOID: Borat.

BOARD SHORTS

WHAT IT SAYS ABOUT YOU: laidback, a surfer, one of the crowd.
WHAT YOU NEED TO PULL IT OFF: a good tan, long legs and a surfboard.
WHAT YOU'RE AIMING FOR: Mike Hynson in *Endless Summer*.
WHAT TO AVOID: Tony Blair.

TIGHT SHORTS

WHAT IT SAYS ABOUT YOU: serious, tough and slick.
WHAT YOU NEED TO PULL IT OFF: smooth lines, sharp colours and a harpoon gun.
WHAT YOU'RE AIMING FOR: Daniel Craig in *Casino Royale*.
WHAT TO AVOID: David Hasselhoff.

FIVE BEST WINDSURFING DESTINATIONS

Maui, Hawaii
Where the world's best windsurfers strut their stuff at Ho'okipa and Jaws, before heading to Mama's Fish House in Paia afterhours. For more sailing and surfing, there's also Kanaha or Spreckelsville too.

•

Jericoacoara, Brazil
A laidback fishing village boasting sensational windsurfing, capoeira and abundant caipirinhas.

•

Dahab, Egypt
This cobalt-blue lagoon on the Sinai Peninsula offers some of the easiest and most reliable flat-water windsurfing all year round.

•

Gnaraloo, Australia
Virtually impossible to get to and featuring a dust-blown, facility-less car park but the waves are to die for…

•

Brandon Bay, Ireland
Blessed with wondrous conditions for every level of windsurfer all year round (if you don't mind the cold in winter), it is fast becoming one of the UK and Ireland's biggest windsurfing destinations.

Beyond Skiing: New Challenges

HELI-SKIING

What it is: avoid the over-crowded pistes and try out areas of virgin powder snow, inaccessible to those limited to the confines of ski lifts. This is where the best snow, best conditions and most exciting runs can be found. It's also far enough from the crowd to add that element of exclusivity and danger.
Where to do it: Revelstoke, Canada.

SPEED FLYING

What it is: like paragliding but on skis. Start at the top of a mountain with a small wing and then, relying on gravity, hurtle down the mountain spending ten per cent of the time on the ground, the remainder in the air. Perhaps the most extreme form of skiing possible.
Where to do it: Les Arcs, France.

SKI JUMPING

What it is: unleash your inner Eddie 'The Eagle' Edwards by accelerating from 0–60mph in three seconds down a 90-metre, 1:1 slope, towards an eventual take-off speed of 80mph and a hidden landing zone below.
Where to do it: Calgary, Canada.

SPEED SKIING

What it is: reaching speeds of over 125mph, speed skiing is one of the fastest sports in the world. Skiers set themselves into a tuck then simply head downhill in a straight line. While technique is important to prevent falls, this is much more a test of bravery.
Where to do it: Les Arcs, France.

KITESKIING

What it is: popular on wide, open fields and, particularly, on frozen lakes, kiteskiing is fast becoming popular in snowy but non-mountainous landscapes. Cling onto a large kite and harness the power of the wind to reach high speeds, perform jumps, or simply hang in the air.
Where to do it: Bergsjø, Norway.

DOG SLEDDING

What it is: requiring massive upper-body and arm strength (train on a rowing machine), dog sledding is more reliant on fitness than experience at first. Being towed behind a team of sled-pulling dogs is often the only way to see spectacular and nearly inaccessible snowy landscapes.
Where to do it: Lapland, Finland.

BOBSLEIGHING

What it is: invented in the town of St. Moritz in Switzerland, bobsleighing's natural home is the Cresta Run. Travelling headfirst at speeds of up to 80mph for 1,000 metres, while descending 156 metres, the run is as breathtaking as it is legendary.
Where to do it: St. Moritz, Switzerland

SKIING *vs* SNOWBOARDING

Always the younger, cooler, yet more uncouth brother, snowboarding will never be able to claim either the same respect or sense of heritage as skiing. While one retains an air of elegance, the other – with its baggy clothes, slang and ski-bum connotations – will forever be the outsider. Most ski instructors recommend grasping the basics of skiing before attempting snowboarding. The skills learned on two skis, they say, can be transferred more easily onto the snowboard than vice versa. Snowboarding, however, is easier to learn.

THE FOUR BEST COMPETITIVE SKI RACES IN THE WORLD

{1} THE INFERNO, MÜRREN, SWITZERLAND

What it is: a total bun-fight, in which 1,800 racers charge down from the summit of the Schilthorn, departing at twelve-second intervals. Speed is the aim of the game, rather than technical ability or stamina, though there are some uphill climbs and treacherous bends and gullies. You must be a member of a club to join in.

When is it: annually in January.

{2} PATROUILLE DES GLACIERS

What it is: perhaps the toughest Alpine event in the world, it's a 53-km (31.8-mile) day-long race, with 4,000 metres' worth of elevation changes, on foot and skis across the Haute Route from Zermatt to Verbier – a route that takes most people six days to complete. You must bring an avalanche transceiver, head-torch, survival blanket, rope, shovel and harness.

When is it: biennially in April.

{3} THE VILLARS 24-HOUR RACE, VILLARS

What it is: set up by racing driver Jacques Villeneuve, and known as the Le Mans of skiing, teams of four to six people compete in a relay to see who can travel the furthest in a 24-hour period. While the skiing is not the most demanding, the stamina required is daunting.

When is it: annually in January.

{4} THE WHITE THRILL, ST. ANTON, AUSTRIA

What it is: similar to The Inferno, 500 people all set off at exactly the same time in a race from the Valluga to the village of St. Anton. Skill is less necessary than good elbows to blast past your fellow competitors and an almost suicidal obsession with downhill speed. The record for the 9-km (5-mile) course is just under eight minutes.

When is it: annually in April.

> "THE PATROUILLE DES GLACIERS IS PERHAPS THE HARDEST THING I'VE EVER DONE IN MY LIFE. CERTAINLY, IT WAS HARDER TO COMPLETE THAN REACHING EITHER OF THE POLES."
> – *Tom Avery, Polar Explorer*

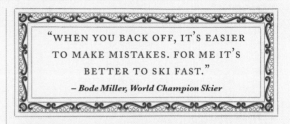

> "WHEN YOU BACK OFF, IT'S EASIER TO MAKE MISTAKES. FOR ME IT'S BETTER TO SKI FAST."
> – *Bode Miller, World Champion Skier*

THE TEN MOST DIFFICULT SKI RUNS IN THE WORLD

Corbet's Couloir Jackson Hole, Wyoming, USA

•

Vallée Blanche Chamonix, France

•

The Hahnenkamm Kitzbühel, Austria

•

La Chavanette (The Swiss Wall)
Les Portes du Soleil, French-Swiss Border

•

Tortin Verbier, France

•

S&S Chute Jackson Hole, Wyoming, USA

•

Courchevel Couloirs Courchevel, France

•

Big Couloir Big Sky, Montana, USA

•

The Marte Face Las Leñas, Argentina

•

Ruby Bowl Whistler Blackcomb,
British Columbia, Canada

ESSENTIAL OFF-PISTE EQUIPMENT

AVALANCHE AIR-BAG

AVALANCHE TRANSCEIVER

HELMET

PEN-KNIFE CAPABLE OF FIXING SKIS

PROBE

SHOVEL

SKINS

WATER BOTTLE

WALKIE-TALKIE

COUNTRY	'THANK YOU'	RESTAURANT TIP	TAXI TIP	CURRENCY
Australia	Thank You	10%	R.Up	Australian Dollar
Bahrain	Thank You or Shukran (Arabic)	10%	10%	Bahraini Dinar
Belguim	Dank U	R.Up	R.Up	Euro
Canada	Thank You	15–20%	15%	Canadian Dollar
China	Xie Xie (Mandarin) or M goi (Cantonese)	Optional 3–5%	R.Up	Chinese Renminbi
France	Merci	5–10%	R.Up	Euro
Germany	Danke	R.Up or 5%	R.Up	Euro
Hong Kong	Thank You or M goi (Cantonese)	S.Chg + 10%	R.Up	Hong Kong Dollar
India	Dhanyavaad	10%	R.Up	Indian Rupee
Italy	Grazie	S.Chg + 5–10%	5–10%	Euro
Japan	Arigatou Gozaimasu	Never	Never	Japanese Yen
Malaysia	Terima Kasih	S.Chg only	R.Up	Malaysian Ringgit
Mexico	Gracias	10–15%	Never	Mexican Peso
Qatar	Thank You or Shukran (Arabic)	S.Chg or 10%	Never	Qatari Riyal
Russia	Spasibo	10–15%	Never	Russian Rouble
Spain	Gracias	5–10%	10–15%	Euro
Saudi Arabia	Thank You or Shukran (Arabic)	10–15%	10%	Saudi Riyal
South Africa	Thank You	10%	10%	African Rand
Sweden	Tack	5–10% or S.Chg	R.Up	Swedish Krona
Taiwan	Kam Sia	Never	Never	New Taiwan Dollar
Thailand	Korp Khun Krap (M speaker) Korp Khun Kah (F speaker)	10–15%	R.Up	Thai Baht
UAE	Thank You or Shukran (Arabic)	10%	Never	Emirati Dirham
UK	Thank You	10–15%	10–15%	Pound
USA	Thank You	15–20%	15%	US Dollar

N.B. R.Up = Round Up; S.Chg = Service Charge; M = Male; F = Female

MIDDLE EASTERN MANNERS

- NEVER expose the soles of your feet.
- NEVER cross your legs when sitting in a chair.
- NEVER point at anyone or make the thumbs-up sign.
- NEVER touch anyone on the head.
- NEVER wear shoes when entering a mosque or holy place.
- NEVER use your left hand for eating, shaking hands, making gestures, etc.
- NEVER give gifts depicting images of women (be careful about giving books).
- NEVER give anyone alcohol unless you know the recipient drinks.
- NEVER take photographs – particularly of women – without first asking permission.
- NEVER photograph bridges, airports, military installations or government buildings.

VERY SUPERSTITIOUS...

{1} In Korea, never use red ink as writing someone's name in red indicates that they are either dead or you want them dead.

{2} In Australia, always make eye contact when chinking glasses in a toast. If you fail to do so, it is claimed that you will suffer from seven years' bad sex.

{3} In Daghestan, men advertise their sexual prowess by setting out water buckets on their porches in which they will wash after that evening's sexual encounter. The bigger the bucket, the greater their presumed sexual prowess – some men even set out two.

{4} Never whistle in a Kazakhstani house as it will bring poverty to the owner.

{5} Do not give scissors, knives or other cutting utensils to a Chinese as they indicate that you wish to sever the relationship; clocks, handkerchiefs or straw sandals are also taboo as they are associated with death and funerals.

{6} Crossing your fingers may be a good luck symbol in Britain, but in Vietnam it is considered obscene.

Business Etiquette

FAR EAST

As a foreign business person, you should be the first to offer your card. Use both hands (never just your left hand), with the card the right way up (type facing the recipient). Study the card presented to you for a few moments before placing it in a pocket (never your back pocket). Have your business cards printed on one side in the local language (this is not necessary in India or Malaysia). Include as much information as possible, including business title, qualifications and any formal titles. Never write on someone's business card.

When attending business meetings, you will find that those familiar with Western customs will shake hands with you; wait for your associate to extend a hand first. Each country has their own traditions so take your lead from your host. For example, in Japan you may be greeted with a long, low bow; the Chinese nod or bow slightly but handshakes are also common; in South Korea you should bow both at the beginning and end of a meeting. Avoid eye contact during the handshake.

MIDDLE EAST

Never present the card with your left hand (except Israel). Have some printed on one side in the local language and make sure you hand it to your counterpart with the side with their own language facing them.

Throughout the Middle East you should generally wait and observe your business counterpart and follow their lead. Handshakes are customary in Egypt, but you may also be greeted with a kiss on both cheeks. In the Gulf States say *salaam alaykum*, then shake hands while saying *kaif halak*. Wait until your counterpart releases your hand. Your host may then place his left hand on your right shoulder and kiss you on both cheeks. Do not be surprised if your hand is held while you are being led somewhere. Holding hands among men is common and does not carry the same connotations as it does in the West.

THE AMERICAS

In North America business cards are generally exchanged during introductions. However, they may also be exchanged when one party is leaving. In Latin America it is a courteous gesture to have business cards printed on one side in the local language, but present it with the English side facing your counterpart.

In North America, offer a firm handshake, lasting 3–5 seconds, with direct eye contact, on greeting and leaving. In Latin America, handshakes have become customary. But be aware that conversations may be held at much closer proximity than you are used to. Moving away is considered unfriendly, and should be avoided. In some parts of Latin America, notably Venezuela, you receive an *abrazo*, a brief hug, which may be accompanied by a kiss on the cheek. Be sure to reciprocate.

EUROPE

Business cards are usually exchanged. Include any educational qualification above bachelor degree level. In countries such as Greece, Spain and Portugal, have your business cards printed on one side in the local language. Present it with the local language side facing up. In Italy, usually the more important someone is, the less they will have printed on their business card.

Handshakes are common throughout Europe and – with the exception of the UK – are usually exchanged both before and after meetings. Keep your handshake brief and simple; no pumping, back-slapping or arm-grasping. A handshake in Germany may be accompanied by a subtle nod of the head.

THE PACIFIC AND AUSTRALIA

Present a business card on introduction, but don't necessarily expect one in return.

Shake hands at the beginning and end of a meeting. Expect less formality in Australia. Call your hosts by their first name or you will be accused of pretension.

JAPANESE BOWING

In Japan, bowing can be used in greeting, as an apology or to express thanks. Men bow with arms straight, palms flat and touching their legs; women bow with their hands slightly cupped, clasped in front of their thighs. At the full extent of your bow, your eyes will be looking at the floor. This, however, causes a problem as you need to ensure that the depth of your bow corresponds to the depth of their bow. For 'equals', the depth and length of the bow must be the same. For someone of superior status, your bow should be lower than theirs to indicate deference. If someone holds their bow for longer than expected, you should bow again. They will probably respond, and you may become involved in a long exchange of bows that get progressively smaller until they peter out altogether.

CHEERS!

CHINESE: Gan bei!
DUTCH: Proost!
FRENCH: A votre santé!
GERMAN: Prost!
ITALIAN: Salute!
JAPANESE: Kampai!
RUSSIAN: Na zdorovye!
SPANISH: Salud!

EXTREME ON SCREEN

Eyeball soup and chilled monkey's brains
Indiana Jones and the Temple of Doom

Whole stuffed sheep's head
Octopussy

"I WON'T EAT RAT. OR LIVE MONKEY BRAINS. ONE HAS TO DRAW THE LINE SOMEWHERE. THAT'S MY LINE." –*Anthony Bourdain*

Dice with Death

The Japanese *fugue* fish – also known as blowfish or pufferfish – contains a powerful poison over 1,200 times stronger than cyanide that, if wrongly prepared, can cause instant death. With over 100 different species, many with varying poisonous parts, only licensed chefs are allowed to prepare and cook *fugue*. Specially trained chefs undergo years of training and written exams; to qualify, they also have to eat *fugue* that they have prepared themselves. There is a process of approximately 30 steps to prepare *fugue*, and it is usually served raw in paper-thin slices, with a minute yet safe amount of the poison left in the flesh. This creates a tantalising sensation for the diner – numbing and tingling of the lips, perhaps even an awareness of the respiratory system – enhancing the adrenaline-fuelled experience of dicing with sudden death. There is no antidote to *fugue* poison, and it is estimated that 70–100 people die a year from ingesting it. Restaurants that are allowed to serve *fugue*, called *fugu ryotei*, are recognisable by the blowfish lantern hanging outside.

SIX EDIBLE INSECTS

Cockroaches
Crickets
Grasshoppers
Scorpions
Silkworms
Tarantulas

Four Rare Delicacies

{1} KOBE BEEF, JAPAN
This is the highly prized and highly marbled beef from the Tajima-ushi breed of Wagyu cattle. It is rumoured that the animals drink beer and receive massages.

{2} KOPI LUWAK COFFEE, INDONESIA
This unusual coffee is made from excreted beans found in Sumatra. Coffee berries are eaten by Indonesian civet cats (known as 'luwaks'). The still intact, digested beans are gathered from the forest floor, cleaned and roasted.

{3} LA BONOTTE POTATO, FRANCE
These nutty flavoured potatoes are so delicate that they are gathered by hand. Only found on Noirmoutier Island, they benefit from the sea water and native salt plains.

{4} WHITE TRUFFLE, PIEDMONT, ITALY
This very rare, uncultivable type of mushroom grows underground and is sought out by professional truffle hunters with dogs. The prized treasures – also known as white gold – are then sold at auction.

> "FOREIGNERS CANNOT ENJOY OUR FOOD, I SUPPOSE, ANY MORE THAN WE CAN ENJOY THEIRS. IT IS NOT STRANGE; FOR TASTES ARE MADE, NOT BORN. I MIGHT GLORIFY MY BILL OF FARE UNTIL I WAS TIRED; BUT AFTER ALL, THE SCOTCHMAN WOULD SHAKE HIS HEAD AND SAY, 'WHERE'S YOUR HAGGIS?' AND THE FIJIAN WOULD SIGH AND SAY, 'WHERE'S YOUR MISSIONARY?'"
>
> – *Mark Twain*

DURIAN FRUIT

This large, spiny tropical fruit is renowned for its pungent smell. Its aroma has been likened to vomit, sewage and dirty socks but, to many, it is considered a delicacy and its distinctive scent is all part of the treat. In South-East Asia, it is banned on most forms of public transport, aeroplanes and in hotels and hospitals. The fruit, also an aphrodisiac, is called 'the king of fruits'.

French Orlotan

This tiny bird, known in the UK as a bunting, is hunted illegally in France. Once caught, its eyes are removed and it is placed in a dark cage or box. An orlotan will then gorge itself on food and become larger. It is then drowned in Cognac or Amangnac, plucked and roasted. The heads are removed and the birds eaten whole – the sharp bones cause bleeding gums – the blood adds a salty taste that complements the flavour of the flesh. Traditionally, the eater wears a napkin over their head to hide the shame of this cruel act; some say this also retains aromas that intensify the flavour and experience.

SNAKE BLOOD

In many parts of Asia, such as Thailand, Indonesia, Vietnam and Cambodia, snake blood is considered to be an aphrodisiac that increases male virility. The blood is drained from the snake while it is still alive and often mixed with alcohol to improve the taste. Famously, the snake's tiny heart is also often served up too – while it is still beating.

MISS DEBRETT *Travelling with a Man*

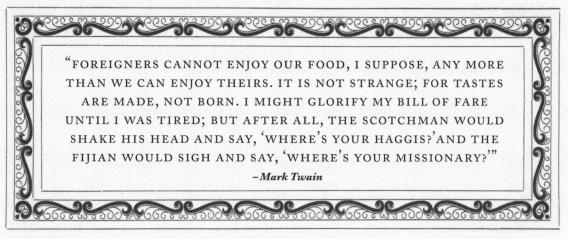

WHEN WE TRAVEL WITH A MAN we're looking, first and foremost, for a good companion; someone who is convivial and courteous, open to new experiences, tolerant of difficulties. We will appreciate it if, when travelling, our own tastes and disposition are taken carefully into consideration; a non-stop programme of adventures and dangerous sports will be anathema to a sedentary, sun-loving female. Compromise is all-important.

WHILE WE WILL APPRECIATE an air of *savoir faire* (linguistic aptitude, knowledge about transport, tipping, sites and restaurants) this can be taken too far. We don't want to be with a show-off, eager to demonstrate his travelling credentials; nor do we want someone who affects an air of jaded *ennui* – we won't be impressed by how well-travelled you are, just depressed that it has taught you nothing.

WE WILL BE EMBARRASSED if you choose to demonstrate your man of the world status by belittling the local culture and customs; we expect your good manners to extend to the locals. Don't assume that we must be looked after at all times. Remember, we are well-travelled too – we don't need to be wrapped in a smothering blanket of 'gentlemanly' behaviour.

BUT KEEP ON YOUR TOES; we may need your protection if local men become a little too interested, or if we unwittingly cause offence.

GASTRONOMY

Bottle Storage

WINE SHOULD BE STORED in constant conditions, in the dark, at a temperature of 12–13°C (55°F).

SUDDEN CHANGES in temperature – such as rapid increases and decreases caused by central heating – can damage wine.

BOTTLES SHOULD BE LAID on their side; this keeps the cork moist. If it dries out, the cork may fail.

SCREW TOPS are becoming more frequent, especially for white wine, but it is generally accepted that very fine wines will always have corks.

PROFESSIONAL STORAGE is recommended for fine wines. This will ensure optimum conditions, and usually the addition of humidity to ensure the cork remains moist.

Facts and Figures

SERVE RED WINE at the 'old-fashioned' pre-central heating room temperature of 17–18°C (63°F).

FINE WHITE WINE only needs 20 minutes in the fridge (including Sauternes); too much chilling will hide the complexity of serious wines. It's best, however, to chill cheaper bottles right down.

ICE BUCKETS are more effective when filled with a mix of ice and water, rather than just ice.

A WINE GLASS should be only one third full. It is better to underfill, rather than overfill, a glass.

REDS SHOULD BE SERVED in a large glass with a bigger bowl to release the bouquet. Whites are served in a smaller, narrower glass that should always be held by the stem to avoid warming the wine.

KNOWLEDGE THE A–Z OF WINE

ACIDITY a necessary component taste of wine to ensure it tastes lively and fresh. A wine with insufficient acidity can be referred to as 'flabby'.

BALANCE a well-balanced wine has good levels of alcohol, fruit, tannin and, especially in whites, acidity.

CORKED when a wine is 'off' and it smells musty.

DRY the opposite of sweet; wines that contain little sugar.

ELEGANT a well-rounded, balanced wine.

FINISH the aftertaste in your mouth; fine wines have a longer finish (also called length).

GRAPE-VARIETY the type of vine plant used, e.g. Cabernet Sauvignon, Chardonnay.

HERBACEOUS wine with a distinctive, herbal aroma.

INTENSITY a wine that has depth, and is extreme in degree, strength or effect.

JAMMY the flavour of intense, ripe fruit.

KNOW-ALL someone who thinks that they're a real buff.

LEGS where wine 'sticks' and runs down the inside of a glass.

MW Master of Wine: a qualification from the Institute of Masters of Wine. There are just over 260 MWs worldwide.

NOSE also called bouquet, this is the smell of the wine.

OAKY the flavour of a wine when it's taken on the taste from the barrel in which it was aged.

PERFUMED the aroma of fragrant white wines.

QUAFFING the act of consuming an easily drinkable wine.

ROUND when a wine is well-balanced in the mouth.

SOMMELIER the wine expert in a restaurant.

TANNIN the bitter taste mainly detected in red wine, originating from the skins, pips and stalks of the grapes.

ULLAGE the distance between the wine and the cork in an upright bottle.

VINTAGE the year the grapes were grown.

WOODY when there's too much oak in a wine.

XENOPHOBIA don't be afraid to try different wines produced around the world.

YOUNG when a wine is underdeveloped and hasn't reached its full potential.

ZINFANDEL a Californian grape; perfect barbecue wine.

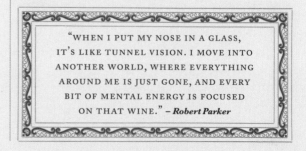

"WHEN I PUT MY NOSE IN A GLASS, IT'S LIKE TUNNEL VISION. I MOVE INTO ANOTHER WORLD, WHERE EVERYTHING AROUND ME IS JUST GONE, AND EVERY BIT OF MENTAL ENERGY IS FOCUSED ON THAT WINE." – *Robert Parker*

WINE RULES

{1}
White before red.
{2}
Light before heavy.
{3}
Cheaper before better.
{4}
Dry before sweet.
{5}
Complex food, simple wine.
{6}
Simple food, complex wine.
{7}
Don't be a bore.
{8}
Know when it's corked.

TASTING NOTES

Swirl the wine in the glass. Give it a sniff and say "that's fine" to the waiter to indicate that you're happy.

Amateurs or the under-confident should also take a small sip.

Remember, it's not to see if you like it, but just to check it's not corked.

If the wine is corked, it will smell musty, a bit like an old dishcloth.

Bits of cork (or sediment) in the wine are not a reason to send it back and don't mean that it's corked.

Never smell the cork; it is there for you to see the information on it.

Put your glass down between sips.

THE IMPORTANCE OF DECANTING

The process of decanting a red wine allows it to breathe. It separates mature wine from the sediment; it mellows and 'brings out' younger reds. Contact with the air livens it and, in a sense, 'accelerates' the ageing process. Decanting should take place a couple of hours before drinking but less, perhaps, for older wines that can fall away through the shock of air contact. Before decanting, ensure that the glass decanter is clean and soap-free. Pour the bottle at a reasonably rapid rate, being careful towards the end to ensure that any sediment remains in the bottle. Simply removing the cork from the bottle will not have the same (if any) affect.

EN PRIMEUR/IN BOND

When wine is bought *en primeur* (called 'futures' in the USA), it is literally in France, in a barrel. People buy wine like this to secure the best price; value can change considerably if a particular vintage gains status. The buyer can also rest assured that it is being perfectly stored. Additionally, the exact size of bottle desired can be ordered, from half-bottles to double magnums, jeroboams and imperials. Wine 'in bond' is when bottles are being stored in a bonded warehouse; it really refers to a tax status as the wine is VAT and duty-free at that stage.

THE PRO ROBERT PARKER

One of the most important wine critics in the world, American Robert Parker's influence on the wine industry is considerable. His famous 100-point scale, published in *The Wine Advocate*, ranks wine between 51–100 based on its appearance, bouquet, flavour, finish and overall quality and potential. His scores have a significant effect on both prices and market demand around the world – many Bordeaux producers don't release their prices until Robert Parker has released his ratings.

KNOWLEDGE PHYLLOXERA

In the late 1800s, a pest insect called Phylloxera destroyed much of Europe's grapevines, notably in France. As a result, many of the vines in Europe today are grafted vines; that is *Vitis vinifera* (Common Grape Vine) grafted onto American Phylloxera-resistant rootstock. Experts continue to debate whether wine from ungrafted, self-rooted vines is superior to wine from grafted vines. Pre-Phylloxera wine is highly-prized and rare.

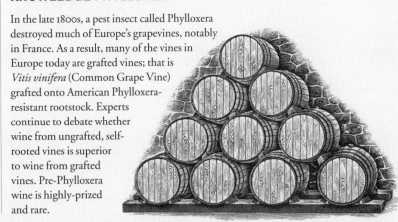

MAJOR WINES AROUND THE WORLD

FRANCE

France is generally considered to be the most important wine-producing country in the world. The main regions are Bordeaux and Burgundy.

{1} **Bordeaux:** the majority of wine from Bordeaux is red; in the UK, red Bordeaux is called 'Claret'. The region is divided by the confluence of the Dordogne and Garonne rivers with the Gironde Estuary; there are two main areas – the Left Bank and the Right Bank. The wines are generally blended from Cabernet Sauvignon and Merlot grapes. Iconic vintages: 1982, 1986 (Left Bank), 1990, 2000, 2005.

{2} **Burgundy:** famous for red and white wines; the whites are seen by some by as the best in the world. The region's complex geography and geology, along with numerous producers and vineyards, mean that the wines vary in style. Principal grape varieties are Pinot Noir for red and Chardonnay for white. Iconic vintages: 1978, 1985, 1990, 1996, 1999, 2002, 2005.

ITALY

Tuscany yields some of the country's best wines – especially Chianti, mainly made from Sangiovese grapes. Vino Nobile de Montepulciano is an impressive red. Also look out for Barolo from the Piedmont region.

SPAIN

Rioja is a full-bodied, chunky red. Alternatively, look out for reds from Ribera del Duero, made from Tempranillo – the most prestigious estate in the area is Vega Sicilia. For either, the grandest tend to be the Reservas or Gran Reservas.

CALIFORNIA

Californian viticulture is blessed with good geographical conditions and they produce huge quantities of wine. The key grapes are Cabernet Sauvignon, Pinot Noir, Zinfandel and Chardonnay.

AUSTRALIA

Home of commercial 'New World' wines, the key reds are Cabernet Sauvignon and Shiraz; the white, once again, is Chardonnay.

NEW ZEALAND

New Zealand's climate and geography provide perfect growing conditions and, as a result, the country produces some excellent wines. Its Sauvignon Blanc is considered to be amongst the finest white wines in the world; also look out for outstanding Pinot Noir.

SOUTH AFRICA

Over half of the wine produced in South Africa is Chenin Blanc. The country also boasts its own speciality, Pinotage, a spicy red well worth trying.

SOUTH AMERICA

When it comes to South America, many claim that red is the best way to go.

{1} **Chile:** with a viticulturally perfect climate, Chile's wines are good quality and well priced. The key red grape is Cabernet Sauvignon.

{2} **Argentina:** the home of excellent – and again, well priced – reds, look out for Argentinian Malbec.

BORDEAUX MATTERS *Want to Know your Wine? Then Know your Bordeaux…*

{1} Ten Bordeaux Châteaux
Château Ausone
Château Cheval Blanc
Château Haut-Brion
Château Lafite Rothschild
Château Latour
Château Lynch Bages
Château Margaux
Château Mouton Rothschild
Le Pin
Pétrus

{2} Six Dream Bordeaux Bottles
Once in a lifetime vintages to try:
Château Lafite Rothschild 1953
Château Haut-Brion 1961
Château Latour 1982
Château Mouton Rothschild 1986
Pétrus 1989
Château Margaux 2005

Recommended by the Fine Wine Expert at Berry Bros & Rudd

{3} Sweet Tooth
Sauternes in southern Bordeaux produces some of the best sweet wine in the world. The area's mists and sunshine encourage the growth of *botrytis cinerea*, a mould that dehydrates and, in the process, sweetens the grapes. Aside from being a classic dessert wine, Sauternes is an excellent accompaniment to foie gras – Château d'Yquem 2001 is one of the finest bottles available.

CHAMPAGNE MISCELLANY

HISTORY: it is rumoured that a monk, Dom Pérignon, in the village of Hautvillers in the Champagne region, northern France, first invented champagne in 1668.

GRAPES: champagne is made from a combination of Chardonnay, Pinot Noir and Pinot Meunier grapes.

MÉTHODE CHAMPENOISE: the process of creating the bubbles; adding a solution of sugar and yeast to wine creates a second in-bottle fermentation.

GENUINE ARTICLE: only champagne made from the Champagne region is allowed to be called 'champagne' on its label.

GLASSES: serve champagne in tulip-shaped flutes; hold the glass by the stem. Glasses must be scrupulously clean – even the most minuscule remains of washing-up liquid can cause the champagne to lose its fizz.

GO VINTAGE?

VINTAGE champagne comes from the crop of a single year. A vintage bottle, therefore, always has a date on its label. A champagne house will only produce vintage champagne from very good years, and will typically release it after about six years. N.B. a bottle should last about 20 years if stored correctly.
Try: Dom Pérignon or Krug. For something special, try Pol Roger Cuvée Sir Winston Churchill. Classic champagne vintages: 1988, 1989, 1990, 1996, 2002.

NON-VINTAGE champagne is blended from the crop of different years; therefore there will be no date on the label. It can vary in quality; good non-vintage champagne demonstrates the skills of the cellar-master as a blend of a consistently high standard is difficult to achieve.
Try: Pol Roger Brut Réserve or Bollinger Special Cuvée.

EXPERT TIP The sign of a good champagne is a consistent stream of small bubbles, that create a light froth around the edge of the surface. This is called the 'mousse'.

HOW TO OPEN A BOTTLE OF FIZZ

Ensure that it hasn't been shaken.

Peel off the foil over the cork.

Point the bottle away from you.

Remove metal cage over the cork.

Hold the cork in one hand.

Hold the bottle in the other.

Gently twist the bottle (not the cork).

Aim for a sigh not a pop.

SIZE MATTERS

Magnum 2 bottles

Jeroboam 4 bottles

Rehoboam 6 bottles

Methuselah 8 bottles

Salmanazar 12 bottles

Balthazar 16 bottles

Nebuchadnezzar 20 bottles

GET IT RIGHT: PORT

Port is a sweet, fortified wine from the Douro region of Portugal. It is traditionally drunk with cheese or after a meal but, if you're feeling hollow-legged, it can be a delicious aperitif when served chilled.

There are two styles of making port. Bottle-aged port is just that: it spends little time in a cask. Cask-aged ports mature in wooden barrels until they are ready to drink, a famous example of this is Tawny port. It is wine to be laid down, as a cask-aged port that spends two years in a barrel will last 20–40 years in a bottle. It is best to drink vintage port. *Try: Taylor's 1977 Vintage Port.*

In formal situations, such as dinners, a port decanter will be placed on the table. You should help yourself and then pass it on, always to the left. If the decanter passes you by without your glass being filled, never attempt to ask for the decanter, thereby making it change direction. The decanter must return to the host without being put down – a Hoggett decanter has a round bottom, making it impossible for guests to put it down.

The tradition of passing the port originates from naval dinners where the port was always passed 'port to port' around the table – i.e. to the left.

TEN COCKTAIL RULES

{1}
Read up. Old cocktail books from the 1850s to 1900s will provide guidance on classic, authentic recipes and ingredients.

{2}
Use clean, dry and chilled glasses.

{3}
Pack the glass with ice – make sure you use plenty so that it stays frozen and doesn't dilute the drink by melting.

{4}
Sugar syrup is a vital ingredient; always use one made from cane sugar.

{5}
Egg white binds and emulsifies the citrus and alcohol in citrus drinks.

{6}
Make sure garnishes and citrus juices are fresh and made on demand.

{7}
Use seasonal fresh fruits.

{8}
Be authentic and choose spirits carefully. As a general rule, avoid anything introduced after 1985.

{9}
Choose classic liqueurs, and trust the iconic, recognised brands.

{10}
Experiment. Keep an eye out for unusual, locally produced spirits when you are abroad.

EXPERT TIP Ice is one of the most important ingredients in a cocktail. Use a domestic ice machine and make sure it's properly frozen and not starting to thaw before you start mixing.

Glassware

Choose simple, classic designs, and make sure the glass isn't too thick.

Collins (or highball glass)

Rocks glass (or tumbler)

Cocktail glass (v-shaped)

Liqueur glass (small, stemmed tasting glass for sipping)

Small cocktail glass (or sour glass)

Coupette glass (or Margarita glass)

ESSENTIAL MARTINI MUSTS

{1} Always chill your glassware to frozen.

{2} Know if you want gin or vodka.

{3} Choose a vermouth or fortified wine that works with your spirit.

{4} The less vermouth used, the drier the drink.

{5} Don't be afraid of vermouth as it is the making of a fine martini.

{6} Know your ratios.

{7} Know your preferred garnish.

{8} Request bitters (Angostura or orange) if you like extra complex cocktails.

{9} Always have it stirred (except for the Vesper, which is shaken, as per Bond's specifications).

Vintage Cognac

True cognac fans should try a rare, vintage pre-Phylloxera variety (dating back to before 1872). These intensely flavoured and highly-priced cognacs are an experience; really, you are drinking a piece of history.

ESSENTIAL EQUIPMENT

MANHATTAN THREE-PIECE SHAKER (the traditional one)

BOSTON SHAKER (big glass and a big tin)

HAWTHORNE STRAINER (one with a spring)

FINE STRAINER (or a tea strainer)

ZESTER (or a potato peeler)

MUDDLER (or a rolling pin)

HAND SQUEEZER (for fresh fruit)

SHARP KNIFE (for fresh fruit)

ELECTRIC BLENDER (more useful than you'd think)

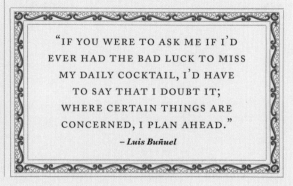

"IF YOU WERE TO ASK ME IF I'D EVER HAD THE BAD LUCK TO MISS MY DAILY COCKTAIL, I'D HAVE TO SAY THAT I DOUBT IT; WHERE CERTAIN THINGS ARE CONCERNED, I PLAN AHEAD."

– Luis Buñuel

THE ULTIMATE HOME COCKTAIL BAR

VODKA

MAIN TYPES

Wyborowa (100% rye)
Luksusowa (100% potato)
Stolichnaya (100% wheat)
Authentically flavoured varieties:
Żubrówka (Bison Grass Vodka)
Cytrynowka (Lemon Vodka)
Wisniowka (Cherry Vodka)
Krupnik (Honey Vodka)

INFO: go for authentic vodka.

RUM

RHUM AGRICOLE

Cachaça 51 or Pitú (Brazil)
Rhum Clément (Martinique)

SELECTED ASSORTED RUMS

Havana Club (Cuba)
El Dorado (Guyana)
Appleton Estate (Jamaica)
Mount Gay (Barbados)

INFO: have a selection of rums, aged
to the following amount: 0–3 years;
5–7 years; 12–15 years; 20+ years

OVENPROOF RUM

Overproof Wray & Nephew (Jamaica)

DARK RUM

Doorly's (Barbados)
Gosling's (Bermuda)
Myers's Dark Rum (Jamaica)

BRANDY

COGNAC

VS Cognac
VSOP Cognac
XO Cognac

OTHER BRANDIES

Pisco (Peruvian brandy)
Metaxa
Spanish Brandies

INFO: experiment and bring a
bottle home from your travels.

TEQUILA

MAIN REGIONS

Los Altos (Don Julio)
Valley of Tequila (Herradura)

MAIN VARIETIES

Blanco (aged 0–60 days)
Reposardo (2–12 months in oak barrels)
Añjeo (1–3 years in small oak barrels)
Extra Añjeo (3+ years)

INFO: made from the agave plant,
so make sure you buy 100 per cent
agave tequila. Los Altos tequilas are
sweeter varieties from the Valley
of Tequila. Choose a selection
of different ages from each region.

GIN

MAIN TYPES

Beefeater (delicate/complex)
Tanqueray (bold/upfront juniper)
Plymouth (softer/sweeter)

WHISK(E)Y*

AMERICAN WHISKEY/BOURBONS

Jack Daniels (Tennessee Whiskey)
Wild Turkey (Straight Rye)
Buffalo Trace (Rye Bourbon)
Maker's Mark (Wheat Bourbon)

SCOTCH WHISKY

Johnnie Walker (a heavier blend)
Bailie Nicol Jarvis (a lighter blend)

MALT WHISKY

Monkey Shoulder (vatted malt)
Laphroaig (Islay)
The Macallan (Speyside)
Springbank (Cambeltown)
Tallisker (Isle of Syke)
Highland Park (Island of Orkney)
Yoichi (Japan)
Suntory (Japan)

**whiskey with an 'e' is produced
in Ireland or in the USA, while
everywhere else forgoes the extra letter.*

VERMOUTH
AND SIMILAR

Noilly Prat Dry or Martini Extra Dry
(dry vermouth)
Punt E Mes or Dubonnet
(sweet vermouth)
Lillet Blanc (Bond's favourite)

INFO: you need a range of vermouths;
they should be kept in the fridge.

LIQUEURS
AND EXTRAS

Absinthe (distilled, not flavoured)
Amaretto (almond)
Angostura and Orange Bitters
Apricot Brandy (it's not brandy)
Cacao (chocolate)
Campari
Cane Sugar Syrup (such as Tessiere)
Crème de Cassis (blackcurrant)
Crème de Fraise (strawberry)
Crème de Framboise (raspberry)
Crème de Mure (blackberry)
Crème de Pêche (peach)
Frangelico (hazlenut)
Galliano (herbal)
Kahlúa (coffee)
Maraschino Syrup (cherry)
Pastis (such as Ricard)
Sloe Gin (preferably homemade)
Strega (herbal)
Triple Sec (such as Cointreau)

INFO: buy the best fruit liqueurs,
with the highest fruit content.

CLASSIC COCKTAILS
Nine Timeless Recipes to Try

White Lady
40mls Plymouth Gin
20mls Cointreau
20mls lemon juice
One egg white
5mls sugar syrup

METHOD: shake and fine strain.
GLASS: coupette
GARNISH: lemon spiral
INFO: this recipe comes from the
Savoy Cocktail Book, written by
Harry Craddock in London
in 1930. The egg white will bind
the ingredients and provide a
wonderful silky texture.

•

Dark and Stormy
2 lime wedges (squeezed)
50mls Gosling's rum
Ginger beer to top

METHOD: build and stir.
GLASS: highball
GARNISH: lime wedge
INFO: this was drunk by British
sailors in Bermuda. It is often
referred to as 'Bermuda's
National Drink'.

•

El Presidente
30mls Havana Club 3 Años
15mls Cointreau
15mls Noilly Prat Dry
Dash grenadine
Orange twist (spray and discard)

METHOD: build and stir in
a mixing glass, then transfer
to sours glass to serve.
GARNISH: none
GLASS: sours
INFO: from the Vista Alegre in
Havana in the 1920s, for General
Carmen Menocal, president before
Fulgencio Batista.

Toreador
40mls 100% agave tequila
20mls apricot brandy
10mls lime juice
10mls lemon juice
5mls sugar syrup
25mls egg white

METHOD: shake and double strain.
GLASS: v-shaped cocktail
GARNISH: none
INFO: this is based on a
recipe from the *Café Royal
Cocktail Book* (1937).

•

Negroni
25mls Beefeater gin
25mls Campari
25mls best sweet vermouth

METHOD: build and stir in
a mixing glass, then transfer
to rocks glass to serve.
GLASS: rocks
GARNISH: orange slice
INFO: believed to have been
invented at Caffè Casoni in Florence
for Count Camillo Negroni,
who liked his Americano served
with a measure of gin.

•

Sweet Manhattan
40mls rye whiskey
20mls best sweet vermouth
Spoon of maraschino syrup
Dash Angostura bitters

METHOD: stir in a mixing glass.
Strain. Spray oils from orange
peel over drink.
GLASS: v-shaped cocktail
GARNISH: cherry
INFO: it is widely believed that
this was invented for Jennie Churchill
(mother of Sir Winston) at a party at the
Manhattan Club in 1874.

Vesper
60mls Gordon's gin 47.3%
20mls Russian vodka
10mls Lillet Blanc

METHOD: shake and strain.
GLASS: cocktail
GARNISH: lemon twist
INFO: created for Ian Fleming at Duke's
Hotel, London; featured in *Casino Royale*.

•

Pisco Sour
50mls La Diablada Pisco
25mls fresh lime juice
15mls sugar syrup
Dash Angostura bitters
One egg white

METHOD: shake and double
strain, or blend.
GLASS: sours/flute
GARNISH: dots of Angostura bitters
INFO: this drink is indigenous to Peru.

•

La Bodequita del Medio Mojito
50mls Havana Club 3 Años
25mls fresh lime juice
15mls sugar syrup
4 mint sprigs
Soda water

METHOD: muddle mint and sugar in glass,
add lime/rum, mix, then add soda and ice.
GARNISH: mint sprig
GLASS: highball
INFO: from the legendary Havana
grocer's store where Hemingway drank.

MARTINIS TO TRY

{1} Equal parts Plymouth gin and
Lillet Blanc, orange bitters and
a lemon twist.

{2} One part Beefeater gin, two parts
sweet vermouth, a dash of Angostura
Bitters and a lemon twist.

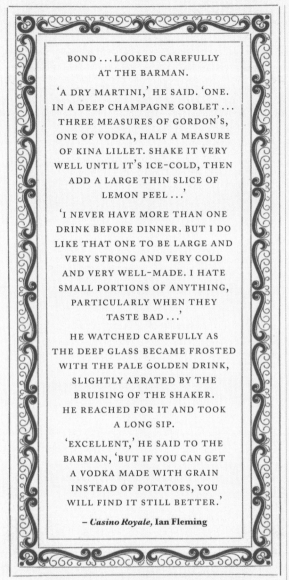

BOND ... LOOKED CAREFULLY
AT THE BARMAN.

'A DRY MARTINI,' HE SAID. 'ONE.
IN A DEEP CHAMPAGNE GOBLET ...
THREE MEASURES OF GORDON'S,
ONE OF VODKA, HALF A MEASURE
OF KINA LILLET. SHAKE IT VERY
WELL UNTIL IT'S ICE-COLD, THEN
ADD A LARGE THIN SLICE OF
LEMON PEEL ...'

'I NEVER HAVE MORE THAN ONE
DRINK BEFORE DINNER. BUT I DO
LIKE THAT ONE TO BE LARGE AND
VERY STRONG AND VERY COLD
AND VERY WELL-MADE. I HATE
SMALL PORTIONS OF ANYTHING,
PARTICULARLY WHEN THEY
TASTE BAD ...'

HE WATCHED CAREFULLY AS
THE DEEP GLASS BECAME FROSTED
WITH THE PALE GOLDEN DRINK,
SLIGHTLY AERATED BY THE
BRUISING OF THE SHAKER.
HE REACHED FOR IT AND TOOK
A LONG SIP.

'EXCELLENT,' HE SAID TO THE
BARMAN, 'BUT IF YOU CAN GET
A VODKA MADE WITH GRAIN
INSTEAD OF POTATOES, YOU
WILL FIND IT STILL BETTER.'

– Casino Royale, **Ian Fleming**

GIN AND TONIC

A COLLINS GLASS, CRAMMED
FULL OF GOOD ICE

•

A SLICE OF FRESH LEMON OR LIME

•

50MLS BEEFEATER GIN

•

100MLS SCHWEPPES TONIC

FERNET BRANCA: MIRACLE CURE?

Fernet Branca is a bitter, aromatic, dark-coloured Italian spirit that many swear by as a miracle hangover cure. Along with the minty (and more palatable) variation, Brancamenta, it is well known to aid the digestion and fortify the stomach.

Made from a secret recipe dating back to 1845, Fernet Branca includes 27 herbs – including aloes, gentian root, rhubarb, gum myrrh and red cinchona bark – picked in four continents and aged in oak casks for over a year.

It is rumoured that Napoleon gave his troops a shot of Fernet Branca every morning to strengthen their will for battle.

Hangovers: Prevention or Cure?

{1} PREVENTION: sensible drinkers curb the effects with a bit of forward planning. They eat something (preferably stomach-liningly fatty) before they start; they drink water as well as just booze; they indulge in a cheeky late-night snack to mop up the excess; most importantly, they remember to neck that pre-bed pint of water.

{2} CURE: as Frank Sinatra said, "I feel sorry for people who don't drink. When they wake up in the morning, that's as good as they're going to feel all day." Everyone has their own idiosyncratic hangover trick, but there are a few classic tactics to soothe the hangover. Rehydration is key, so drink plenty of water. A fry-up usually helps or, if you're short of time, a bacon or sausage sandwich. A strong coffee will perk you up, as will a can of Coca-Cola. If things don't improve, an over-the-counter remedy may sort you out. If all else fails, there's the hair of the dog ... see above.

COFFEES AROUND THE WORLD

CARIBBEAN

Mild and sweet, the beans of Jamaica are grown on the slopes of the Blue Mountains. They often compare less favourably to those of Central America, but beans from Cuba and Puerto Rico are generally subtle, dark and intoxicating.

CENTRAL AMERICA

The coffee grown in Costa Rica and Guatemala is all, the story goes, descended from a single tree imported by explorer Gabriel Mathieu de Clieu in 1723. The well-respected beans are now praised for their fine balance between acidity and sweetness.

ETHIOPIA

Where many believe coffee was first grown, Ethiopian beans often have a wild and fruity taste. Two types of Ethiopian coffee tend to be available: Harrar, generally considered to be finer of the two, and the gamy Djimmah. Beans from neighbouring Yemen are of similar taste and often excellent quality.

KENYA

More acidic than most, Kenyan beans are grown at altitude giving them a full-bodied flavour. Generally, Kenyan coffee is of a consistently high standard.

INDONESIA

Earthy, full-bodied and powerful, Indonesian coffees can be unreliable. When they're right, however, they are magical. Coffee from Java was once considered to be amongst the world's finest, but most experts now agree that intensive farming has ruined Javanese produce.

SOUTH AMERICA

This is, perhaps, the most famous coffee-growing area in the world. The most consistently excellent are from Brazil and Colombia where the beans are rich and sweet. They are usually a safe bet, but often are not the most exciting coffees on the market.

COFFEE HOME BASICS

BEANS: to keep coffee fresh at home, buy beans and, if possible, grind them as you need them. Find a supplier who can tell you where your beans are from and how they were roasted. It is also important to check when they were roasted – if it is more than a week ago or your supplier can't answer, don't buy them.

GRINDING: a good grinder is essential at home; bad grinding is the simplest way to ruin coffee. If you don't have one, ask your bean supplier to grind your beans for you – it won't be as fresh but it will improve your coffee.

STORAGE: store your coffee in a dark, air-tight container. Oxygen and light will ruin the flavour (and a bean's flavour will dissipate after ten days at room temperature). Store in a fridge or freezer for best results – there is no need to defrost them before use.

Decaffeinated Decoded

THERE ARE TWO MAIN DECAFFEINATION PROCESSES:

{1} **WATER-PROCESSED:** the beans are steamed and soaked in water vats, removing both caffeine and flavour. The liquid is then drained away, the caffeine removed and the beans resoaked in the flavour-filled water. Inevitably, some of the flavour is lost along the way, making this a safe but not entirely satisfactory method.

{2} **CHEMICAL-PROCESSED:** coffee beans decaffeinated by chemicals taste far better because more flavour is left intact. While some have worried about the effects of drinking coffee treated in this way, it is now generally agreed that the amount of chemical residue left in the coffee is so minimal that it can do very little harm.

Home Brewing

A cup of coffee is 98 per cent water. A true coffee perfectionist would use filtered or bottled water, not tap.

Always brew your coffee on demand – never leave it sitting in a jug on a hot-plate as the flavour will disappear.

Never add boiling water to coffee; ensure that it is several degrees under boiling point or the intense sudden heat will damage the bean.

Pressure is the single most important thing in a home espresso machine. The higher it is, the better the coffee.

Aside from an espresso machine, a cafetière provides some of the the richest coffee at home. Use dark roast beans – two scoops of coarse ground coffee per person.

As a mainstay in most Italian homes, stove-top espresso makers could not come more highly recommended. Quick and easy – but not as good quality as an espresso machine – they require fine-ground beans.

Capsule or pod machines can make excellent coffee; they are clean, quick and convenient. You get what you pay for, however, and you can only use the coffee the manufacturer provides, not your own beans.

Coffee cups should be warm, but not hot, and only filled up to two thirds capacity. The cup itself should be the shape of half an egg.

COFFEE TERMINOLOGY

AMERICANO: an espresso topped up with water.

BARISTA: Italian for the person operating an espresso machine.

BLEND: a mixture of beans originating from different areas.

CAFÉ CRÈME: French coffee served with milk (similar to café au lait).

CAFÉ AU LAIT: French coffee mixed with boiled (not steamed) milk, usually drunk at breakfast time .

CAPPUCCINO: an espresso topped up with the same amount of steamed milk and then a similar amount of foamed milk. Sometimes, chocolate powder is shaken on top. In Italy, it is strictly a breakfast drink.

ESPRESSO: hot water is forced, at high pressure, through ground beans, creating the purest coffee.

FLAT WHITE: the Australian for latte.

FRENCH ROAST: a very dark roast coffee.

ITALIAN ROAST: a dark roast coffee, though not as dark as a French roast.

LATTE: an espresso topped up with steamed or foamed milk. Just like cappuccino, it's not to be drunk after breakfast time.

MACCHIATO: an espresso with a small amount of milk – sometimes a couple of tablespoons, sometimes an equal volume to the coffee itself.

MOCHA: a drink that includes both coffee and chocolate. Mocha is also an extremely rare and fine bean from Yemen.

TURKISH COFFEE: made by boiling finely ground beans with sugar; the sediment then settles in the cup. It is made in a *cezve*.

CREMA

DEFINITION: A LAYER OF FOAM THAT FLOATS ON TOP OF ESPRESSO COFFEE.

An espresso is not an espresso without an oily, golden crema. It should be able to support the weight of half a teaspoon of sugar for at least a few seconds.

Crema is, however, notoriously elusive to achieve at home. Always ensure that beans are fresh and, ideally, dry-processed (washing can remove vital oils).

Crema should not be yellow or creamy. An off-white and thin crema indicates that the beans need to be more coarsely ground and packed more tightly into the machine. A dark, burnt-looking crema means that the beans are probably too coarsely ground and packed too tightly.

Coffee Trivia

Mocha got its name from the port of Al Mukha, on the Arabian Peninsula, from where Europe received coffee from Africa. When chocolate arrived in the New World, its taste was compared to coffee. Any drink combining coffee and chocolate is called a mocha.

THE ESSENTIAL COOK'S KITCHEN

COOKWARE
Frying pans (big and small)
Griddle pan
Saucepans: large, medium, small, spare
Roasting tin
Sauté pan (high-sided frying pan)
Wok
·

ELECTRIC
Coffee bean grinder
Electric scales
Espresso machine
Four-slice toaster
Kettle
Food processor
·

FABRIC
Apron
Cloths
Oven gloves
Tea towels

UTENSILS & EQUIPMENT
Can-opener
Cheese grater
Chinese bamboo steamer
Chopping boards
Colander
Japanese bamboo-wood spoons
Knives (see p.CLVIII)
Measuring jug
Measuring spoons
Oil brush
Palette knife
Peeler
Pestle and mortar
Potato ricer
Rolling pin
Rubber spatula
Scissors
Sieve
Tongs
Whisk (flat and balloon)

ON A ROLL
Baking parchment
Cling film
Freezer bags
Kitchen roll
Tin foil
·

IN THE FRIDGE
Butter (French, unsalted)
Cheese (such as cheddar)
Chillies (red, green)
Cream or crème fraîche
Eggs (free-range)
Fresh herbs (including basil,
thyme, flat-leaf parsley,
mint and coriander)
Ginger (root)
Lemons (fresh)
Milk (semi-skimmed or whole)
Pancetta
Parmesan (block for grating)

The Foodie's Cupboard

ANCHOVIES (in olive oil)
BAKED BEANS (Heinz)
CAPERS (in salt)
CHOCOLATE (70% cocoa solids)
COCOA POWDER (70% chocolate)
COUSCOUS (or quinoa)
FLOUR (plain, corn)
GARLIC (whole bulb)
HP SAUCE (Heinz)
LEA & PERRINS WORCESTERSHIRE SAUCE
LIQUID SAUCES (soy, oyster, fish)
MARMITE (unless you hate it)
MUSTARD (English, Dijon, wholegrain, powder)
NOODLES (dried)
OILS (olive oil [extra virgin and standard], sunflower, sesame)
OLIVES (black)
ONION (white and red)
PASTA (penne, spaghetti, linguine, tagliatelle, orecchiette)
PEPPERCORNS (whole black for grinding)
PICKLE (Branston)
PLUM TOMATOES (whole, tinned)
PORCINI (dried mushrooms)
RICE (Arborio [for risotto], Basmati, long grain)
SALT (Maldon Salt and sea salt for grinding)
SUGAR (brown, white, caster)
TOMATO KETCHUP (Heinz)
VEGETABLE BOUILLON POWDER (stock)
VERMOUTH (Noilly-Prat Dry)
VINEGAR (balsamic, malt, red and white wine)

KNOWLEDGE FLAVOUR AND UMAMI

Humans have hundreds of dedicated receptor cells for the different elements of taste. For hundreds of years, taste was recognised as comprising four elements: sweet, sour, salty and bitter. It is now recognised that there is a fifth – umami. In 1908, Japanese professor Kikunae Ikeda first used this odd word to describe the 'heartiness' found in foods containing glutamate. Umami is that 'meaty' and intense savoury flavour found in Chinese food (often containing lots of glutamate, or MSG) that can't be created with seasoning or rich ingredients. Also found in Parmesan, cured hams and shitake mushrooms, it is an essential element in creating a memorably tasty dish.

 EXPERT TIP For the ultimate cooker, go for a dual fuel range with electric double oven, grill and five burner gas hob, including a wok burner.

SEVEN BOOKS
FOR FOODIES

Kitchen Confidential Anthony Bourdain
A warts-and-all account of what really goes on in a restaurant kitchen. And why you should never order the chef's 'special'.

•

McGee on Food and Cooking Harold McGee
The book that turned Heston Blumenthal into a boffin. A peerless guide to the science behind the stove.

•

Nose to Tail Eating Fergus Henderson
From roast bone marrow to rolled pig's spleen, waste-nothing recipes from a restaurant Mecca for carnivores worldwide, London's St. John.

•

An Omelette and a Glass of Wine Elizabeth David
Timeless food writing from the remarkable woman who single-handedly shifted olive oil from the bathrooms to the kitchens of Britain.

•

The Man Who Ate Everything Jeffrey Steingarten
A former lawyer who makes a forensic case for the danger of salad and why horse fat makes for the perfect chip.

•

Leiths Techniques Bible Susan Spaull and Lucinda Bruce-Gardyne. Need to clarify a consommé or make the perfect pastry? This ultimate reference book should be every cook's best friend.

•

Eating Up Italy: Voyages on a Vespa Matthew Fort
A former *Guardian* restaurant critic explores Italy's history, culture and geography through its food.

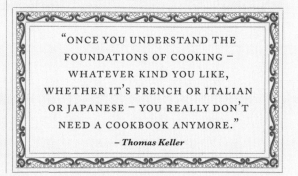

"ONCE YOU UNDERSTAND THE FOUNDATIONS OF COOKING – WHATEVER KIND YOU LIKE, WHETHER IT'S FRENCH OR ITALIAN OR JAPANESE – YOU REALLY DON'T NEED A COOKBOOK ANYMORE."
– *Thomas Keller*

HOW TO SHARPEN A STEEL-BLADED KNIFE

CHEFS NEVER WORK WITH BLUNT KNIVES AND NEITHER SHOULD YOU.
A KEEN BLADE IS CRUCIAL FOR PRECISE, EASY CUTTING. IGNORE GADGETS, AND
EQUIP YOURSELF WITH THE PROPER KIT: A WHETSTONE TO GRIND A FINE EDGE
PERIODICALLY AND A STEEL TO MAINTAIN IT REGULARLY. OPT FOR THE SAME
BRAND AS YOUR KNIVES, OR THE BRAND RECOMMENDED BY THE MANUFACTURER.

{1} WITH A WHETSTONE

Whetstones come in different levels of abrasion, generally divided between rough, medium and finishing. Good results can usually be achieved with just a medium stone, although a finishing stone will elevate the sharpness noticeably. Rough stones should be used before medium stones, for sharpening blades that are chipped or in bad condition.

To use, leave the stone to soak in water for a few minutes (not required for ceramic varieties).

Put on a flat surface then place the heel (handle) end of the blade on the stone at an angle of 20 degrees, facing away from you.

Push away in a long, sweeping arc across the stone and up to the tip of the blade, ensuring you keep a consistent angle.

Repeat evenly and equally on both sides of the knife until the blade is really sharp.

{2} WITH A STEEL

Steels won't sharpen a blunt blade, but they will maintain a sharp blade on a home cook's knife for several months, if used regularly (ideally before each use of the knife).

Hold the steel vertically with the tip placed on a surface. Place the heel of the blade at a 30 degree angle against the top of the steel and sweep the blade downwards.

Maintain the same angle and apply light pressure in a smooth arc. Repeat several times on each side of the blade.

 EXPERT TIP Ceramic blades may stay sharper than those made of steel, but they can be brittle and may chip, crack or even shatter. Specialist expertise and equipment are also required for sharpening. For general home use, it is advisable to opt for steel blades.

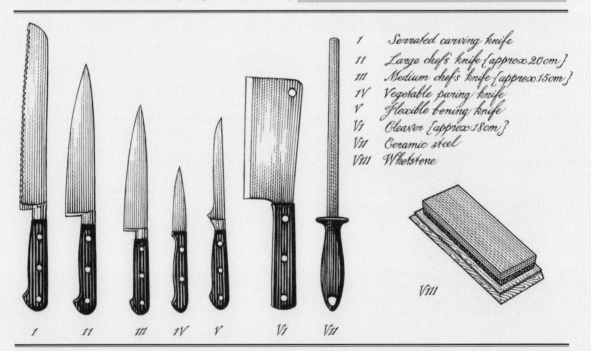

1   Serrated carving knife
11   Large chef's knife {approx 20cm}
111   Medium chef's knife {approx 15cm}
1V   Vegetable paring knife
V   Flexible boning knife
V1   Cleaver {approx 18cm}
V11   Ceramic steel
V111   Whetstone

MISS DEBRETT *Food to Impress*

IF YOU ARE SEEKING to impress us with your culinary prowess, the secret is to make it look easy. We will be appreciative of a simple meal, well cooked and beautifully presented. But do not attempt *haute cuisine* unless you have proven culinary credentials. Certainly, a magnificent gourmet meal, prepared with ease and panache, cannot fail to impress. But if we hear you crashing about in the kitchen, swearing and muttering, as we wait patiently for our overdue first course, we will conclude that you have been over-ambitious. Your inability to match your own grandiose expectations will inevitably frustrate you, and you may well become tetchy and morose. This will not impress us.

CULINARY SKILLS APART, we will always approve of efforts on your part to cater for our tastes. It is never a good sign when a man serves a woman an unswervingly macho meal – slabs of red meat, flaming hot chillies, mountains of potatoes and not a salad leaf in sight. Going too far in the opposite direction – artful concoctions, miniature helpings and exquisite arrangements of colour and texture – is distressingly effeminate; leave that to the professionals.

FINALLY, WHILE YOU MAY well enjoy eye-wateringly spicy take-aways or grease-laden fry-ups, it is probably best to keep these tastes to yourself for the time being. We will be very wary of food that we associate with unhealthy bachelors.

HOW TO CHOP AN ONION LIKE A PRO

Hold the onion on its root end and cut vertically in half.

Take one half and peel off brown papery layers, working from the top towards the root, until the flesh is exposed.

Trim off the pointed end but not the root (this will hold the onion together until it's fully chopped).

Place on a board cut-side down, and make a series of parallel cuts that stop just short of the root.

The finer the required dice, the closer together the cuts should be.

Then make a horizontal cut (with your knife parallel to the board) though the middle of the onion half, again stopping just short of the root.

Finally, make a series of cuts across the onion at right angles to the earlier cuts, right up to the root.

The diced flesh will fall away. As before, the finer your slices, the finer the dice.

Repeat on the other half.

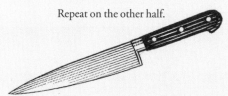

HOW TO FLAMBÉ

Meaning 'flamed' in French, flambé is a cooking technique in which alcohol is added to ingredients in a hot cooking pan and ignited.

The complex reactions that take place are said to develop new flavours, although the spectacle of combusting liquor vapours have theatrical appeal on their own.

Flambé is historically popular for dishes served tableside (think Crêpes Suzette in grand French dining rooms of yesteryear). But it's still used as a kitchen trick by chefs wanting to burn off the booze from a pan at speed.

Fanning a few flames of your own is certainly going to impress upon guests your culinary prowess, but only if you retain your eyelashes in the process.

The hotter the pan, the higher the fire, so make sure it's down to a low-to-medium heat.

Pour 1–2 measures of a 40 per cent spirit (cognac works well with both sweet and savoury) into a glass and then, at arm's reach, into the pan.

Retaining your distance, quickly strike a match and move it to the lip of the pan.

Once the alcohol ignites, leave it for a few seconds and then give the pan a shake to coax out any of the final vapours.

Check out your admiring audience.

BUYING MEAT: *What To Look For*

BEEF: hung for a minimum of 14 days (preferably for 28 days) • dark red meat • marbling of fat in the flesh

LAMB: lean cuts • cream, not yellow, coloured fat

PORK: firm white fat • light grain of fat in the meat

CHICKEN: always free-range • preferably organic • firm flesh and well-developed thighs • scent-free, fresh meat

N.B. Always try to buy the best quality meat available.

KNOWLEDGE GAME GUIDE

In an age of increasing concern about intensive farming and fatty food, meat doesn't come much more free range and lean as wild and semi-wild game.

Age is a crucial factor to bear in mind during the purchase process, since it determines tenderness and cooking methods. A young roast grouse in the weeks that follow the Glorious 12th is a real treat. But it toughens up as autumn wears on, when it might be better in the casserole pot.

Hanging time also has a distinct influence on the texture and flavour of game. The era's gone when the more robust palates would wait for virtual putridity, and a good thing too. But appropriate hanging, which depends on the beast and the weather, certainly contributes positively to the end result.

The best advice for all things to do with game is stick to the seasons and buy from a reputable source.

 EXPERT TIP Unlike meat which generally benefits from ageing, offal is highly perishable so freshness is paramount.

GET IT RIGHT: STEAK

When it comes to steak, there's a trade-off to be made between tenderness and taste.

Fillet, the most expensive of cuts, is rightly revered for its melt-in-the-mouth texture rather than its flavour.

Sirloin, rib eye and rump require an increasing amount of jaw work, but reward the tastebuds more in return for the extra effort.

APPROXIMATE TIMES FOR PAN-FRYING STEAK, ABOUT 2CM THICK:

BLUE: 1 minute per side

RARE: 1.5 minutes per side

MEDIUM-RARE: 2 minutes per side

MEDIUM: 2.5 minutes per side

MEDIUM-WELL: 3 minutes per side

WELL-DONE: 3.5 minutes per side

The precise times will depend on the efficiency and heat of your pan, as well as the temperature of the meat when you start. Room temperature steak will have a significant head start on steak straight from the fridge.

Experienced chefs tend to rely on feel, rather than exact timings, to judge the degree to which a piece a steak is cooked. When prodded with a finger, the more giving the meat, the rarer it is.

Don't forget to season the meat before you cook it. A generous rubbing of Maldon Salt and some ground black pepper will make your steak a noticeably tastier piece of meat.

Once you've cooked your steak, leave it to rest for a few minutes before you eat it.

 EXPERT TIP When cooking steak in a griddle pan, rub the meat, not the griddle, with oil to avoid a smoking pan.

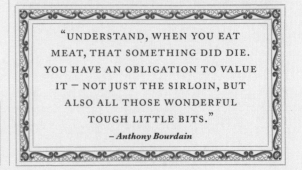

"UNDERSTAND, WHEN YOU EAT MEAT, THAT SOMETHING DID DIE. YOU HAVE AN OBLIGATION TO VALUE IT — NOT JUST THE SIRLOIN, BUT ALSO ALL THOSE WONDERFUL TOUGH LITTLE BITS."
– Anthony Bourdain

OFFAL *More Than Muscle*

When you eat meat, you are eating a muscle of one sort or another. But the animal kingdom also offers a wide range of additional tastes and textures in the form of what the British call 'offal' – a cheap, delicious, highly nutritious and somewhat misunderstood foodstuff.

A derivation of 'off falls' (Americans call it 'variety meats'), offal describes the internal and external edible parts that are removed between slaughtering and butchering an animal.

KIDNEYS: lambs' kidneys are the best. If preparing, remove the membrane, cut in half and use scissors to snip out the fatty core. If cooking or eating, make sure they are pink. Multi-lobed ox, calves' and veal kidneys are strong flavoured. Keep the ox for a tasty pie. The other two benefit from a robust mustard sauce.

LIVER: calves' liver is the most highly-prized, followed by lambs'; both are best eaten medium-rare (ask for it 'pink'). Pigs' liver, often the choice of school cooks, is best reserved for paté. Poultry livers also make for good paté (and, in the case of some ducks, foie gras), although pan-fried they make the basis of an excellent warm salad. Again, pinkness is the order of the day.

SWEETBREADS: it's a more enlightened butcher, not a bakery, where you'll find these thymus and pancreas glands of lambs and veal. Gourmets opt for the latter, but both come off well when sautéed or braised.

BRAINS: somewhat of a rarity today, due to the PR double-whammy of BSE and Hannibal Lecter, but brains (usually calves') have a rich heritage in French cuisine.

PIG PARTS: no animal is more versatile than the pig. The head forms the basis of the traditional jellied meat dish, brawn, but also supplies such porcine derivatives as ears (often braised and deep fried until crispy) and cheeks (braised and fried to make Bath chaps). Also look out for trotters, tails and blood (in the form of black pudding).

OTHER INNARDS AND EXTREMITIES: in an order of decreasing likelihood of appearing on modern menus: tongue, heart, tripe (stomach), chitterlings (intestines), lights (lungs), fries (testicles – probably for the more daring).

Meat Roasting Times

BEEF: 20 mins at 220°C, then 10–15 minutes per 450g/1lb at 190°C for rare, 20 mins per 450g/1lb for medium and 25 minutes per 450g/1lb for well-done. Rest for 30 minutes.

LAMB: initial 20 mins at 220°C, then 20 mins per 450g at 190°C. Allow the meat to rest for 30 minutes before carving.

PORK: initial 20 mins at 220°C, then 35 mins per 450g at 190°C. Check the juices run clear and rest for 30 minutes.

CHICKEN: 20 mins per 450g/1lb at 190°C, plus 20 minutes extra. Most small birds take under an hour: turn the heat up to 220°C for the final fifteen minutes to crisp off the skin. It is essential to check that the juices run clear. Rest for 30 minutes.

These are guidelines: the timings will depend on the efficiency of your oven, as well as the temperature of the meat when you start.

Pink Pork

Pork was always thoroughly cooked to prevent the parasitic disease *trichinellosis*, caused by feeding pigs infected raw meat – a practice now banned in the UK. If you are sure of the provenance of your pork, it is potentially safe to eat it slightly pink. It is not, however, a widely accepted practice.

MISUNDERSTOOD: MUTTON

Mutton is often seen as a poor-man's meat, inferior to lamb. For hundreds of years, however, it was the only sheep eaten in Britan. Poor quality, tough meat available during World War II contributed to mutton's bad image. Well-hung (for about 10–12 days) and cooked very slowly, this full-flavoured meat is delicious when roasted or used in stews and casseroles.

ETIQUETTE: EATING SEAFOOD

FISH ON THE BONE: work down one side of the spine at a time, from head to tail, easing off mouthful-sized pieces. Never flip the fish over – lift the bone up and gently ease off the flesh from beneath. When in doubt, order a fillet.

LOBSTER: a whole lobster in its shell is usually served already cut into two halves. Eat with a knife and fork, or just a fork while holding the shell steady with your other hand. The big claws generally come already cracked but, if not, you will need to use special lobster crackers. Once you've cracked the claws, pull out the meat with a fork. Use a lobster pick to get meat out of the smaller attachments. The body also contains the tomalley (the lobster's edible green liver that is considered to be a delicacy) and, in the female lobster, coral roe, which is also edible.

MUSSELS: either use your fork or an empty mussel shell as a pincer to extract the mussels from their shells. Put all empty shells on the spare plate provided.

OYSTERS: they should come already shucked (i.e. detached), but use your fork to prise the flesh from the shell if any sticks. Squeeze over some lemon juice, bring the shell to your lips, tilt and slide the oyster into your mouth. Don't chew; swallow it in one. Oysters are best eaten in the months which contain the letter 'R' – when the sea is at its coldest.

PRAWNS: pull off the head and tail, then peel off the shell around the body starting from the underside where the legs meet the body. Remove the black thread from along the back and then eat the flesh in your fingers.

AT A GLANCE CAVIAR

CAVIAR IS THE ROE of the sturgeon fish. It is best eaten as simply as possible, served at room temperature. Sour cream, onions and lemon are popular additions, but a connoisseur would never disguise the true taste of caviar.

THE AVERAGE PORTION is approximately 30 grams; it should be enjoyed in small quantities. Good caviar should not taste salty. Test its freshness by placing a small amount on the fleshy part of your hand between your thumb and index finger – it should not smell.

A GLASS OF VODKA or champagne is caviar's perfect partner.

 EXPERT TIP The best scallops are hand-dived and sold in their shells. If bought out of their shells, make sure they haven't been stored in water at the fishmonger's.

BUYING FISH: *What To Look For*

Bright, convex eyes • dark red gills • shiny and moist skin • flesh that's firm to the touch • a smell of the sea, not fish

GET IT RIGHT: SUSHI

The preparation and consumption of sushi is highly ritualistic – basic principles should be observed.

Pour soy sauce into your saucer and mix in some wasabi. Never smear wasabi directly onto the fish.

Sliced ginger cleanses the palate – eat between dishes.

Dip sashimi (sliced raw fish on its own) into the sauce with your chopsticks and eat.

Sushi rolls and nigiri (blocks of rice with fish on top) should be eaten whole.

Place nigiri in your mouth fish-side down – the fish warms on your tongue and releases flavour.

Never point with your chopsticks.

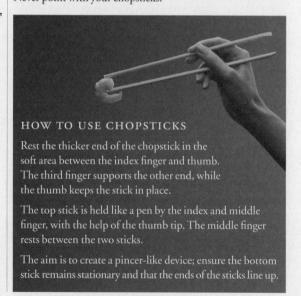

HOW TO USE CHOPSTICKS

Rest the thicker end of the chopstick in the soft area between the index finger and thumb. The third finger supports the other end, while the thumb keeps the stick in place.

The top stick is held like a pen by the index and middle finger, with the help of the thumb tip. The middle finger rests between the two sticks.

The aim is to create a pincer-like device; ensure the bottom stick remains stationary and that the ends of the sticks line up.

Mark Hix's Soft Boiled Goose Eggs with Asparagus Soldiers (SERVES 2)

Simple yet sophisticated – this is a dish to impress. Try dipping thick asparagus spears into the yolk like toast soldiers.

500g medium to thick asparagus, woody stems removed
2 goose eggs
Maldon Salt

{1} Have two pots of water boiling; one salted for the asparagus and one for the eggs.
{2} Carefully place the eggs into the pan of unsalted water with the help of a slotted spoon.
{3} After ten minutes, remove the eggs from the water and set aside on a plate.
{4} At the same time, put the asparagus into the other salted, boiling pan. This will take about 5 minutes to cook while you remove the tops from the eggs.
{5} With a small knife (you can use a special egg top remover), carefully remove the tops from the eggs and then place them back on to keep the eggs hot. Put the eggs into egg cups on pre-warmed plates.
{6} Check if the asparagus is tender by cutting a little off a thick end. Drain in a colander, and arrange in bundles next to the eggs.
{7} Spoon a little pile of Maldon Salt on to each plate and serve.

Instant Summer Pudding

Impress guests with a twist on the traditional bowl of strawberries. Add a sprinkling of black pepper, or a slug of sweet, top-quality balsamic vinegar. Do one or the other – never both – to enhance the berries' sweetness and flavour. Obviously, leave the cream.

ETIQUETTE: EATING VEGETABLES

GLOBE ARTICHOKES: eat the tender tips of the leaves one by one, dipping them into the butter or sauce as you go. At the centre, the smaller leaves and hairy choke are cut away and the heart eaten with a knife and fork.

ASPARAGUS: eat asparagus in your fingers, unless it is a vegetable served with a dish, or covered in sauce. Pick up each spear towards the end of the stem, dip it in any accompanying sauce and eat bite by bite. Leave any woody ends of the stems on the side of your plate.

PEAS: avoid turning over your fork and using it as a scoop in public; instead, squash the peas on to the back of the fork. Utilise any aids on your plate – such as mashed potato.

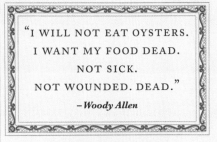

> "I WILL NOT EAT OYSTERS.
> I WANT MY FOOD DEAD.
> NOT SICK.
> NOT WOUNDED. DEAD."
> – *Woody Allen*

SEASONAL EATING

A selection of foods at their best:

ASPARAGUS May–June
STRAWBERRIES June–July
BROAD BEANS June–August
CHERRIES June–August
COURGETTES June–September
BEETROOT June–October
MACKEREL June–October
SEA BASS June–December
RASPBERRIES July–August
FRENCH BEANS July–September
TOMATOES July–September
WATERCRESS July–September
LOBSTER July–November
SCALLOPS July–November
PEACHES August–September
PLUMS August–September
GROUSE August–December
PEARS September–October
MUSSELS September–December
LEEKS September–February
KALE September–April
PARTRIDGE October–January
BRUSSELS SPROUTS October–February
PARSNIPS October–February
APPLES (COX) October–March
PHEASANT November–January

CURRY: A TEMPERATURE GUIDE

MILD

Korma
Tikka Masala
Pasanda

MEDIUM

Dopiaza   Karahi
Rhogan Josh   Biryani
Kashmir   Massala
Bhuna

HOT

Jalfrezi
Dhansak
Madras

VERY HOT

Phal
Vindaloo

GEAR INDIAN SPICE KIT

The ultimate spices you need for Indian home cooking:

ASAFETIDA
CARAWAY SEEDS
CARDAMON
CAYENNE PEPPER
CHILLI POWDER
CHILLIES (fresh)
CINNAMON STICKS
CLOVES (whole)
CORIANDER SEEDS
CUMIN SEEDS
FENUGREEK SEEDS
FENNEL SEEDS
GARAM MASALA
GINGER (fresh)
MUSTARD SEEDS
NUTMEG (and mace)
SAFFRON
SESAME SEEDS
TURMERIC

SPICY TIPS

Try to buy spices from an ethnic grocer,
rather than the supermarket.

Spices usually need to be roasted
or ground to taste their best.

Roast spices by dry-frying them in a frying
pan or griddle; be careful not to let them
burn as they will spoil and go bitter.

Grind spices in a pestle and
mortar or electric grinder.

THE SCOVILLE SCALE

In 1912, Wilbur Scoville developed a method to determine
the heat level in chilli peppers; the greater the number of
Scoville Heat Units, the hotter the chilli.
*N.B. it is extremely difficult to measure the exact rating of
a chilli as it is a natural product and therefore varies greatly.*

SCOVILLE HEAT UNIT (SHU)	TYPE OF CHILLI PEPPER
350,000–580,000	Red Savina Habanero
100,000–350,000	Habanero, Scotch Bonnet
100,000–200,000	African Birdseye
30,000–50,000	Ají, Cayenne, Tabasco
5,000–23,000	Serrano
2,500–8,000	Jalapeño
1,000–1,500	Poblano
500–2,500	Anaheim
100–500	Pimento
0	Bell pepper

Capsaicin, the compound found in chillies that creates
the heat, is fat-soluble. Some milk or yogurt is therefore
the most effective solution to a fiery mouthful; water will
not really help and may increase the burning sensation.

The heat in chillies make you feel good. It stimulates the release
of endorphins – the 'happy' chemical produced by the pituitary
gland that is also released during strenuous exercise and orgasm.

Trivia: HP Sauce

In the late nineteenth century, Edwin Samson Moore,
founder of the Midlands Vinegar Company, visited
a grocers in Nottingham that owed him money. He
discovered the grocer, FG Garton, brewing a distinctive
smelling sauce called Garton's HP Sauce, so named after
Garton heard a rumour that it had been served in the
restaurant at the Houses of Parliament. Moore took the
recipe in lieu of Garton's debt and developed the sauce,
launching it in 1903. Still made from a secret recipe, one
in four households consumes a bottle of HP every year.

The 10am 30-minute Full English Breakfast (SERVES 2)

4 top-quality pork sausages
4 rashers of dry-cured back bacon
2 slices of English black pudding
2 field mushrooms
1 can of baked beans
1 tomato, halved
2 eggs
2 slices bread
Vegetable oil
Butter
Salt and pepper
Sauce of choice (tomato ketchup, brown sauce,
English mustard)

METHOD

10:00 Set the oven to 100°C, turn the grill to high and put a large frying pan over a low-to-medium heat. Put two plates in the oven. Gather the ingredients.

10:05 Add the sausages and a dash of oil to the pan. Prick them if you want to please your doctor more than your taste buds. Quarter-turn every few minutes.

10:10 Put the baked beans in a saucepan over a low heat. Stir occasionally.

10:15 Season the tomato and mushrooms with salt and pepper, and top with a knob of butter. Place under the hot grill. Add the bacon to the pan.

10:20 Divide the evenly-browned sausages between the plates in the oven. Turn the bacon and add black pudding. Turn the pudding after three minutes.

10:25 Divide the mushrooms, tomato, bacon and black pudding equally between plates in the oven. Toast the bread. Wipe out the pan with some kitchen roll, add a fresh splash of oil and crack in the eggs.

10:30 Remove the plates from oven and add the baked beans and fried eggs. Butter the toast, cut in half and add to the side of the plate. Serve with preferred sauce.

FIVE MARMITE FACTS

The basic ingredient of Marmite is brewers yeast.

•

The illustration on the label is of the earthenware pot in which Marmite was once sold.

•

Marmite was included in soldiers' ration packs in the First World War.

•

It was also used as a dietary supplement in prisoner of war camps.

•

It is vegetarian and virtually fat-free.

BARBECUE RULES

{1}
Ensure that the barbecue is properly lit and ready before guests arrive.

{2}
Provide enough seats; no one wants to be juggling food and drink while standing.

{3}
Make sure there's plenty of chilled beer, cider and wine, as well as Pimm's and lots of ice.

{4}
Be aware of your neighbours; check the wind direction in relation to their windows.

{5}
Cook food properly and thoroughly – you don't want to poison your guests.

{6}
Don't make an exhibition of the cooking. Your guests should not feel coerced into applauding a one-man show.

{7}
No comedy aprons, chef's hats or swaggering machismo as the meat hits the grill.

BASIC TABLE MANNERS

YOUR TABLE MANNERS say a lot about you – women, colleagues and clients will notice your table behaviour and draw conclusions. We all indulge in less-than-perfect behaviour in private, or in very familiar company, but it is important to get it right when it matters.

THE CARDINAL dining crime is eating noisily; nothing is more likely to get you noticed.

KEEP YOUR MOUTH CLOSED while chewing and take care not to overfill it – you will then be able to breathe steadily.

NEVER TALK while there is food in your mouth – even when you have a conversational gem up your sleeve. If you're asked a question mid-chew, try to finish as quickly as possible.

EAT AT A RELAXED PACE, and keep an eye on your fellow diners' progress. Companions will feel exposed if you gobble your food, and you will feel awkward if you finish well ahead of the table.

WAIT UNTIL EVERYONE has been served before picking up your cutlery. When dining in a group, assist your neighbour. Offer and hold communal dishes and check they've got everything they need.

ELBOWS SHOULD NOT rest on the table. Napkins should be dealt with when you sit down, and placed on your lap.

SOUP STYLE

Push your soup spoon from the front of the bowl away from you to catch a mouthful. Bring this to your mouth and tip the soup in from the side of the spoon; don't suck or slurp. Tilt the bowl away from you in order to get the last few spoonfuls. Bread may be dipped in the soup. Put your spoon down while you use your fingers to break off pieces of bread, dip and eat them. Leave your spoon in the bowl when you have finished.

Finger Bowls

Finger bowls – small bowls of warm water with a slice of lemon – are usually provided if your food is to be eaten with your fingers, such as shell-on prawns.

Dip your fingers in the bowl one hand at a time, rub gently to remove any stickiness and then dry them on your napkin.

"I'M STARVING"

Refrain from proclaiming "I'm starving" at the first twinge of hunger. You are not starving, and other people are unlikely to be interested in regular updates on your appetite. If hunger is making you tetchy, do your best to control your temper.

Table manners are important at all times so don't forget them when you're very hungry. There's no excuse for wolfing down your food without stopping for breath.

When you have finished your meal it is bad form to announce "I'm stuffed" or even "I'm full". If you do feel the need to give those around you a report, a more polite way of phrasing it is simply: "I've had plenty".

STYLE GUIDE CUTLERY

A KNIFE should be held firmly in your right hand, with the handle tucked into your palm, your thumb down one side of the handle and your index finger along the top (but never touching the top of the blade). It should never be eaten off or held like a pencil.

A FORK, when used with a knife or spoon, should be held in the left hand, similarly to the knife, with the tines facing downwards. On its own, it is held in the right hand, with the tines facing upwards, resting on the fingers and secured with the thumb and index finger.

A SPOON is held in the right hand, resting on the fingers and secured with the thumb and index finger. Food should be eaten off the side of the spoon; it should never be used at a right angle to the mouth.

CUTLERY should be rested on the plate/bowl between bites, and placed together in the bottom-centre when you are finished. Never gesture with your cutlery.

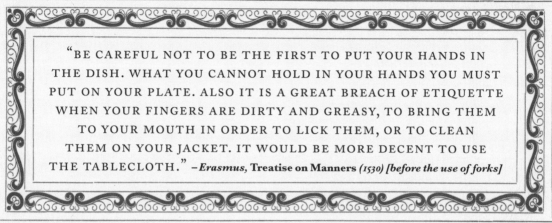

"BE CAREFUL NOT TO BE THE FIRST TO PUT YOUR HANDS IN THE DISH. WHAT YOU CANNOT HOLD IN YOUR HANDS YOU MUST PUT ON YOUR PLATE. ALSO IT IS A GREAT BREACH OF ETIQUETTE WHEN YOUR FINGERS ARE DIRTY AND GREASY, TO BRING THEM TO YOUR MOUTH IN ORDER TO LICK THEM, OR TO CLEAN THEM ON YOUR JACKET. IT WOULD BE MORE DECENT TO USE THE TABLECLOTH." *–Erasmus,* **Treatise on Manners** *(1530) [before the use of forks]*

MANAGING CANAPÉS

{1} ALWAYS try and eat a canapé in one mouthful, but avoid overfilling your mouth or having to chew vigorously mid-conversation.

{2} TIMING is everything – don't tuck in if you are about to be introduced to someone.

{3} AVOID challenging or messy varieties if you're in impressive company.

{4} IT'S POOR FORM to take two canapés at a time.

{5} NEVER put sticks or spoons that you've eaten off back on a tray unless it's empty.

{6} NEVER double dip your canapé in the sauce.

BREAD ROLL RULES

{1}
Bread rolls are eaten from the side plate,
to the left of a place setting.
{2}
You should break your roll into bite-sized
pieces that are eaten individually.
{3}
Break off a new piece for each mouthful, rather than
dividing the roll into numerous chunks in advance.
{4}
Butter, if desired, is taken from the butter
dish and placed on the edge of your side plate.
{5}
Each new piece, or mouthful,
is then individually buttered.

THE CUTLERY ARSENAL

{1} THE RANGE OF CUTLERY WILL DEPEND ON THE FORMALITY OF THE OCCASION, BUT THE RULE IS ALWAYS THE SAME: SIMPLY WORK FROM THE OUTSIDE INTO THE MIDDLE.

{2} THE LAYOUT SHOULD ALWAYS BE THE SAME – FORK TO THE LEFT, KNIVES AND SPOONS TO THE RIGHT AND PUDDING IMPLEMENTS ABOVE THE PLACE SETTING. A KNIFE FOR BUTTERING BREAD SHOULD BE PLACED ON OR NEAR THE SIDE PLATE (TO THE LEFT OF THE PLACE SETTING).

{3} GLASSES SHOULD BE PLACED TO THE RIGHT OF THE SETTING, AND DIFFERENT GLASSES SHOULD BE PROVIDED FOR RED WINE, WHITE WINE, WATER AND, IF APPLICABLE, CHAMPAGNE.

{4} IF YOU FEEL OVERWHELMED, JUST HANG BACK AND WATCH WHAT EVERYONE ELSE DOES.

NEW CHIVALRY

21st-Century Chivalry

CHIVALRY: the courteous behaviour of a man towards a woman. But what do 'modern' women want? When is chivalry out-dated and patronising, and when is it appropriate and well-mannered?

Modern chivalry is all about the natural gesture, striking a balance between treating a woman like a lady, but respecting her independence. It is about good manners that come instinctively, rather than contrived gestures that feel out-dated.

New chivalry requires a man to have a natural confidence, but he is never arrogant. He understands the appropriate gesture but, most of all, he makes women around him feel at ease.

CHIVALROUS GESTURE: STANDING FOR A WOMAN

A MAN SHOULD STAND UP to greet a woman when she enters the room for the first time. There is no need, however, to be like a jack-in-the-box every time she goes to the loo, goes to get a drink, and so on.

Money Matters: Who Pays?

THERE IS ONE abiding rule – the person who requests the pleasure, pays for the pleasure. So, as a simple point of etiquette, you should pick up the tab if you have invited the other person. Life isn't simple, however, and all too often the awkwardness around paying the bill is all about gender.

IT IS MORE LIKELY than not that the man has been the one to invite his date out to dinner, so he should be the one to pay. But it's unfair if he has to pay every time – and some women are actively insulted if men always insist on picking up the bill. On the other hand, if he doesn't make the gesture, then he could all too easily be judged ungentlemanly.

MEN SHOULD BE PREPARED to pay every time, but equally ready to concede under the following conditions: if she is adamant she must pay her way; if it is your birthday or a special occasion on which she wants to make the gesture of paying for you; or if you're both trying to introduce a take-it-in-turns policy.

DO NOT BE TEMPTED by the compromise solution: splitting the bill. The greatest spoiler to romance is Going Dutch.

CHIVALROUS GESTURE: HOLDING DOORS OPEN

HOLDING THE DOOR open for a woman is still a chivalrous gesture, even in our less gallant times. If, however, a woman arrives at the door first and goes to open it, don't awkwardly rush in front of her with grand exclamations of "I'll get that!".

IT IS COURTEOUS for a man to open the car door for a woman, letting her get in first, before walking around the vehicle and getting in himself.

Compliments

Only offer compliments when you believe them, and don't over-compliment – you will look like an insincere flatterer. Stick to specifics; vague, over-generalised compliments are easily devalued. Never damn with faint praise, or give a compliment with one hand and take away with the other. Try and give the compliment in a timely manner – don't wait until the end of the evening to comment on her dress, for example, do so when you first meet up. A spontaneous response always feels more genuine.

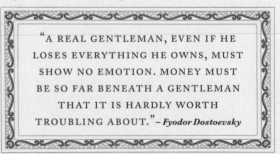

"A REAL GENTLEMAN, EVEN IF HE LOSES EVERYTHING HE OWNS, MUST SHOW NO EMOTION. MONEY MUST BE SO FAR BENEATH A GENTLEMAN THAT IT IS HARDLY WORTH TROUBLING ABOUT." – *Fyodor Dostoevsky*

CHIVALROUS GESTURE: OFFERING YOUR SEAT

IN THE PAST it was always considered courteous for a man to offer his seat to a woman. It is now a more tricky matter of personal judgement. There is no need to jump-up on the train or underground every time you see a woman standing. Exceptions to this are the pregnant (if you are totally sure she's expecting) and the elderly, when it is a definite requirement.

THE RULES OF SOCIAL KISSING

Social kissing is a potential minefield. It is dependent on situation, age, background, and profession. As a general rule, don't kiss colleagues/clients but, if it's expected, here's how to do it with unfailing style and confidence…

{1}
Usually it's right cheek first, but prepare to change direction at the last minute.

{2}
One kiss or two? Two can seem over the top in a professional environment.

{3}
Use humour to deflect embarrassment over the meet-in-the-middle mix-up.

{4}
Cheek skin must make brief, light contact.

{5}
Avoid sound effects, air kissing and saliva traces.

{6}
Don't linger, and keep hands strictly above the waist.

CHIVALROUS GESTURE: WALKING ON THE KERBSIDE

A MAN SHOULD WALK on the kerbside of the street. If, however, a woman naturally falls in step on the kerbside and seems comfortable with it, then it would be clumsy for him to start dodging around her to try and walk on the outside.

THE PERSONA OF THE CHIVALROUS MAN

He has an air of sociability and hospitality.

•

He is unrushed, calm and always has time.

•

He is in control of life, and never stressed.

•

He is naturally charming to everyone he meets.

He rarely loses his temper, and never in public.

•

He can seemingly handle any situation that is thrown at him.

•

He is patient, and left unruffled by life's daily irritations.

•

He is modest, yet confident, and cultivates an air of ease.

Chivalrous Conversation

The most important element of conversation is balance – establishing a perfect mix of talking and listening. Clever conversationalists pick up threads as they go along. They create a multi-layered conversation and a sense of intimacy.

It is important to set the conversation off well. Try to think of an alternative to the usual "How are you?" or "What do you do?". Gentle humour, flattery and the occasional well-placed compliment all oil the wheels of conversation.

There is a fine line between interest and intrusion. Familiarity comes with time, so be aware of unspoken barriers. Avoid strong opinion or stark honesty; the odd frisson is interesting, but controversial views may offend. Never talk about money, illness or death. Don't bluff, lie, name-drop or brag.

DATING THE BASICS

IT IS DEEPLY FLATTERING to be asked out – remember that no one will ever hate you for it, even if they refuse.

TAKE CHARGE. Ask her out by phone or face-to-face. Decide the date and venue – make sure it's somewhere with a good atmosphere – and the time of day.

ALWAYS BE PUNCTUAL. If you are running late, call ahead – never send a text.

HAVE A BACK-UP PLAN in case things go wrong (another choice of venue if the place you were going is shut, somewhere indoors if it starts to rain on an outdoor date).

PLAN ON THE OFF CHANCE that things go really well (a late bar to go on to after dinner, clean sheets in case she wants to go home with you).

NEVER ANSWER CALLS or send text messages during the date. Give her your undivided attention.

Looking Good

The aim is to look as though you have thrown together a stylish look without too much effort. You must also feel comfortable in what you're wearing; this isn't the time to experiment with your look. At a minimum, you must be clean, smell good and look tidy.

You need to dress to fit the occasion – is it a smart dinner or the theatre, a few drinks in the pub or a walk in the park? Look the part and choose an appropriate outfit.

However, the most important thing is that a woman will remember what you wore on the last date and the date before that, and the date before that, so try not to wear the same outfit twice in quick succession.

CANCELLING A DATE

The clear-cut rules for cancelling a hotel reservation can be applied for dating cancellations. If you pull out more than a month beforehand, there is no penalty at all; between a month and two days' beforehand, there are varying but small amounts of fallout; anything less than 48 hours and you start to incur hefty charges; and if you cancel on the same day or, rudest still, fail to show up altogether without good reason, then you have to pay the full price (you will probably never see her again). Good reasons: contagious illness, family crisis, hospitalisation; bad reasons: working late, sport-related excuse, hangover; unforgivable reason: no reason at all.

DATING WITH KIDS

DO Warn your date that you're bringing your kids: no unexpected surprises.

DO Choose something your kids would like to do: a daytime trip to an adventure park, a family movie and pasta lunch, a day by the seaside.

DO Make your kids feel that this is a day out for everyone; not that they're being dragged along on a date.

DO Ensure that your date spends time with your kids: send them off to buy ice creams, or let them walk ahead together. That way, they'll strike up a conversation and get to know each other.

DON'T Resist the temptation to choose adult activities, regardless of your children's taste, patience or endurance (art galleries, theatres, shopping). It will only lead to trouble.

DON'T Beware of over-compensating for the fact that you'd rather be alone with your date by spoiling your children with sweets, ice creams, presents etc.

DON'T Only having eyes for your partner isn't fair to your kids: never make your children feel like gooseberries.

DON'T On the other hand, don't ignore your date because you're so preoccupied by your children's needs. They won't want to come along and play families with you again if you do.

INTERNET DATING

Use a realistic (but flattering) photograph to illustrate your online profile.

Get to know each other over email; you can then progress to text messaging and phone calls before you arrange a date.

Do an internet search for their name, and check out their profile on social networking sites.

 EXPERT TIP On a date, never discuss your ex-girlfriends or salary; politics and religion are also risky topics.

FIRST DATE RULES

{1}

Drinks or lunch are a good option; you can test the water without having to spend an entire evening together.

{2}

Avoid venues that are too noisy, pretentious or intimate.

{3}

Try to slip some well-timed compliments into the conversation.

{4}

Make an effort to ask her questions (and listen to the answers).

{5}

Pay the bill, unless she insists. Don't Go Dutch.

{6}

You should try to kiss her (if it's gone well).

{7}

You should not try to get her into bed (take the lead from her).

NEXT STEPS...

TEXT OR EMAIL the day after a first date. Wait two to three days before ringing to arrange the specifics of meeting up again.

AFTER A COUPLE of evening dates, try a day date (art gallery, picnic) or an activity date (golf lessons, ice-skating) to check you get along without low-lighting and a bottle of wine.

THREE DATES or more and you can say that you are 'seeing someone' (this doesn't necessarily mean exclusively); six dates or more and you need to decide if you want things to get more serious or stop seeing each other.

WHEN YOU ARE introducing her to friends while you are dating, you should say "This is (Susan)" rather than assuming too much – e.g. "This is my girlfriend". Never presume that she is your girlfriend without asking (she will appreciate the opportunity to put things on a more formal footing).

Blind Dates

BLIND DATES should be approached with caution and realism – the hit rate is often low because a third party is trying to direct Cupid's arrow.

ESTABLISH CONTACT to make the necessary arrangements. Email is a convenient (and suitably anonymous) method of communication. Drinks are a more flexible option than dinner. Establish a way of recognising each other: for example, it could be decided that both of you will be carrying or reading a copy of the same newspaper.

IF THE MATCH proves to be disastrous, you should still stick around for two drinks. An early departure is humiliating and ungentlemanly. Send an email within a few days, letting the other party down gently. If the evening goes with a bang, exchange numbers, send a text message and plan more dates. Don't forget to thank the matchmaker.

SPEED DATING

Make sure you look good and have some attention-grabbing opening lines and interesting questions ready.

Although you feel you are on display, try not to treat the evening as a performance – don't deliver a monologue or give a false impression.

As time is short, don't be coy if you are attracted to someone. If you like them, flirt.

Every minute counts: you need to be memorable and leave her wanting more...

Lonely Heart Acronyms

BBW	big beautiful woman
BHM	big handsome man
NSA	no strings attached
NTW	no time wasters
OHAC	own house and car
RPG	role-playing games
SF	super friendly
SNAG	sensitive New Age guy
SOH	sense of humour
TDH	tall, dark and handsome
WLTM	would like to meet

FAMOUS LOVE POEMS
A BLUFFER'S GUIDE

How do I love thee? Let me count the ways.
I love thee to the depth
and breadth and height
My soul can reach.
How Do I Love Thee…
Elizabeth Barrett Browning (1806–61)

•

Had we but world enough, and time,
This coyness, Lady, were no crime.
To His Coy Mistress
Andrew Marvell (1621–78)

•

I crave your mouth,
your voice, your hair.
Silent and starving,
I prowl through the streets.
Love Sonnet XI
Pablo Neruda (1904–73)

Let me not to the marriage of true minds
Admit impediments. Love is not love
Which alters when it alteration finds.
Sonnet 116
William Shakespeare (1564–1616)

•

When you are old and
grey and full of sleep,
And nodding by the fire…
When You Are Old And Grey…
W.B. Yeats (1865–1939)

•

Nothing in the world is single;
All things by a law divine
In another's being mingle –
Why not I with thine?
Love's Philosophy
Percy Bysshe Shelley (1792–1822)

Love at the lips was touch
As sweet as I could bear;
And once that seemed too much;
I lived on air…
To Earthward
Robert Frost (1874–1963)

•

Lay Your Sleeping head, my love
Human on my faithless arm…
Lullaby
W. H. Auden (1907–73)

•

I ne'er was struck before that hour
With love so sudden and so sweet,
Her face it bloomed like a sweet flower
And stole my heart away complete…
First Love
John Clare (1793–1864)

SIX FOODS OF LOVE

Aphrodisiac n. *A food, drink or drug that stimulates sexual desire.*

{1}
ASPARAGUS: nineteenth-century French bridegrooms were required to eat several helpings at their pre-nuptial meal.

{2}
COFFEE: perhaps it's more about the energy boosting caffeine…

{3}
CHOCOLATE: the chemicals phenylethylamine and serotonin in chocolate stimulate the pleasure points in the brain. Chocolate is banned in some monasteries.

{4}
FIGS: the Ancient Greeks are said to have celebrated the seasonal crop of figs with ritual copulation.

{5}
OYSTERS: apparently Casanova ate 50 for breakfast.

{6}
TRUFFLES: highly-prized, highly-priced, highly-scented.

TEN CLASSIC
ROMANTIC MOVIES

Gone With the Wind (1939) *Clark Gable*

•

Casablanca (1942) *Humphrey Bogart*

•

Brief Encounter (1945) *Trevor Howard*

•

An Affair to Remember (1957) *Cary Grant*

•

Breakfast at Tiffany's (1961) *George Peppard*

•

The Umbrellas of Cherbourg (1964) *Nino Castelnuovo*

•

Doctor Zhivago (1965) *Omar Sharif*

•

Annie Hall (1977) *Woody Allen*

•

An Officer and a Gentleman (1982) *Richard Gere*

•

When Harry Met Sally (1989) *Billy Crystal*

Say It With Flowers

Flowers are the perfect impromptu present, but follow these basic guidelines to ensure that you get it right:

MIXED BOUQUETS can look cheap if they aren't of a decent size and well-styled. Instead, buy just one type of bloom, or go for just one colour.

GREENERY is also important – it's there to bulk up the bouquet and complement the flowers.

DON'T PANIC and just pick the first blooms you recognise. Consider her tastes and style. Classic or contemporary? Minimalist or vintage? Talk to the florist. Explain the style you're after and the occasion.

BE PREPARED to spend – you can never economise on flowers.

BUY HER FLOWERS on her birthday, on Valentine's Day, on your anniversary and on no particular occasion.

USE THE CARD that accompanies the bouquet to its full potential. For example, include details of a surprise date: 'See you in the bar of the ABC Hotel at 7pm'; tell her something you find hard to say: 'Thank you for being there for me'; state the obvious: 'I love you'.

NEVER ORDER cheap arrangements online; never buy bunches from the supermarket or the garage; never buy carnations or chrysanthemums (the kiss of death); never send flowers as an apology without some verbal backup.

Flower Trivia

During Victorian times, different types of flower were understood to represent a feeling, so the choice of flower could convey one's sentiments at a time when men and women couldn't be so upfront with each other. For example: Jasmine, elegance; Lily of the Valley, sweetness; Orchid, love; Red Rose, passion; Tulips, a declaration of love. The study of the meaning of flowers is called *floriography*.

SEVEN
ROMANTIC NOVELS
THAT WOMEN WILL LOVE

Doctor Zhivago (1957) Boris Pasternak

•

Far from the Madding Crowd (1874) Thomas Hardy

•

Gone with the Wind (1936) Margaret Mitchell

•

Lady Chatterley's Lover (1928) D.H. Lawrence

•

Rebecca (1938) Daphne du Maurier

•

The English Patient (1992) Michael Ondaatje

•

Wuthering Heights (1847) Emily Brontë

HOW TO BUY UNDERWEAR

FIND OUT HER SIZE. Have a look at the label in her bra and knickers.

CHOOSE SOMETHING she'll like; don't just buy your fantasy.

WOMEN USUALLY HAVE everyday underwear, and then sexier sets for special occasions. Look at both of these styles and keep them in mind when choosing.

ASK FOR HELP. The assistant will be used to helping men choose – take their advice.

WHEN YOU FIRST BUY her underwear, don't go too risqué. The message you'll give her may distract from the gesture.

START off by buying a classic bra and knicker/thong combination.

SAVE SUSPENDER BELTS, teddies and items with intimate bits missing until you are very confident in your lingerie purchasing skills and your knowledge of her tastes.

THINK ABOUT WHAT COLOURS she likes; black is the default.

GOOD QUALITY UNDERWEAR can be expensive, but it fits and looks better, so is always worth the investment.

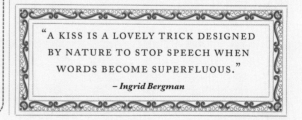

"A KISS IS A LOVELY TRICK DESIGNED BY NATURE TO STOP SPEECH WHEN WORDS BECOME SUPERFLUOUS."
– *Ingrid Bergman*

EIGHT THINGS MEN SHOULD KNOW ABOUT WOMEN

{1}

She can multitask (solution: don't claim that you can).

{2}

She's endlessly fascinated by other people's relationships (solution: feign interest).

{3}

She expects you to know why she's upset (solution: pretend you do).

{4}

She will ask you "Do I look fat?" (solution: don't answer).

{5}

She likes to talk on the telephone (solution: live with it).

{6}

She will nag you (solution: ignore it).

{7}

She'll ask you if you fancy her best friend (solution: lie).

{8}

She will be upset if you look at attractive women (solution: carry on – it's only natural).

Is Platonic Possible?

Women make great friends and are useful for giving you the female low-down. But remember: you can only be platonic friends if neither of you fancy each other.

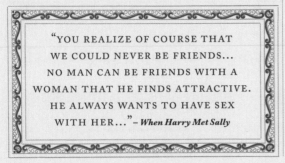

"YOU REALIZE OF COURSE THAT WE COULD NEVER BE FRIENDS... NO MAN CAN BE FRIENDS WITH A WOMAN THAT HE FINDS ATTRACTIVE. HE ALWAYS WANTS TO HAVE SEX WITH HER..." – *When Harry Met Sally*

FRIENDS' EXES CAN YOU GO THERE?

DATING SOMEONE ELSE'S EX is generally not a good idea and likely to cause you problems. Make sure the relationship between your friend and his ex is completely over (and they both realise this) before you get involved. If it's just a fling, it may be best to keep it to yourselves – devious, but less damaging.

IF YOU HAVE TRUE FEELINGS and want a proper relationship, let your friend know yourself – you don't want them to hear it from someone else. Don't be affectionate in front of them, and tone down your honeymoon-like behaviour.

DON'T FORGET that other mutual friends could also find the situation difficult. You could lose your friends over it – make sure the woman in question is worth it before you go public.

COMMITMENT: 'ME' *vs* 'US'

IT'S ALL GOING TERRIBLY WELL. You're finishing each other's sentences and laughing at each other's jokes and, before you know it, the C-word crops up. Commitment. But what does it actually mean? It means growing up, sorting out priorities and making choices – it also means a radical shift from 'me' to 'us'.

THE FEAR, FOR A LOT OF MEN, is that it means the end of fun. The fear is natural but, if you view commitment purely as a restriction of your freedom, then you're probably not ready for it.

COMMITMENT MEANS SAYING goodbye to your single lifestyle. A lot will be depend on your age. Look around you – are your friends still largely out there, dating an unending stream of women and notching up marks on the bedpost? Or are they gradually pairing off and setting up homes with baby alarms and lawnmowers? It may be that the single life you all enjoyed together has said goodbye to you.

YOU'LL KNOW THE TIME is right for commitment when you feel lucky and excited about this new stage in your life, when the sense of momentum is irresistible. Commitment has its charms – the future should feel like adventure.

Ex Management

HER EX: remember that she could not be faithful to you *before* she met you, so excessive jealousy is unreasonable. Remember that there is a good reason why she is not with him anymore; the actual threat he presents is therefore negatively rated. That said, any overt displays of affection or uncharacteristic flirting should be viewed suspiciously.

YOUR EX: if you bump into her, don't ignore her; say hello at least. Be civil and don't be too flippant – you can't ignore history. If your new partner is present, keep the meeting as brief as possible but make sure you introduce them. Avoid deep discussions and never flirt with her unless you think you've both changed your minds.

GREEN-EYED MONSTER

JEALOUSY is a hugely destructive emotion; it makes women feel smothered, rather than loved.

IT ISN'T necessary to know what your partner is doing/who she is speaking to every minute of the day.

INSECURITY breeds mistrust and, if you can't trust her, she'll start to question the relationship.

BY ALL MEANS 'claim' your girlfriend in a social group, but make it an affectionate rather than an aggressive gesture.

TRY NOT to view her male colleagues or friends as 'rivals'.

IF YOU FEEL jealous of someone, tell her rather than letting it explode into a big, lingering problem.

POSSESSIVENESS is not a cure for jealousy.

BUT IF YOUR girlfriend is outrageously flirting with someone else, then the green-eyed monster is allowed an outing.

Never do or say . . .

Never comment on what she eats.

Never be financially dependent upon her.

Never mention hormones.

Never criticise her driving.

Never flirt with her friends.

GET IT RIGHT: THE END

"Why do you have to break up with her? Be a man. Just stop calling." Joey, Friends

After an extended relationship (6 months+), breaking up deserves some care and forethought.

It should be done face-to-face, not via text message or email.

Do not break up with someone if she has just received bad news or is in a stressful situation.

Do not break up with someone just before Christmas, her birthday or Valentine's day.

Once you've decided to end it, however, do the deed before things become too much like living a lie.

Choose somewhere private; make sure she's close to home.

Try to be honest, but don't be excessively hurtful.

Give the break-up the dignity it deserves and keep a low profile for a while. You need to look like you're suffering too.

If the boot's on the other foot and she dumps you, don't try to change her mind or persuade her otherwise.

Don't spread rumours about her or bad-mouth her. It's never wise to burn your bridges.

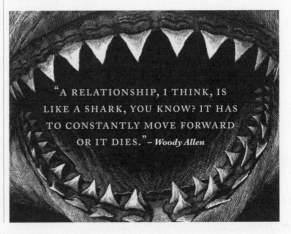

"A RELATIONSHIP, I THINK, IS LIKE A SHARK, YOU KNOW? IT HAS TO CONSTANTLY MOVE FORWARD OR IT DIES." – *Woody Allen*

SUCCESSFUL SEDUCTION:
TEN THINGS TO REMEMBER

{1}

A woman's decision to sleep with
you will largely be based on trust.

{2}

Environment is crucial: choose somewhere
private, relaxed and intimate.

{3}

Lighting is very important. Switch off that overhead bulb.

{4}

Try rushing her and you'll undo all your good groundwork.

{5}

She needs to feel comfortable:
an ounce of sleaze and she'll run for the door.

{6}

Staying the night doesn't necessarily
mean she wants to sleep with you.

{7}

Just because she's on your sofa and it's
late doesn't mean she won't call a cab.

{8}

Never, ever beg or plead. She will pity you.

{9}

If you are at her place, never leave straight
afterwards or sneak off during the night.

{10}

Never say "Thank you" – it's not like
she's just made you a cup of tea.

AT A GLANCE: FLIRTING

Do a background information check – is your target single, married, straight; is your best friend also interested in her?

A few secret smiles and some careful eye contact (no staring) is a good starting point.

Conversation should be kept fun, amusing and light.

Introduce a few teases and gentle physical contact (a touch of the arm, a light nudge), but don't overdo it.

Successful flirts recognise when to stop and move on – but they also know how to leave someone wanting more (of them).

Chat-Up Lines

*"If I said you had a beautiful body,
would you hold it against me?"*

CHAT-UP LINES can easily backfire. Do you really want to be remembered for second-hand conversation? If you resort to clichés, you'll look like someone who's been round the block too many times. Instead, master the art of refreshingly flirtatious conversation.

REMEMBER THE BASICS: eye-contact, confidence and a large dose of well-timed (appropriate) humour. The rest of the battle is to keep her interested long enough to get a number (or something more…). Ask her questions. Remember what she tells you. Make her laugh. Be interested and interesting. Never try to move things along too quickly or jump the gun: *"Is it hot in here or is it you?"*

ON SCREEN
KISSES IN THE MOVIES

Longest kiss in screen history *three minutes between Regis Toomey and Jane Wyman in You're in the Army Now (1941)*

Best wartime kiss *Lauren Bacall and Humphrey Bogart ("Kiss me as if it were the last time") in Casablanca (1942)*

Forbidden love *Burt Lancaster and Deborah Kerr ("Nobody ever kissed me the way you do") in From Here to Eternity (1953)*

Love on a train *Cary Grant and Eva Marie Saint in North by Northwest (1959)*

Urban anxiety *Woody Allen and Diane Keaton ("What are you doing?") in Manhattan (1979)*

MISS DEBRETT *In the Bedroom*

WHEN THE BEDROOM DOOR is closed, and the stage is set for seduction, be aware that your every move will be subject to forensic scrutiny. If the seduction is anticipated you will have prepared meticulously: clean bedlinen, flattering lighting, any troubling signs of sad bachelordom (discarded underwear, games consoles, top-shelf magazines) ruthlessly excised.

ENSURE THAT YOUR BEDROOM does not bear the traces of previous occupancy (photographs, stray items of lingerie, cosmetics). No woman is going to be interested, or impressed, by the notches on your bedpost.

COMING ON TO A WOMAN like a second-rate lothario is an instant turn-off: we're not seduced by your Casanova-style antics, just depressed to find ourselves the last in a long line of 'conquests'. It is so much better to relax and take it slowly, and be guided by us. You won't need a crystal ball to know when we're giving you a green light; but if proceedings have stalled at amber, or worse, have ground to a halt at red, remember that 'no' really does mean 'no'.

Accept our decision with good grace, and never, ever try to change our minds. Pleading and sulking will convince us that we've made the right decision. A gentlemanly response to refusal will earn you brownie points, and may even ensure you have better luck next time.

IF ALL GOES WELL, remember that your behaviour in the immediate aftermath and on the following morning is absolutely crucial. Women like pillow talk and tenderness; turned backs, neanderthal grunts and snores are an instant turn-off.

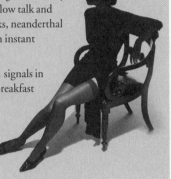

SHOW SOME POSITIVE signals in the cold light of day – breakfast in bed and affectionate gestures – and there's every chance that we'll be coming back for more.

HOW TO MAKE A PASS

Remember that this is a high-risk activity that is not always successful.

Don't pretend to be something you're not; high octane come-ons may backfire.

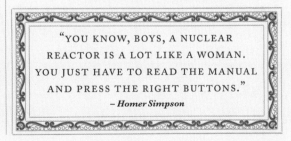

If the object of your desire is taken by surprise, she may consider your actions indelicate, or worse, disrespectful.

If you suspect there is potential for action, show your intentions with some very relaxed but unmistakable flirtation.

Give her the opportunity to consider the prospect and to make her feelings clear – whether positive or negative.

If you are rebuffed, a regretful smile and a gracious withdrawal will leave the one that got away feeling flattered (and then she may change her mind).

Most importantly, your dignity remains intact.

SEDUCTION TRACKS

Sexual Healing Marvin Gaye

•

Just The Way You Are Barry White

•

Je T'aime…Moi Non Plus Serge Gainsbourg and Jane Birkin

•

Love To Love You Baby Donna Summer

•

I Wanna Touch You Baby Roy Ayers

•

Simply Beautiful Al Green

•

Try A Little Tenderness Otis Redding

•

La Femme d'Argent Air

•

I Want A Little Sugar In My Bowl Nina Simone

•

The Look Of Love Dusty Springfield

> "YOU KNOW, BOYS, A NUCLEAR REACTOR IS A LOT LIKE A WOMAN. YOU JUST HAVE TO READ THE MANUAL AND PRESS THE RIGHT BUTTONS."
> – *Homer Simpson*

KNOWLEDGE: DIAMONDS *The Four 'C's*

Diamonds can be a tricky business. Before you buy, it is important to understand the four 'C's: carat, clarity, colour and cut.

CARAT

The size of the diamond. The larger the stone, the greater the carat weight. The greater the carat weight, the more expensive the diamond. There are 100 points to a carat; 1 carat = 0.2g or 200 milligrams.

CLARITY

Clarity refers to the marks or inclusions in the stone. Fewer inclusions mean greater clarity. The greater the clarity, the greater the brilliance (sparkle) and value. A diamond is viewed under 10x magnification by a professional gemmologist to determine its clarity.

F	Flawless	Extremely rare – a diamond with no imperfections.
IF	Internally flawless	Rare – a diamond with no internal inclusions.
VVS1, VVS2	Very, very slightly included	An excellent diamond – contains inclusions that are extremely difficult to see under magnification.
VS1, VS2	Very slightly included	A diamond that contains small inclusions that are hard to see under magnification.
SI1, SI2	Slightly included	A diamond containing visible inclusions under magnification.

COLOUR

The colour is graded alphabetically. Letters towards the beginning of the alphabet are the best, colourless diamonds, starting with D. Generally, stones should be of H quality or higher.

D E F	G H I J	K L M	N O P–Z
Colourless (and best)	Near colourless	Faint yellow	Very light – light yellow

CUT

The cut is the angles and proportions of a stone. A well-cut diamond is neither too shallow nor too deep – this allows the stone to sparkle as the light reflects off the perfectly cut facets.

The grades of cut are excellent, ideal, very good, good or fair. The shape of a diamond is also often referred to as the cut. This is a matter of personal choice and does not generally affect the price. There are many different shapes to choose from: round, oval, pear, princess (square), marquise (oval with pointed ends), emerald (rectangular) and asscher (square with rounded edges) are all commonly seen. Round cut diamonds are the most usual and popular. A single diamond set alone is referred to as a solitaire.

BRITISH WEDDING ANNIVERSARIES

1 PAPER

2 COTTON

3 LEATHER

4 FLOWERS, FRUIT

5 WOOD

6 SUGAR

7 WOOL, COPPER

8 BRONZE, POTTERY

9 WILLOW, POTTERY

10 TIN

11 STEEL

12 SILK, LINEN

13 LACE

14 IVORY

15 CRYSTAL

20 CHINA

25 SILVER

30 PEARL

35 CORAL

40 RUBY

45 SAPPHIRE

50 GOLD

55 EMERALD

60 DIAMOND

70 PLATINUM

PROPOSALS: RULES

{1}
Plan ahead. It's an occasion that
will be recalled time and time again.

{2}
Proposals demand once in a lifetime romance.
Don't hold back.

{3}
Remember that the location will
become a place of great significance.

{4}
Timing should be carefully thought through.

{5}
Be flexible: the best-laid plans
can go awry if the mood isn't right.

{6}
Get down on one knee.
You may feel foolish, but she'll love it.

{7}
Pop the question confidently and clearly –
she doesn't want to be guessing if she's heard correctly.

{8}
Remember, there can be no truly offensive
or wrong way to ask someone to marry you.

{9}
Before you propose, it's traditional
to ask her father (or a parent) first.

GET IT RIGHT: THE RING

In an ideal world, you are supposed to drop to one knee and whisk out a box containing the sparkler of her dreams. In reality, you may not know your solitaires from your emeralds, and the idea of picking the right ring fills you with fear.

You're not alone. Many choose to propose without a ring and opt for a different token such as a bracelet or necklace instead. The couple then hit the shops together. She won't think badly of you for it – there aren't many women who would sneer at a day of diamond shopping. A ring should be on her finger within a reasonable time; have a chat about budget before you shop to ensure that there are no unrealistic demands on your wallet.

If you decide to take the plunge and choose a ring in advance, then make sure you listen to the jeweller. Take advice and ask questions – it's a complicated business. Don't worry too much about making sure it fits right as you can always have it altered. Traditionally, an engagement ring should cost approximately twice your net monthly salary, but you should just buy the best you can afford. Make sure you insure it for the correct amount; ask the jeweller for an insurance receipt.

The Refusal

She may need a moment to take it all in after you've popped the question, but if she ponders for more than a moment it's not a good sign. If she says "No" then keep your dignity and temper. Don't grovel, and never try to persuade her – a refusal on her part would be no light decision. If you have proposed with a ring, she should offer to give it back – it's up to you if you want to take it or not. Most jewellers will give you a refund.

SPREADING THE NEWS

It is usual to tell both sets of parents first, depending on who knew beforehand. Then tell your friends, and the news will spread like wildfire – expect a champagne-fuelled social whirlwind for the subsequent few weeks.

Traditionally, the bride's mother puts a public announcement in the 'Forthcoming Marriages' column of a local or national newspaper. Wording should read:

Mr P Jennings and Miss K Ashton-Smythe

The engagement is announced between Peter, eldest son of Mr and Mrs Simon Jennings of Lewes, East Sussex, and Katherine, only daughter of Mr and Mrs John Ashton of Godalming, Surrey.

Friends should send a letter or card of congratulations. Correctly, the letter should be addressed either to the bride-to-be or her fiancé but never jointly, even if they are living together – well-wishers should write to the person they were friends with first or are related to. Nowadays, however, many people know the couple equally, so this old rule may not apply. Either way, it's good form to send a card.

If It All Goes Wrong

If an engagement is called off, there is usually no need to give any detailed explanation as to why. If wedding invitations have already been sent out, informal notes or printed cards should be sent to each guest announcing that the ceremony will not take place. The bride-to-be should return the engagement ring. Any wedding presents received should be returned with a letter of thanks.

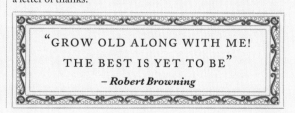

"GROW OLD ALONG WITH ME!
THE BEST IS YET TO BE"
– *Robert Browning*

The Best Man's Duties

Arranging a stag-do.

Making sure the ushers have the correct clothes and know what is expected of them.

Meeting up with the bride and groom's parents, and the bridesmaids before the day.

Visiting the ceremony and reception venues. Becoming familiar with their layout and the timetable of events.

Attending the rehearsal and introducing people that might not know each other.

Staying with the groom the night before the wedding.

Running through the day with the groom and checking that he has everything he needs (not forgetting the rings).

Accompanying the groom to the ceremony venue in good time and staying with him in the lead-up to the service.

Casting an eye over the venue and checking that family and guests are being seated correctly.

Handing over the ring(s) at the critical moment.

Ensuring that the bride and groom are ready to have their photographs taken; getting them into the car (or equivalent) that will take them to the reception.

Liaising with the bridesmaids and ensuring that everything is going to plan.

If there are any problems, remaining calm and quietly sorting them out.

Delivering the best man's speech. The best man shouldn't drink too much until the speeches are over.

Ensuring that the first night/honeymoon luggage, tickets and passports are in the correct get-away vehicle.

After the wedding, arrange for any suits to be cleaned and returned.

HANDLING THE IN-LAWS

WHEN IT COMES to your partner's relations, the laws of probability are not on your side. At best you've swelled their ranks, further dividing the pot of love and attention; at worst you've stolen their beloved daughter/sister, stealing them away from the family nest like the cuckoo they know you are.

EVEN WONDERFUL in-laws can create problems. If they're warm, uncritical, unfailingly supportive, always pleased to see you and generous at Christmas-time, this will play merry hell with your relationship with your own less-than-perfect parents or siblings.

IF YOU INHERIT toxic in-laws, comfort yourself with the thought that your partner chose to leave the bosom of his/her family and create a new family with you. Sit tight, behave immaculately and trust that there will be no doubt about which family is the better bet.

REMEMBER that old-fashioned chivalry of the door-holding and standing-up kind can go a long way with critical mothers.

AS FOR PERFECT in-laws, don't make the mistake of boasting about them to your own family (that way lies perdition). Instead just secretly enjoy the fact you've bucked the trend.

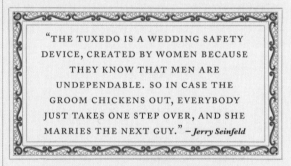

"THE TUXEDO IS A WEDDING SAFETY DEVICE, CREATED BY WOMEN BECAUSE THEY KNOW THAT MEN ARE UNDEPENDABLE. SO IN CASE THE GROOM CHICKENS OUT, EVERYBODY JUST TAKES ONE STEP OVER, AND SHE MARRIES THE NEXT GUY." – *Jerry Seinfeld*

Are you a Mummy's Boy?

She buys your underwear.

•

She does your washing and irons your socks.

•

She never likes your girlfriends/partners.

•

You need her approval before going out with a girl.

•

You still live at home.

•

You can do no wrong in her eyes.

•

You're afraid of her reaction to how you decide to live.

N.B. Women will view the relationship you have with your mother as a sign of how you may treat them in the future.

GET IT RIGHT: THE BEST MAN'S SPEECH

Speak for between five and fifteen minutes – don't go on for too long.

If you are not used to public speaking, keep it brief and heartfelt.

Make sure you include mentions and stories about both the bride and the groom.

Your speech should celebrate the groom and his bride, not humiliate them.

Never be rude about their families.

Moderate the stories: keep it appropriate and clean.

Don't discuss the groom's former conquests or girlfriends.

Embarrass the groom with genuine wit and good humour.

Avoid *risqué* jokes.

If you're struggling, include a joke at your own expense to make the guests laugh.

Never, ever make personal jokes about the bride.

End with a toast to the bride and groom: 'Mr and Mrs X'.

Remember, there is more to being a best man than making a side-splitting speech. You will need organisational ability, an attention to detail and plenty of charm.

SIX STAG-DO RULES

{1}
The groom should never pay.
{2}
The groom should be humiliated –
but not so much the wedding is called off.
{3}
Find out the party's budget –
don't go abroad if no one can afford it.
{4}
Check if your chosen venue allows stag parties.
A lot of clubs don't.
{5}
Don't arrange the stag-do on the night before the wedding.
{6}
What happens on the stag, stays on the stag.

 EXPERT TIP If you're best man, make a copy of the speech and try it out on a friend – ideally one who knows both the bride and groom and can gauge their reaction on the day.

THE GODFATHER

A CHILD TRADITIONALLY has three godparents: a boy has two godfathers and one godmother, and a girl has two godmothers and one godfather.

WHILE TRADITION also dictates that a godparent is expected to become the legal guardian of the child should anything happen to the parents, this scenario is unlikely today.

BEING ASKED to be a child's godparent is a huge honour. Before accepting, ask yourself honestly whether you are prepared and able to fulfil the role.

SOME ADULTS COLLECT godchildren like stamps; they end up with an impressive collection but never do anything with them. If you haven't got the time or interest, then be honest and decline the role.

TRY TO UNDERSTAND what the parents want from you. You must be ready and willing to have regular contact with the family: don't enter into this relationship knowing that you will be one of those godparents who no one has seen for years.

ASK YOURSELF WHY you were asked to be a godparent in the first place – what makes you different from the parents and other godparents: culture, glamour, sporting prowess, sociability? Play up to that reason.

AS GODPARENT, you can be in the uniquely gratifying position of being the child's first grown-up friend and confidant. Treat them as your equal, and never judge or nag your godchild.

MAKE YOURSELF ACCESSIBLE; when they're old enough, give the child your mobile number and let them know that they always can call you for a chat.

GIVE THEM slightly unsuitable presents from time to time – it may drive their parents mad but it will show your godchild whose side you are on.

NEVER, EVER FORGET a birthday or Christmas. Send postcards from holidays; always let them know that they are in your thoughts.

A GUIDE TO PAGE NUMBERS

REFERENCE · *Index*

REFERENCE · *Index*

REFERENCE · *Credits*

THANKS TO:

Andrew Harper, luxury travel expert
Andy Watt, Bentley Mulliner
Ashutosh Khandekar, *Opera Now*
Bill Dawes, *Boards*
Bill Eliot
Bob Lyell, Steve Moore
    and Richard Charlesworth, Bentley
David Cavill
E. Jane Dickson
Henry Besant, Worldwide Cocktail Club
Hurlingham Polo Association
James Aitchison
Jonathan Irby, West London Shooting School
Joss Fowler, Berry Bros & Rudd
Mark Hix
Matt Bryant Personal Training
Nick Foulkes
Susannah Jowitt
The English Tiddlywinks Association
Thinkfish
Tom Avery
Will Andrews, Proctor & Gamble